In the Line of Duty

20th Anniversary Edition

Jeff Davis Duty, Jr.

Edited by

Diana Duty West

Cover Photograph: Author and Binney at their digs in Passfield Hall on Endsleigh Place, London, England, on the occasion of Binney's release from quarantine, March, 1958

Nan Press | New Jersey

Biography & Autobiography / Personal Memoir

First edition, first printing: August, 1994
Twentieth anniversary edition, first printing: December, 2014

ISBN-13: 978-0692343616
ISBN-10: 069234361X

Published in the United States by Nan Press, Long Valley, New
Jersey.

Printed in the United States of America.

3 4 5 6 7 8 9

Cover design by Alexander West and Diana West
Pink Bunny illustrations copyright © 1962, 2014 by Patricia Ellis
Marti

ACKNOWLEDGEMENT

With thanks to my daughter Diana Duty West, without whose help this book literally would not have been. With her encouragement she kept me at it, and through her countless hours of selfless labor she gave it birth. It may be my story, but it is as much her book as mine.

I also acknowledge the tremendous contribution of my sister, Carolyn Banks. It was mainly through her efforts that the majority of the genealogical data, especially with regard to the Duty family, was collected and organized.

IN THE LINE OF DUTY

DEDICATION

I dedicate this book with all my love and gratitude first to my mother, Lois White Duty, without whose biological input there would have no story, and without whose inspiration the story would have been much different. Second, to my father, Jeff Davis Duty, Sr., who lent his patience and support so completely when I was young and later became my mentor in the law. Third, to my daughter Diana and my son John, who have always stood by me both as family and friends. Finally, to my grandchildren, born and yet unborn, and their children and their children's children, without end, who I love in anticipation and who I wish to know me as a person, even as I relate to them some details of their family heritage. In this honored clan, I also include my step-granddaughter Nicole Brunson, who was first to try out my lap.

IN THE LINE OF DUTY

Table of Contents

IN THE LINE OF DUTY

Data fata secutus

Duthie

Ancient Duty Crest

IN THE LINE OF DUTY

Coat of Arms

Duty

Modern Duty Crest

IN THE LINE OF DUTY

Be yourself—but be your best self. Dare to be different and to follow your own star.

And don't be afraid to be happy. Enjoy what is beautiful. Love with all your heart and soul. Believe that those you love love you.

Forget what you have done for your friends, and remember what they have done for you. Disregard what the world owes you, and concentrate on what you owe the world.

When you are faced with a decision, make that decision as wisely as possible—then forget it. The moment of absolute certainty never arrives.

Above all, remember that God helps those who help themselves. Act as if everything depended on you, and pray as if everything depended on God.

S. H. Payer

IN THE LINE OF DUTY

Preface

A Duty to Perform

It has occurred to me on numerous occasions that too much of one's family history, the little things that make a family unique, are lost with the passing of each generation. We hear stories and listen to reminiscences which bring our ancestors to life and give our family a living dimension. What we forget, though, is that this is all in our own heads, and when we shuffle off of this mortal coil, most of it goes with us. As time passes, more and more is lost. Therefore, I have decided to put down on paper something of the picture which I have in my own mind of my family history. I will try to bring this down through my own life so that my children and grandchildren who remember me in the flesh will feel a direct link with their past. Then perhaps someone in later generations will add to the chronicle and keep our family's history alive.

Of course, it will not all be fact. Much of it will be subjective; therefore, other than a living history, it may be more of a living legend. Still, it will at least satisfy the curiosity of those who come after and perhaps make them just a little proud of their heritage. I begin this project in love and sincerely hope that it will be read in love and some day be perpetuated. After all, love of one's family and one's children is the great bond that links us together as a race throughout all history, both written and unwritten. Without wanting to sound too much like Tiny Tim in Dickens' *A Christmas Carol*, I hereby bequeath you my story and say to you, "God bless you, one and all."

IN THE LINE OF DUTY

Chapter 1

Origin of the Species
400 AD-1900

Although there is no direct proof, evidence and logic indicate that the name "Duty" is an Anglicization (and some would say a corruption) of the Scottish name "Duthie," and even earlier the Irish "Dubthe." The Duthies are a subset of the Scottish clan "Ross." Some evidence to bear this out came to light when I was in England in 1958. I went to Summerset House, the great British repository of official records, and looked up the Duty family. The only Dutys which I could find were located in Yorkshire. Since Yorkshire is in the far north of England, just south of the ancient border with Scotland, this would seem to lend credence to the conjecture that they did indeed spring from the clan Duthie and simply Anglicized their name when they took up residence among the Sassenach.

Former Duthie Home in Scotland

Later inquiries turned up an indication that the Scottish Duthies came from the island of Iona and the town of Tain, a village on the West Coast of Scotland. Reconstruction of events from legends, myths, and some historical facts indicates that these early Duthies, known as Dubhachts, were a clan or perhaps merely a Druidic Christian religious sect who emigrated from Ireland. Traces of the Dubhachts go back to the rise of the High Kings of

Ireland in Armagh. Most famous of the Dubhachts was a pagan warrior hero of the "Red Branch" who served the High Kings, but eventually, after a civil uprising, led his clan to Connaught. Another (from whom I suspect that we actually descend) was Dubhacht of Illster who served the High King as bard during the advent of Patrician Christianity. Legend tells that he was actually converted from Druidism to Christianity by St. Patrick and later became a saint. His daughter, Brigid (to whom sainthood has also been attributed), served as abbess of a settlement of Christian Druids (called the Culdees) at Kildare. Apparently, from this community came the Culdeen settlers who founded Tain in the 5th or 6th century AD on the West Coast of Scotland in a region called Dalriada (Claim of the King). They established a church dedicated to St. Dubhacht. It is unclear whether these Culdee families became known as the Duthies because of their dedication to St. Dubhacht or whether a direct family link actually existed between the Dubhachts subset; and it was

SPIRITWALK

I know where I walk now
others may not go
For all my wandering talk
others do not know
There's a sadness in my heart,
a yearning in my head
A power born of hollow hills
gold and twilight led

I know where I walk now
beauty is not dead
I know that my way there
won't be always kind
Yet I have been this way before
root, leaf, and vine
If I speak of love now
it's of my loving quest
to gather in the harvest
(I'll reap some bramble, too)
But my own way to go now
leads into the west

There was a guiding star once
O! How it did shine!
There've been so many stars
beckoning along the way
But I hear the faerie music
and I see the moonpath glow
Someone's calling me softly
Now it's time for me to go

Bridgid Con Dubhacht

only a short step across the border from the Clan Ross territory, centered around Moray Firth, to Yorkshire in England, where the name Duty first appears.

Although the actual facts of the Duty origins are buried in the mists of time and can only be glimpsed and guessed at from myths and legends, the "Spiritwalk" poem does add some personal credibility. The original was in ancient Gaelic and was attributed to Brigid Con Dubhacht herself.

What is more certain is the tradition that the family has been noted for its poets, historians, philosophers, lawyers, judges, and doctors. Interestingly enough, these same intellectual tendencies seem to have continued to grace the family, even in their migration to the New World, as evidenced by the numerous lawyers, doctors, and judges named Duty. The family also had its roots deeply imbedded in the soil of religion, first as Druids and later as converted Christians. Besides the St. Dubhacht described above, two other St. Dubhachts have been identified. Hopefully, these attributes have also been passed down through the generations. Incidentally, the name Dubhacht seems to come from the Old Celtic word "dubh" meaning dark—shadowy— veiled—mystery (perhaps artistic?) and "acht," meaning forked—angled— writing; in other words, a person with arcane skills in writing or communication, such as a bard, poet, philosopher, or historian. This also fits in with what can be pieced together about our earliest forebearers. Besides dark and mysterious skills, dubh may also have referred to a dark haired or dark complected appearance; physical characteristics which still pop up in the family from time to time.

The next step of direct interest to our family, following our Irish-Scottish origins, is our transition to the New World. The first known record of a Duty in American is William Duty, who was born on August 5, 1658, in Rowley, Massachusetts. He married Elizabeth Hidden on May 1, 1684. She was born on December 19, 1665. William became a Selectman in Rowley and owned a ship chandlery in Boston. William and Elizabeth had nine children: Mary, William, Sarah, John, Matthew, Samuel, Andrew, Moses, and Joseph. William died on April 11, 1738, and Elizabeth died on February 7, 1743. Both are buried in Rowley, Massachusetts.

Our line proceeds through William and Elizabeth's eight child, Moses Duty, who was born on September 2, 1700. He married Mary Palmer on May 1, 1741. She was born on June 1, 1717, and they had six children: Moses, Jr., Mary, Eunice, Mark, William, and Sarah. Moses Senior was a farmer and brewer. He died on April 20, 1778, in Exeter, New Hampshire. His wife Mary died on November 2, 1763, in Exeter, as well, where they are both buried.

The Battle of Bunker Hill by John Trumbull

About 1765, the family moved to Hanover, New Hampshire. Moses and Mary's fourth child Mark, born October 16, 1747, was living in Derryfield, New Hampshire when the Colonial rebellion against England broke out. He and his brother William joined a regiment of the New Hampshire militia commanded by Mark's father-in-law, Andrew Woodbury, and fought at the Battle of Bunker Hill. (It is believed that Mark and William were specifically depicted in the famous painting of Bunker Hill by John Trumbull.)

Mark and Abigail Woodbury, who was born on August 3, 1746, in Salem, New Hampshire, married on March 1, 1770. They had four children: Andrew, Hannah, Mark, Jr., and Ebenezer. Mark Senior died on May 27, 1836. Abigail died in 1774. They are buried in Derryfield, New Hampshire.

As a matter of peripheral interest, it should be noted that Joseph Smith, founder of Mormonism, was the grandson of Mark Duty, Sr.'s sister Mary, who was born on October 11, 1743. She married Asael Smith, and when the family learned of it so much displeasure was expressed that Mary and her new husband moved to Topsfield, Massachusetts, where Joseph was born. Oral tradition also tells us that in later years when Joseph was revelling in the first flower of his new church in Illinois, his grandmother visited him. When she learned what was going on, she excoriated him publicly and disowned him on the spot. Duty women, of the blood, have always been a touch puritanical.

In the aftermath of the Revolution, at least part of the family migrated to Virginia. It was in that state in 1791 that Mark's and Abigail's oldest son Andrew Woodbury Duty, who was born on July 18, 1772, in Derryfield, New Hampshire, married Mary Dowell, who was born in 1773 in Hillsborough, New Hampshire.

Andrew first came to Virginia at the seaport of Occoquan. Later, the family would move to Culpepper and eventually to that part of Virginia which split off as West Virginia at the time of the Civil War. They settled in what is now Doddridge County near the county seat of West Union. Upon Andrew's death in 1823, he was buried in Tyler County, Virginia. Mary returned to Massachusetts and died in 1847 in Lowell, where she is buried.

Their son Andrew Woodbury Duty, Jr. was born on November 29, 1808. He married Martha Ankrom on August 14, 1823. She was born on January 14, 1799, and was able to trace her ancestry back to Scottish Earls. They had nine children: Hiram Nelson, Mary, Joseph, Elizabeth, John Randolph, Andrew Woodbury III, Hamilton, Ebenezer, Martha, and Jessie. Andrew, Jr. owned and operated the Bearsville Milling Company. He died on February 17, 1869, and Martha died on June 3, 1873. Both are buried in Tyler County, West Virginia.

Joseph Harrison Duty was the third child of Andrew, Jr. and Martha, born on May 26, 1827. He was married to Christianna Martha Davis, born 1828, by Rev. William Cooper, a Methodist minister, on May 2, 1844. Joseph and Christianna had fifteen children. Their names are Lenora Susan, Victoria, Andrew Lee, Sylvanus, Landora, John, Phoebe Ellen, Martha, Sidney, Laura May, Ebenezer, Janet, Joseph, Herbert, and Kraft. Joseph was

Uncle John R. Duty
(Drawing from a portrait now lost, made approximately 1860, original drawing owned by Donna Duty Lamp of Akron, OH)

a shoemaker by trade. His politics, however, were not so mundane. He and his brother John Randolph were the only two members of the family to side with the Confederacy during the War Between the States. And as a consequence they were disinherited by their father, thus being cut out of a share in the family mills.

When the Civil War broke out, Joseph went south and enlisted in the Confederate Calvary, becoming a member of the infamous unit known as Morgan's Raiders. In 1863, as the Confederate forces marshalled for their last great advance northward which would end at Gettysburg, a call was sent out for fresh supplies of horses. Joseph knew, of course, the location of most of the prime horses in Doddridge County, which were hidden in a secret corral in the cane breaks. Indeed, it was not surprising that he knew where they were since one of his brothers operated a livery stable in West Union and had been instrumental in hiding the stock. Answering the call of duty (no pun intended), Joseph passed along his information to his superiors. Eventually, it culminated in Joseph leading his unit into Doddridge County where they burned the train station and court house in West Union and then relieved his family and neighbors of most of their horses. Naturally, this did nothing to heal the rift between Joseph and his family, nor did it make him or his family popular in

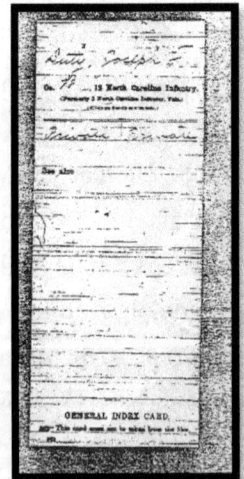

Joseph's enlistment record
(All men enlisting for service in the Tennessee Field were registered as members of North Carolina)

Doddridge County for many years after the war.

Soon after the raid on Doddridge County (possibly during the retreat with the horses), Joseph was captured by Union Forces and imprisoned at Camp Chase, Ohio. After six months, he escaped, though, and made his way back across the Ohio River to West Virginia and went into hiding. He had lost his health while imprisoned and required some time to recuperate. Eventually, he recovered enough to rejoin the Confederate forces in Tennessee before the war ended.

After the cessation of hostilities, Joseph returned to his family in Doddridge County, but finding the climate decidedly unfriendly, he left his family and moved with his co-Confederate brother John Randolph to Marietta, Ohio, where he died on January 26, 1900. Finding herself alone with so many children to feed, Christianna turned their home into a boarding house for railroad workers.

Sad to say, the other members of Joseph's and her families never forgave Joseph for his transgressions during the war. Even though they were quite well off, they never gave up their grudge and allowed Christianna and her children to struggle on for years in privations. She died around 1880 in Ritchie County, West Virginia, only in her fifties, but worn out by hardship, hard work, and heartache.

Our current family began to take shape in the 1850s. In July 1855, my great-grandmother Helen Bond was born in Doddridge County, West Virginia. In August 1851, her future husband and my great-grandfather Andrew ("Andy") Lee Duty was born nearby to Joseph and Christianna. (As an interesting footnote, Andy's tombstone shows his birth year as 1848, although the US census of 1870, using information provided by Christianna, reflects a birth year of 1851. Indeed, his sister Victoria was born in 1848. One can only conjecture that the discrepancy was Helen increasing the difference between their ages.).

There is also an apocryphal story that when Helen and Andy

Andrew Lee Duty (left) and his brother-in-law Oliver Bond *(Mammy Duty's younger brother)* **Circa 1880**

decided to marry, they were forced to elope, barely making it across the river into Ohio ahead of Helen's furious brothers. Obviously, there was still a stain on the Duty name. Apparently, however, the Bonds reconciled themselves to Andy, because the couple soon returned to West Virginia where they had two sons, John Randolph, born May 17, 1882, and Claude Joseph born in 1888.

Perhaps it was due to Joseph's lingering legacy, or perhaps it was simply a matter of seeking greener pastures, but sometime around 1890 Andrew and Helen took their boys and moved across the Ohio River to Marietta, Ohio, where they were well received by Andrew's uncle John Randolph and his family. After all, Uncle John had shared in Joseph's politics and thus his disgrace.

In Marietta, Andrew and Helen, following in Christianna's footsteps, opened a boarding house for railroad workers, while Andrew worked in some capacity with his uncle. In December 1892, a baby girl was born in their boarding house to a woman named Blake. Nothing else is known of the circumstances, except that the child was named Laura and was taken by Helen and Andrew to raise as their daughter.

Around 1900, Andrew and Helen were seemingly caught up in the restlessness which saw so many Americans migrating westward following the Spanish American War. Helen made a trip to Arkansas, ostensibly to visit a friend who lived in what was then Pleasant County located in the northwest corner of the state (later Pleasant County would be subdivided into several counties, including Benton where the Dutys settled).   In hindsight, it seems obvious that Helen was actually on a scouting trip to find a new home for their family. Fortuitously, she arrived in Arkansas at a time of ample rainfall and beheld a vista of green and fertile farmland. She immediately wrote to her family to prepare to move.

Helen returned to Ohio to collect her brood, and in 1901 led them south by covered wagon. By this time, Helen was being called Mammy and Andrew Pappy.

Somehow, in their meandering journey, they passed through Western Oklahoma. They probably crossed the Arkansas River from Fort Smith to swing west in order to avoid the Boston Mountains. In any event, they paused for a time in Tulsa, where Mammy set up a food service for railroad workers. In addition, she and son John taught at an Indian school. Then, sometime in 1901, they arrived and took up a farm near Pea Ridge in Benton County, Arkansas. Their decision to settle near Pea Ridge was influenced by the fact that the town boasted a community college, and Mammy was set in her determination that her children would receive good educations. Both John and Claude did, in fact, attend the Pea Ridge Academy.

Mammy and Pappy Duty's Gravestone

Chapter 2

The Benton County Dutys
1903-1945

Around 1903, Mammy's and Pappy's eldest son, my grandfather John R. completed college and began teaching school. Over the next few years, he taught in various (mostly rural) schools at such diverse locations as Rocky Comfort, Dug Hill, Mountain View, Garfield, and Springdale. While he was teaching at Garfield, Mammy and Pappy moved there from Pea Ridge, probably to be near their fast-arriving grandchildren.

John Randolph Duty

In 1905, John R. married Rella Lee Cooper, born on October 4, 1884, in Kansas, the daughter of David Cooper of Hiwassee, who was also of

Benton County. At the time, Rella was 20 years old and John was 25. Family legend has it that John met Rella when he called upon Mr. Cooper, who was the superintendent of the county schools, to ask for a teaching position. He rode his horse into the Cooper yard and saw what he later was claimed to have described as "the prettiest girl in the world" standing by the well. She gave him a cup of cold well water and he promptly gave her his heart.

Rella "Mama" Duty

John and Rella had five sons: Jeff Davis, Charlie Ross, Ralph Wendell, Ireland, and John Junior (who was known as "Baby John," but died of pneumonia in 1934). John and Rella also raised Lee Dean, the son of their adopted daughter Laura, after her death in 1927.

Students and teachers at the Garfield Academy taught by John R. Duty in 1906

Several years before, Laura had married Walter Dean of Avoka, a railroad junction just north of Rogers. They had two children: Lee Andrew Dean and Mary Dean. Daunted by his loss, Walter never remarried after Laura's death. Instead, he became committed to his career as a police officer for the city of Rogers. Eventually, he became the Police Chief and until the mid-1940s he *was* the police force.

John reached the pinnacle of his teaching career about 1908 when he was called to be the Superintendent of Schools in Springdale. Rella and

Mammy Duty, 1925

John moved to Springdale, but Rella was pregnant with Charlie and it was decided to leave Jeff in the temporary care of Mammy and Pappy in Garfield. In some respects, I have always believed that it was because of this time spent with them that he later felt so emotionally close to his grandparents.

During summer vacations while living in Springdale, John began reading law at the McGill-Lindsey law offices. Sometime around 1910, he passed the Arkansas Bar, whereupon he and Rella and their growing brood of sons returned to Garfield. Once there, John promptly established a law office and son Jeff rejoined the family.

Pappy died of blood poisoning from a barbed wire cut in 1910. The following year, in 1911, John R. loaded the rest of the family in a wagon and moved to Rogers. The story is told that while making the slow dusty trip two-year old Lee kept asking, "Are we there yet?" Finally, after several repetitions of the same question, four-year-old Charlie answered, "Lee, we will be there when we get there!" I have always thought that wise statement might well serve as a good family motto.

Mammy Duty, 1933

The Duty & Duty Law Firm

Once settled in Rogers, John R. opened a law office on north First Street. Soon thereafter, Claude joined John to establish the firm of Duty & Duty, Attorneys at Law. For the next few years while their families grew, John R. and Claude proceeded at first to struggle and then to firmly establish themselves as one of the premier law firms in the area and as leading lights at the Bar.

Claude became known as a "fixer"; someone who could solve problems no matter what it took. He was a pillar of the First Methodist Church in Rogers, and it was his conviction that many disputes could be worked out between the parties without having to resort to the courts.

John R. can be described, at 6'2" and over 200 pounds, as a large, reserved, pipe-smoking, dignified individual. He

Duty & Duty (left-right): Miss Sackett (secretary), Ralph Duty, Jeff Duty, Claude Duty, John R. Duty

dominated his surroundings wherever he went. Apparently, it might be said that he was bigger than life. Indeed, everyone I ever heard speak of him, especially his own family, referred to him with awe. To this day the younger generation refers to him as, "the late, great John R.," and this is done, not in derision, but with great respect. His persona and his career were both impressive as John became one of the foremost constitutional lawyers in the region and took a lively interest in public affairs and politics. Consequently, he was elected to the Arkansas Senate in 1916.

Over the years, the name Duty & Duty became almost synonymous in the area with the practice of law. It became such a common household term, in fact, that upon one particular occasion, while participating in a prayer service at the Methodist Church, Claude was called upon to deliver the closing prayer. He did so with great eloquence and at some length. Finally, he closed his peroration with the immortal words, "...and now, Oh Lord, we ask all these things in the name of Thy Son, Jesus. Yours very truly, Duty & Duty."

The firm managed to survive the 1929 crash and in the early 1930s regained sufficient prosperity to begin construction of their own office building. The Frisco Railroad had recently abandoned a round-house in Rogers and John and Claude bought the used brick. With it, using a plan from a structure in colonial Williamsburg, they erected a highly distinctive building on a tree-shaded quarter block at the southwest corner of the intersection of south Second and Elm streets. This was probably the high-water mark of the Duty & Duty firm.

Unfortunately, John R. died suddenly of a ruptured spleen in 1936, almost at the same time the new

We Wish You
A Merry Christmas and
A Happy New Year

Mr. and Mrs. John R. Duty

building was completed. Mammy preceded her son John R. in death by only one year, dying in early 1935 at the ripe old age of 86.

John R.'s son Jeff (who had joined the firm in 1930) continued to practice with Claude and were later joined by John R.'s son Ralph. Jeff left the firm in 1941 when he was elected prosecuting attorney for the old Fourth Judicial District. Ralph departed to join the Marine Corps during World War II. No longer requiring a building designed for a large firm, Claude sold the building to a group of young doctors. They converted it for medical offices and established what later became known as the Rogers Medical Center. (For historical interest, their names were Hollis Buckaloo, John William Jennings, Stuart Wilson, and Larry Collette.)

Claude continued to practice law in Rogers. About 1956, Jeff rejoined him to resurrect the Duty & Duty law firm in offices upstairs in the Golden Rule building, located on the southeast corner of Walnut and Second streets. It is interesting to note that this suite of offices was essentially the same as the one occupied by Claude and John R. just prior to moving into their own building.

Claude and Jeff continued to practice together until Claude's death in December, 1961. Claude was survived by his wife Opal Cowie Duty and by two sons, C.J. Duty of Springfield, Missouri, since deceased, and James Andrew Duty of Rogers.

Jeff and his wife Lois White Duty continued to live in Rogers, where Lois taught school until 1973 and Jeff continued to practice law until the present. Indeed, at 88 (at the time of this writing), he is the oldest practicing attorney in the State and was recognized as such at a special banquet held in his honor in April, 1993, by the Benton County Bar Association and the Ozark Legal Services. Over the years, Jeff has refined his practice until now he concentrates primarily upon cases involving the violation of Constitutional

Funeral Service Held Sunday for Mrs. Duty; Burial Near Garfield

Funeral service was held Sunday afternoon at the First Methodist church for Mrs. Helen Bond Duty, 90, who died Saturday afternoon at the home of her son, Claude, South Fifth street, from a long illness of influenza.

Mrs. Duty was a native of Dodridge county, Virginia. Beginning at an early age, she taught school for a number of years. About 1877 she was married to Andrew L. Duty, of pioneer Virginia stock, and the couple moved to Ohio.

In 1901 the family moved from Ohio to Arkansas, settling on a farm near Garfield, where they resided until Mr. Duty's death in 1911, after which she made her home variously with her sons John R. and Claude Duty in Rogers.

Besides her two sons, she is survived by five grandsons, Jeff, Charley, Ralph and Ireland Duty, sons of John R. Duty, and C. J. Duty, son of Claude Duty, all of Rogers; a great niece, Miss Ollie Collins of Little Rock, and two great grandchildren, the children of Jeff Duty.

The Rev. E. J. Gardner, pastor of the First Methodist church, delivered the funeral sermon and a quartet sang hymns which had been favorites of Mrs. Duty.

Burial was made in the Reddick cemetery, near Garfield, beside her husband. Pallbearers were H. T. Penn, E. G. Sharp, Hugh Puckett, W. N. Ivie and J. W. Walker of Rogers and Harry C. Baker of Garfield.

rights. Jeff and Lois are old-style, unreconstructed, liberal Democrats, in the very best of the term. As long as there are citizens like them, a republic built around the rights of individuals will endure.

After some years of widowhood, Jeff's mother Rella met Ivan Gaines of Bentonville and they were married in 1940. Ivan moved into the family home with Rella, where they continued to live until it burned down in 1945. With the insurance proceeds, they built a much smaller, modern home on the site of the earlier structure and lived there the remainder of both their lives.

Rella (always known as "Mama") can best be characterized as a

Mama Duty on a Motorcycle

person with a heart as big as all outdoors. Her whole life was built around giving and nurturing, first her own family, and then her grandchildren. She kept an enormous garden and provided hearty meals for all and sundry. No advance notice or invitation was required to sit down at her table. She was always cheerful, with a ready laugh, and forever humming or singing, mostly hymns. Her favorite went, "...Further along, we'll know more about it. Further along, we'll understand why. Cheer up my brothers, live in the sunshine. Further along, we'll understand why." Mama died after a brief illness on October 29, 1958. Ivan passed away about 1968.

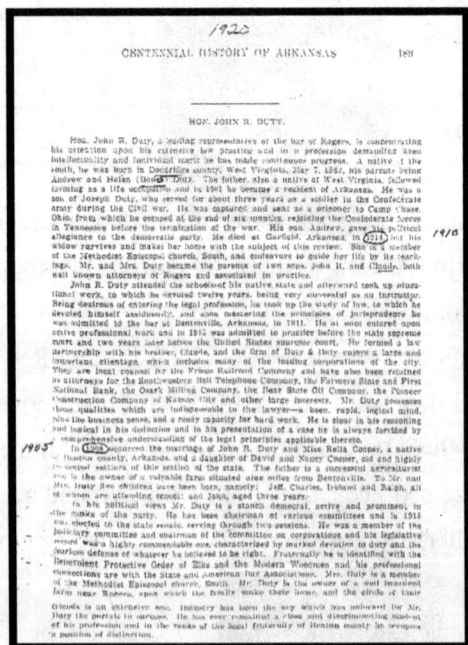

Chapter 3

My Home Town:
A Brief History of Rogers, Arkansas
by Florence Felker, November 1, 1991
Reproduced with the generous permission of the author

When "Old No. 17" puffed into what is now Rogers on May 10, 1881, a crowd of curious spectators, who had travelled for miles in some cases, were on hand to view this new noisy and ugly iron horse. The coming of the railroad, the Frisco, was the beginning of Rogers. Rogers owes its site and its name to the railroad. The site was bought from B.F. Sikes, who had a block of 200 acres to sell, and the town was named for Captain C.W. Rogers, the general manager of the Frisco. He and his wife were active in the Congregational Church of St. Louis. Mr. Rogers visited this new town often in the early years and it was because of her influence that the first church erected here was of the Congregational denomination. It was built where the building known as the Plaza is now.

Walnut Street, Looking East, Rogers, Ark.   Pub. by Rogers Mfg Racket Store

Rogers was incorporated on May 23, 1881. The first election was on June 1, 1881, with a population of 600. Also, it was through the Congregational Church American Home Missionary Society that the first school was built in Rogers, the Rogers Academy, a private school. There were no public schools. The Academy was built on the site now occupied by the Elmwood School. Elizabeth Hall was erected a few years after the main building, and it served as a dormitory for the Academy building. Rogers students attended as day students, of course. Room and board for out-of-town students was $1.50 per week, and students had to furnish their own rooms, except for stove and lamp. A full year at the Academy in 1892 was figured to cost a student $94.00, which included tuition and books. No student would be admitted or retained who used tobacco, and each had to attend church at least once on Sunday.

In 1911, the Congregational and the Presbyterian churches voted to unite in one body and become members of the Presbyterian Synod of Arkansas. It soon was evident they could no longer support the Academy, and in

IN THE OZARKS — LAND OF A MILLION SMILES.

March, 1914, the
transfer of the Academy
to the Rogers Public
School District was
made. The first public
school building was
erected in 1887 on the
site were the First
Federal Savings & Loan
building now stands.
Salaries were low and it was seldom that teachers had a college education.
From this early beginning, our school system has grown until there are now
many public schools in Rogers of high caliber.

If any of you wonder why we have some crooked streets in Rogers,
it is because the original town was laid off parallel to the railroad. Later,
additions were laid off running true north and south.

The first water supply in Rogers was a well in front of what is now
known as the Poor Richard building.

Benton County was named for Senator Thomas Hart Benton of
Missouri, who was one of Arkansas' best friends in the Congress before and
after statehood. Records fail to show the source of the name of Esculapia
Township, but it is of Greek origin and is reminiscent of medicine.[1] There
used to be several springs in the vicinity of Rogers; one in Esculapia Hollow,
now gone to ruin; another called Callahan Springs; and also Electric Springs,
which can still be seen as a small trickle of water on Highway 12 leading to
the Lake area. People thought water from these springs had medicinal value,
and people from Texas used to come here for the Electric Springs water,
especially, and thousands of gallons were distributed around town. There

---

[1] *Author's note*: It refers to the Greek god of medicine.

was a large hotel built near Electric Springs, which was quite popular in the early days. It has long since been torn down. No history of early Rogers can ignore the influence of these many springs.

Mr. W.R. Felker came to Rogers two years after the town was founded and established the first bank in Rogers, the Bank of Rogers, which was first located in the corner of a grocery store. In about 1905, he built and moved his bank into the building now occupied by Television Station 51. He continued to operate this bank until 1914, at which time he sold it. Mr. Felker then organized a company which built the railroad from Rogers to Grove, Oklahoma. This was later sold to the Frisco. Then Mr. Felker's company built a railroad from Rogers to Siloam Springs, running through Cave Springs, and another railroad running through Cave Springs to Fayetteville. Changing conditions slowly brought an end to the once profitable railroad operation and it was abandoned and junked, with only the Grove branch of the Frisco remaining, and that has since been abandoned.

At the same time Mr. Felker built this bank building, Mr. J.E. Applegate built the building next door that is now occupied by Poor Richards for his fine new drug store, he having first had a drug store in another Rogers location. The Applegate home was where the Immanual Church now stands. There were five Applegate sons who followed their father into the drug business. They had two drug stores in Rogers, one in Springdale, and one in Bentonville. A grandson, John Applegate, operated one of the stores in Rogers until he sold it to the Lewis Drug Store, who in turn sold it to Poor

Richards. The other Applegate-owned drug store in Rogers was the Corner Drug Store, now owned by Kenneth Petway. Poor Richards has restored the original Applegate Drugstore to its former handsomeness, with a soda fountain just like the old days.

There has been a Stroud's Department Store in Rogers since 1884. The store where it is now located was built in 1891 and was operated by Mr. A.B. Stroud. Harold Wardlow was later its owner, and now it is owned by H.K. Scott and Bill Crum.

During the Depression, there were three banks in Rogers: the First National Bank on the corner of 1st Street and Elm, now occupied by the Jade Shop; the Farmers State Bank, located where the Television Station is now; and the American National Bank operated by Mr. T.E. Harris and located on the corner of Walnut and First, where the Dixieland Shoe Store is now. The First National Bank and the Farmers State Bank both failed, and the American National, the smallest, was the only one to weather the Depression, thanks to the good management of Mr. T.E. Harris. This was our only bank for a good many years. In 1937, they bought the building in which the television station is now located, and, as they graduated from college, the Harris boys, Lawrence, Gene, and Ray, joined their father in the bank, changing the name of it to the First National Bank. They later built a new bank at their present location and moved into it, and now, of course, it is being greatly enlarged, the present owner being Sam Walton and associates. In 1956, another bank, the Farmers and Merchants Bank, was organized by Charley Garrett as its president and it was located in the

First Methodist Episcopal Church.
Rogers, Ark.

building on Second Street, now owned by Hardy Croxton. Of course, now the Farmers and Merchants Bank is located in their new building.

For many years, the apple growing industry was a big thing in this area. In 1919, Benton County growers marketed 5,000,000 bushels of apples. They sold for an average of $1.00 per bushel. This was the biggest year they had. From then on, profits were not as high, the weather was not as favorable, and there was an increase in diseases which attacked the orchards. There were also at that time many apple evaporators, or drying plants, in the area making dried apples. Also, the vinegar plant took the apples not good enough to ship for use in making apple cider vinegar. For a few years in the early '20s, an apple blossom festival was held in Rogers while the apple trees were in bloom, each town around Rogers sending floats. Queens and maids were elected and this festival became known as the biggest program put on in the State with many hundreds or thousands of visitors. However, it rained so many times on the day of the Festival, ruining all the floats, that after a few years these festivals were discontinued. Too, the bugs attacking the apple trees became immune to all the sprays they had and the trees were dying. This loss of apples almost broke many apple growers, as well as other businesses who sold to or bought from the apple growers. By the late '20s, the apples were no longer king of the county.

The first newspaper appeared four months after Rogers was founded; it was known as the Rogers Champion. There were several other newspapers started and stopped after a time. In 1929, Mr. E.W. Pate (Mary

Ruth Garner's father) bought the Rogers Democrat, a weekly paper, and the Daily Post that Jim P. Shofner had owned. Mr. Pate changed the name to the Rogers Daily News, and he really ran a good hometown newspaper during the years he owned and operated this paper. Due to failing health, Mr. Pate sold the paper in 1955 to a Mr. Nutter of New Orleans whom he thought would continue to operate it as a hometown paper, but this man after a few years sold it to the Donrey Chain, who have operated it ever since. In 1950, Mr. Pate published a mid-century edition of the history of Rogers, from which paper I got a great deal of this information about the early history of Rogers.

Of course, Monte Ne was an interesting place in the early part of the century. William Hope Harvey, whose nickname was "Coin" because of his free silver campaign book, bought several hundred acres in what was known as Monte Ne. He planned to establish a summer resort there. He finally got a railroad built from Lowell to Monte Ne and some hotel

Concrete amphitheater at Monte Ne

buildings erected. Some gondolas were acquired and visitors coming in on the train were met by gondoliers in gondolas, who transported them over the lagoon to the hotels. Also, Mr. Harvey thought a pyramid should be built here to house the secrets of our civilization so people in a few thousand years from now would know about us and how we lived. Work was started on the stone and concrete amphitheater that was to be the base of the pyramid in 1925, and it was built around the big spring. However, ill health and lack of money kept him from ever getting the pyramid built. At the same time he was working on the pyramid, "Coin" Harvey helped to launch the Liberty Party. In 1933, they held their national convention there at the amphitheater, and he was nominated as their candidate for presidency. With a bad defeat in the fall elections, the Liberty Party came to an end. And so did the active part of Mr. Harvey's life. The few years left to him were spent at home, after so many defeats in his life. Of course, the Lake covers now what was Monte Ne, but when the lake is low, the stone and concrete amphitheater can still be seen.

Mr. and Mrs. Hugh Rice, who had lived part of their lives in Rogers, left $50,000.00 for a hospital in Rogers. This was the nucleus of our present hospital. It was started with only 25 rooms and was operated by the City of Rogers, opening on September 25, 1950. The City continued to operate it for a short time, but was going in the hole so badly that they were very happy to turn the entire facility over to the Dominican Sisters, who have continued to operate it in a most efficient way ever since, adding to it many times in the last several years, until now we have a very fine hospital, indeed.

The present Townhouse was built as a hotel in 1929 by Gus Lane of Russellville, and it was quite an event in Rogers when the hotel opened. It was called then the Lane Hotel. However, during the Depression, it went into receivership. Later, Earl Harris, who owned the Harris Bakery, bought it and operated it and lived in it for several years, changing the name to the Harris Hotel. Then Mr. Warren Felker eventually owned it and they

changed the name again to the Hotel Arkansas. This hotel was the center of most of the social activity of Rogers for many years. Finally, after the advent of many motels in the area, Mr. Felker was forced to close it and finally sold it to a religious organization who operated it as a retirement hotel. They have since sold it and it is now privately operated as a retirement hotel.

Mr. O.L. Gregory, who owned the vinegar plant in Rogers for many years, and for whom I worked as his private secretary, had a lot to do with the growth of Rogers. His payroll was pretty large and the vinegar plant furnished a market for the apples not good enough to ship. He lived in the house on Highway 12 in which the Hudsons now live, and he owned as farmland all the area that surrounds the house, with the exception of the Callison house. His farmland included all of Summit Drive Hill, all of Lakeview Drive, and all the land down the hill on both sides of the road to the curve going out to the Lake area. There were no houses except houses he furnished to his farm hands. Ray Harris eventually bought all of this land and has really developed a fine residential area out of all of this, we thought, worthless

farm land of Mr. Gregory's. I have often thought Mr. Gregory wouldn't believe his eyes if he could come back to earth now. During World War II, Mr. Gregory sold at a very cheap price some of his land to the City of Rogers for a lake, with the understanding that it would be named for his wife Atalanta, so that is how Lake Atalanta got its name.

Another big event in the old history of Rogers was the marriage of Betty Blake to Will Rogers. There were seven pretty Blake sisters who lived on the way to Lake Atalanta. Betty and Will's marriage took place in Rogers on November 25, 1908. Betty's family didn't think much of this cowboy from Oklahoma Betty had married, but he ended up supporting her whole

family. He did much for Rogers. During World War I, he gave one third of all his Red Cross donations to the Rogers' branch. And many times he made contributions for the streets and other repairs in Rogers, but it was always given only if they would tell no one. He didn't like that kind of publicity.

Mr. J.W. Walker, Mr. J.E. Felker, and Mr. R.H. Whitlow established the Mutual Aid Union, which later became the Progressive Life Insurance Company, and the built the insurance building at the corner of Second and Walnut, now know as the Plaza. Also, Mr. Felker and Mr. Walker established the Union Life Insurance Company in Rogers, but moved it to Little Rock and it became one of the largest domestic insurance companies in the State. It, after a few years, was sold to Little Rock interests, as was the Progressive Life. But during the early years, many girls in Rogers started their working careers at the Progressive Life offices; they employed quite a large office force.

Another big milestone in the history of Rogers was the completion of Beaver Dam in 1965. Darrow Garner had the vision to see what was possible in the development of a residential area around the

Lake, so he bought a great many acres of land surrounding the Lake. I don't think he even thought so many lovely homes would be built out there and that so many nice new people would move out there. I believe the first nice homes to be built in the Prairie Creek area were the Hilt and the Hudson homes, and from then on the building out there has mushroomed, all of which has been a boon to the city of Rogers, and we old-timers have been delighted that so many fine new people have decided to make Rogers their home.

The first national company to come to Rogers was Munsingwear. However, they pulled out after a few years, and that building is now occupied by Tyson. The second big company to come to Rogers was Daisy, bringing with them several families,[2] which was a big boost to the economy of Rogers. Since then, many new industries have come to Rogers, all of which you know about.

The First Wal-Mart Store
was in Rogers, Arkansas

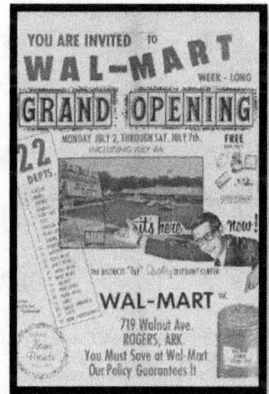

---

[2] *Author's Note:* One of the families brought to Rogers by Daisy was the family of Lanbert "Lanny" West, of whom my son-in-law Brad West is a member.

Summing up, the highlights of Rogers are briefly as follows:

1881   May 20, first passenger train arrived

1881   May 28, Rogers incorporated, named for W.C. Rogers

1881   June 1, first election, population 600

1883   Congregational Church built at Second and Poplar

1884   Rogers Academy built by Congregational Mission

1887   Public school built

1895   First electric lights

1903   First auto owned by W.A. McMillen

1907   First telephone directory, 1 page

1908   Silent moving pictures

1915   Union station built, since torn down

1923   Arkansas Western Gas installed

1950   September 25th, Rogers Memorial Hospital opened

1960   Census, 5,700

1960   March 7, Pea Ridge Park dedication

1963   Rogers Hough Memorial Library opened

1966   Beaver Dam completed

1970   Census, 11,050

1980   Census, 17,429

1991   Census, 24,367 (which, of course, doesn't include residents of Lake

        area and other areas not in city limits)

Chapter 4

The White-Side Story
1872-1974

Although my surname is Duty, I share the histories of both my father and my mother. Therefore, it is most appropriate that the maternal side of my family, of which I am equally proud, should also be told.

Pearl "Dolly" Eleanor
Wetzel White

William James (Will J.)
White

My mother, Lois Elizabeth White, was the youngest of three sisters born to Pearl Eleanor and William James (Will J.) White. Her mother was called Dolly because of her diminutive size, 90 pounds and 5'2½" tall (she wore a size 3 shoe), but was born Pearl Eleanor Wetzel on December 26, 1873, to a prominent farming family near Taylorville, Illinois. I always knew her as Nonny.

Pearl's mother was named Emily Marilla Eaton Wetzel. She married my great-grandfather, Moses Rheem Wetzel, on May 30, 1867. I never knew my great-grandmother Wetzel, as she died before my birth in April, 1927, but my great-grandfather Wetzel was still living when I was a boy. At that time, he had made his home with my grandparents; so I had the rare opportunity to bridge a four-generation gap. I knew him as Grandpa Wetzel. He was born in Cumberland County, Pennsylvania on April 10, 1843, and lived to the ripe old age of 98, passing away on

Moses Rheem Wetzel and Emily Marilla Eaton Wetzel

August 13, 1941, in Rogers, Arkansas.

Grandpa Wetzel's greatest fascination for me was that he had served in the Union Army during the Civil War. At the age of 19, he enlisted in the 158th Pennsylvania Infantry, with which he served for nine months (family legend has it that he was a drummer boy). His regiment

Moses Rheem Wetzel

fought at the Battle of Gettysburg, but his particular company did not participate in the actual fighting. Instead, they had the onerous duty of caring for the wounded. Although his military career was brief, he would always remember his service with great pride.

Following the war, Grandpa Wetzel moved from Pennsylvania to

Illinois, where he met and married my great-grandmother and prospered as a farmer, school teacher, and pillar of the Methodist Church. Although Grandpa Wetzel was living in Rogers, Arkansas, with his daughter (my grandmother Nonny) at the time of his death, the city hall and many of the downtown offices and businesses in his hometown of Taylorville closed their doors in his memory from 2:00 pm to 3:00 pm on the day of his funeral. Both of my Wetzel great-grandparents are buried in the old Stonington Cemetery, Stonington, Illinois.

Moses Rheem Wetzel

MOSE WETZEL OBSERVES HIS 96TH BIRTHDAY

M. R. Wetzel, Well Known Local Civil War Veteran, Dies At Age Of 98 Years

Final Tribute Is Paid Late M. R. Wetzel

Rheem E. Wetzel Sr., Stonington Man Celebrates 100th Birthday Today

Rheem E. Wetzel Sr., a retired farmer of Stonington, is quietly celebrating his 100th birthday today Relatives, neighbors and friends honored him, Sunday, with a potluck dinner in the Old Stonington Baptist Church near Stonington. Present at the affair were many of his 133 descendants, including five children, 26 grandchildren, 78 great-grandchildren and 5 great great grandchildren. A reception was held from 2 until 4 o'clock in the church.

Mr. Wetzel gives credit for his advanced age to "always behaving myself", and "I've never been in the calaboose".

Retiring from farming only years ago, when he was still doing custom work baling hay, he is "taking it easy" now, and spends a great deal of his time watching television Still enjoying good health, he has firm handshake and says he is one oldtimer who isn't anxious for the "good old days". Always one to welcome changes, especially if it held advantages in making a task easier, Wetzel developed and patented a safety valve for steam engines The patent was sold and the valve principles were used for years on steam locomotives. A farmer in the Moweaqua area for most of his life, he constantly worked on mechanical

innovation to do farm work better and faster. A short term as engineer in a canning factory in the 1880s apparently helped him develop some mechanical and engineering skills uncommon to farmers working with horses. Soon after he purchased a threshing machine and steam combine and began long-lasting career of custom threshing business.

Mr. Wetzel was born on a farm near Moweaqua, just one week after the assassination of President Lincoln.

Becoming eligible for social security benefits in 1956, he is one of the oldest social security beneficiaries in this area. As for social security, he says, "It's a dandy thing. I'm for anything beneficial to the human family." Victor Christgau, executive director of the social security administration, Washington, D. C., sent congratulations to Mr. Wetzel.

His five children are: Mrs. Zintka Smith, Mrs. Cecil Thomas,

Mrs. John (Zelda) Sanders Sr., all of Stonington; Mrs. Fred (Nellie) Becker and Gail Wetzel, both of Moweaqua.

Funeral Today Rheem E. Wetzel, 101, Christian County's Oldest Resident

Final tribute to 101-year-old Rheem E. Wetzel of Stonington, Christian County's oldest resident, was held at 2 o'clock this afternoon, in the Old Stonington Baptist Church. The Rev. Billy Howard, pastor, officiated. Interment was in Moweaqua West Cemetery, with the Connolly funeral directors in charge.

The pallbearers were Rheem Wetzel, Jack, Ralph and James Sanders, Keith and Dean Becker, all grandsons of Mr. Wetzel.

Mr. Wetzel died at 9:45 o'clock Saturday morning in Meadow Manor Nursing Home, Route 48 North, where he had been a patient three months. He had been in ill health three months.

A native of Christian County, Mr. Wetzel was born in Prairieton Township, April 21, 1865, the son of B. F. and Sarah Hartwell Wetzel. He was married Feb. 26, 1890, in Prairieton Township, to Pearl Adams, the ceremony being performed by her grandfather, the Rev. C. D. Northcutt. She preceded him in death in 1953.

Mr. Wetzel, a retired farmer, spent his entire life in the Moweaqua—Stonington community.

Mar. 25, 1967

WETZEL, Rheem. E., 101, Stonington, died 9:45 a.m. Saturday, Meadow Manor Nursing Home, Taylorville; leaves sons, Gail, Moweaqua; daughters, Mrs. Cecil Thomas, Mrs. Elwood Pearson, Mrs. John Sanders, all of Stonington; Mrs. Fred Becker, Moweaqua; services, 2 p.m. Monday, Old Stonington Baptist Church; burial, Moweaqua West Cemetery; call after 4 p.m. Sunday, Connolly Funeral Home, Taylorville.

On his 100th birthday, when asked to what he attributed his longevity, he replied. "I've always behaved myself." After his retirement from farming, Mr Wetzel continued to do custom hay baling for a number of years. He always said he was one "old-timer" not anxious for the "good old days;" that he enjoyed and welcomed changes especially if they held advantages in making a task easier. He developed and patented a safety valve for steam engines. During his farming career, he constantly worked on mechanical innovation to do farm work better and faster. A short term as engineer in a canning factory in the 1880's helped him develop some mechanical and engineering skills uncommon to farmers working with horses. Soon after he purchased a threshing machine and steam combine, and began a long career of custom threshing. Mr. Wetzel was a member of the Old Stonington Baptist Church.

He is survived by four daughters, Mrs. Fred (Nellie) Becker Moweaqua; Mrs. Cecil Thomas, Mrs. Elwood (Zintka) Pearson, Mrs. John (Zelda) Sanders, all of Stonington; one son, Gail, of Moweaqua; 27 grandchildren 97 great-grand children; and 1 great great-grandchildren. A son died in infancy, and another son, Bain, died in 1954.

Mr. and Mrs. R. E. Wetzel, Moweaqua

Mr. and Mrs. Wetzel, three miles west of Moweaqua, are celebrating their 50th wedding anniversary Monday with family dinner at noon and open house in the afternoon and evening. Their six children will be with them, and also 26 grandchildren and one great-grandchild.

Mr. Wetzel was born 75 years ago three miles from their present home, and Mrs. Wetzel 69 years ago within two miles. With the exception of four months in Decatur, they have lived their entire lives in the same community. They started housekeeping in a house that was built by Mr.

Wetzel who cut the lumber from the timber which surrounded the location. They have seen the mode of transportation change from covered wagon to stream-lined styles.

Mr. Wetzel was the first to introduce the self-feeder and wind stacker threshing machine in his community and he has served in every public office in the township except that of constable and assessor. They are members of Stonington Baptist church where he is chairman of the board of trustees, a member of the board of deacons, and teaches the men's Bible class.

WILL CELEBRATE 50TH ANNIVERSARY

Eaton Family

Eaton Family Portrait (left-right):
Emilly Marilla Eaton Wetzel, Hattie Eaton Butler, Jordan S. Eaton, Margaret Eaton Clawson, Grandmother Eaton, Dara Eaton Kearns, William Eaton

Wetzel Family Oct 9, 1954 (left-right):
Uncle Earl Wetzel, brother of Dolly; Aunt Muriel Wetzel; Will J. White; Dollie Wetzel White; Eleanor White Davis (sofa); Carolyn Duty Banks (floor); Karen Marie Banks (baby); Lois White Duty (holding Karen); Jeff Davis Duty, Sr; Davis Duty

Left:
Sarah Jeanette
Lymer White

Right:
Grandfather
Lymer
(Sarah's Father)

Left:
Sarrah Stephens
White

Right:
Joseph Bradey
White, Sr.

My grandfather Will J. White (who in later life was known in the community as Uncle Bill) was the second child born to Joseph Brady and Sarah Jeanette Lymer White and was the grandson of Sarrah J. Stephens White and Joseph Bradey White, Sr. (born January 4, 1808). Little is known about my great-great grandparents White, except that Sarrah Stephens was born on August 7, 1806. She married Joseph in 1833, died on March 13, 1850, at age 43 and is buried in the Oak Hill Cemetery in Taylorville, Illinois. They probably made their home somewhere around Pana, Illinois, where Whites are not uncommon, even today. My great-grandfather Joseph Brady, Jr., was born on December 2, 1844. Great-grandmother Sarah Jeannette was born on March 18, 1848. They were married July 4, 1870, in Christian, Illinois.

Before my grandfather White's birth, with the post-Civil War depression still raging, like many of their contemporaries, his parents Joseph and Sarah decided to pull up their roots from where they lived in Pana,

Joseph Brady White, Jr. and siblings circa 1890 (left-right): Mrs. Juanita White Donaldson, Samuel White, J.B. White, Mrs. Ann Gibson.

Illinois, to seek their fortune in the West. This occurred in the summer of 1871, soon after the birth of their first child, a daughter named Jeannette (Nettie) Beatrice. On June 4th, Joseph and his brother-in-law George Lymer made the arduous, overland journey to what is now the State of Washington. They eventually found and homesteaded rich, virgin land in the Yakima Valley in what would become Klickitat County, Washington. There, they established a horse ranch near the town of Goldendale.[3]

---

[3] As a footnote, it should be mentioned here that in a startling coincidence, my daughter Diana's mother-in-law, Sharon West (neé Linse) was born in the Yakima Valley of Washington State and traces the origins of her family's presence there (both her grandparents Linse and Watkins) to approximately the same timeframe. One can only wonder if they knew the White family.

In the following summer of 1872, when it was felt that Nettie was finally old enough to travel, Sarah and the baby embarked upon the road west to join her husband. To reach Joseph and her brother at their new home in Washington, Sarah and Nettie went by train to Salt Lake City. Joseph met her there and they traveled on to Washington by covered wagon. I doubt that we can possibly conceive of the physical and emotional stress that such moves and such conditions would impose.

Only one story survives about that trip, but it speaks volumes. At

Joseph Brady White, Jr. and children Jeannette (Nettie) Beatrice White and William James White

one point, their travel was interrupted when the family woke at their campsite one morning to discover that the mules had strayed during the night. Having no alternative, Joseph was forced to leave his wife and baby alone for almost three days, with only the wagon for shelter, while he went hunting the strayed beasts. One can only imagine the fear felt by Joseph for the safety of his young wife and baby and the fear experienced by Sarah during what must have been the longest three days of her life, there alone in Indian-inhabited wilderness, wondering if she would ever see her husband again. Eventually, Joseph found the mules, though, and the journey continued.

Son Will J. appeared on the scene on August 17, 1873. Except for what limited formal education he received from his parents, his primary learning was of a practical nature such as boys acquired in those days when raised in a pioneer wilderness environment. By the age of twelve, he was spending whole summers alone in the mountains tending sheep. His only companions during such periods were his pistol, his dog, and occasionally some boys from the nearby Yakima Indian village.

Will's mother, who had never been a strong woman, did not thrive in the northwest. By the 1880s, she had developed a full-blown case of tuberculosis. In the fall of 1885, more probably the spring of 1886, leaving Nettie and Will in the care of Uncle George, Joseph took Sarah home to Illinois to seek better medical care then was available on the frontier. Family tradition has it that the White family tended toward the medical profession. It is therefore probable that it was to one of his physician relatives that Joseph took his desperately ill wife. It soon became apparent, however, that Sarah was not going to get better. When there no longer seemed to be any hope, Joseph summoned his children to cross the continent to be with their mother at the end.

William James (Will J.) White

Nettie made the painful decision to stay in Washington. She was soon to marry a neighbor named Schaeffer. They were wed in 1887. Little else is known about Nettie's life expect that she died in childbirth, complicated by a lung infection, on December 6, 1895.

It thus fell to Will to make the journey alone back to Illinois. How daunting it must have been for a thirteen-year-old frontier boy with all his worldly possessions in one small trunk (my mother still has it) to set out all alone on such an odyssey. No one ever said that Will J. lacked courage. He was a tough kid and would never change and thus later became a strong man. He did arrive in time to be with his mother at her death on November 17, 1886. With her passing, a new chapter had opened in Will's life.

Inexplicably, Joseph and Will lingered on in Illinois following

Sarah's death. The reason for this is not altogether clear, although it is probable that Joseph was devoting this time to getting Will raised and launched as an adult. What is known is that in 1889 Joseph married Jeannette (Jenny) Garwood from Stonington in Christian County, Illinois. Soon thereafter, Joseph and his new wife returned to the State of Washington. Will remained behind, probably helping to manage the Garwood farm, which Jenny had inherited, near Stonington. Joseph and Jenny remained in Washington for five years, returning to Illinois about 1895. Joseph died on September 9, 1896. But Jenny survived until 1937, when she died at her home on Cherokee Street, in Taylorville, at the age of 89.

My grandfather always said it was Jenny who actually raised him and for his part he became deeply devoted to her. Indeed, she probably was able to give him the nurturing which Sarah had been unable to provide due to her frail health and frontier hardships.

Will grew to manhood in Illinois. He had very little education and knew only farming, but he was possessed of enormous drive and a will of iron. If his business acumen, and perhaps luck, had been greater, he would have been a millionaire. Alas, he was doomed to a life of struggle against overwhelming odds, continuing to work himself to exhaustion, with very little to show for it.

At the death of his father, Will apparently inherited the prosperous Garwood farm. Since the property had been Jenny's, it was probably part of an arrangement by which Will received the farm in exchange for using what was left from the sale of Joseph's share of the horse ranch of Joseph's brother-in-law George to buy for Jenny the large, comfortable Cherokee Street house in Taylorville.

By 1898, when Will was 24, his prospects were as bright as they would ever be. He even felt secure enough to begin courting Pearl Eleanor

"Dolly" Wetzel, a vivacious young school teacher and daughter of a prominent farming family born on December 26, 1873, who lived not far away, near Stonington. The couple were married on March 28, 1899. Nonny often told the story of how their wedding took place on a rainy, dreary day with the church afloat on a sea of mud. Only in later years was she able to laugh at the memory of her father forgetting to remove his boots, with the result that he escorted her down the isle

Dolly Wetzel and her brother Mack Wetzel

leaving a trail of muddy footprints behind. One can imagine the young bride's chagrin at her father's gaucherie, which was probably made worse by titters from the congregation.

Soon after their marriage, Will sold his farm in Illinois, in favor of a sheep ranch in Texas. This venture only lasted a short time, however, for about 1900 Will and Dolly were settled on a farm near Lamar, Missouri. The neighboring farm was owned by Will's cousin, Albert D. Callison. It was while living in Missouri that the couple began their family. Eleanor was born in 1901, Mary in 1906, and Lois on February 6, 1908.

In 1912, Will J. and his cousin Albert, who was fondly known as Uncle Albert, sold their respective farms and moved to Rogers, Arkansas, where they pooled their resources to establish a funeral home. Lacking any interest in the day-to-day operation of a mortuary, Will J. settled his family on a fruit farm south of Rogers and just south of the site now occupied by the Rogers cemetery. By coincidence, their home was located just about a block east of where my parents now live at the time of this writing, at 1400 South 9th Street.

Sometime later Will sold out his share of the funeral home to Uncle Albert. However, due to unwise investments and reverses in the farming business, Will was eventually forced to sell the fruit farm. He moved his family to a smaller and somewhat less pretentious farmstead north of Rogers on the road that later became State Highway 101, just west of its intersection with US 62. Ironically, their

Will J., Eleanor, and Dolly White

new home was less than a mile north of the large and prosperous farm and homestead of a family named Duty.

In their new location and reduced circumstances, Will and Dolly eked out an existence with blood, sweat, and deteriorating health. In spite of the relentless demands of a hardscrabble Ozark farm, they still found time to be active in the Methodist church, where Nonny taught Sunday school for many years.

In the early 1940s, Nonny and Granddaddy finally had to give up farming and moved to town. With the proceeds of the farm, they bought a newsstand on south First Street and signed the mortgage for a home on north Third. Together, they ran the newsstand, called the In-and-Out Store,

Mary, Dolly, and Lois White

until Will's health became too fragile, about 1950. He was of tough pioneer

Lois, Mary, and Eleanor White

stock, though, and even with his body crippled by strokes, he put in an acre-sized garden each spring and tended a flock of hens. Regardless of the obstacles, Will never stopped trying for as long as he drew breath. Even at the end, on June 1, 1957, he died hard. Whereas some people peacefully slip away in their sleep, Will J. physically wrestled with the Angel of Death until the very end.

As the grandchildren and great-grandchildren came along, Dolly became known as Nonny and remained in reasonably good health, reigning as a grand old lady until her death at 100 on March 16, 1974. Her death was as peaceful and gentle as Will's was difficult. My sister Carolyn and I were there. I remember Nonny as a true gentlewoman with a Christian soul, a sharp sense of humor, and an implacable will to survive. For Granddaddy, I can only say that no man ever worked so hard for so little, never ceasing to exhibit the indomitable spirit of a pioneer adventurer and the sentimental soul of a loving father and husband. They never received all they deserved, but they deserved in overwhelming measure everything that they did achieve.

**Left:
Mary, Dolly, and
Lois White**

**Right:
Lois and Mary
White**

Left:
Lois and
her two
sisters,
Eleanor
and Mary

Right:
Moses
Wetzel,
Dolly, Lois,
and Baby
Davis

Left:
Will J. and Dolly
(1933)

Right:
Will J. and Dolly
(1956)

Left: Lois and Nonny (Dolly) on her
100th birthday with her $100 money tree
Right: Dolly on the Balcutha in
San Francisco (1958)

Chapter 5

A First Hand Account
by Lois White Duty

Reproduced with the generous permission of the author

I am Lois Duty, formerly Lois White. My family moved to Rogers in 1912. I was four years old at that time. When I was five, my parents enrolled me in Miss Nellie Morgan's kindergarten. This was located on the west end of the property on which the Elmwood school is now located. It was a small one-room school building and was a private school. As I remember it, Miss Nellie taught three grades: Kindergarten, first, and second. She had a small enrollment of not more than 15 or 20 students.

At that time, the central grade school of Rogers was located in the old Academy building on the grounds where the Elmwood school is now located. There were two two-story red brick buildings, one immediately behind the other. They faced east and the administration building stood behind the classroom building. Mr. Alcorn was the Principal when I was enrolled in the third grade. He lived with his family in the administration building. My third grade teacher was Miss May Pitts, who later married Clyde Young. A few years later, she became the business teacher at the Rogers High School.

The first and second grades were in the administration building. The third, sixth, seventh, and eighth were in the front building. The fourth and fifth were in the High School building, using the rooms at the east and west ends of the second floor. This building was located on west Walnut Street, where the First Federal and Loan is now.

When I was in the fourth grade, my teacher was Miss Alice Bowen. Later, she married Harvey Tual. My fifth grade teacher was Miss Garnet Dunham, who married Dr. Curry several years later. The first floor of the high school was really the furnace room and work shop, along with rest rooms for the boys. Across the hall from these rooms was a long room that ran full length of the building. This was our play ground in bad weather. The floor was where they had put the cinders from the coal furnaces. It was a dark and gloomy place and was not too clean. Immediately behind the west end of the high school was a veterinarian's home and place of business. All of his veterinarian work was done in a shed-like building and we students could hear the noises from the animals when they were being treated.

For the sixth, seventh, and eighth grades, we were back at the Academy. My teachers were Miss Florence Robinson and Mr. Tommy Locke. Mr. Locke was the Principal. It was during those years when they had May Day celebrations and the school children had an important part in it. We practiced our winding the May Pole for many days before the final celebration. There was a grandstand at the east end of the campus where the bands and important speakers performed. From the school building to the grandstand, there were two rows of large maple trees. They were spaced far enough apart that a large group of children could march to the grandstand. The winding of the May Pole was done on the north side of the trees. One year, it rained on the day of the celebration and I can remember how pitiful we all looked in our cheese cloth dresses clinging to our bodies, but we danced anyway.

I entered high school in 1921. Mr. Jim Oliver was the Superintendent and Mr. Birch Kirksey was the Principal. Mr. Oliver was succeeded by Mr. Charles Baldwin. Mr. Baldwin was the senior English teacher. Mr. Kirksey was the Principal all during my high school years. He taught mathematics and was a splendid teacher. I had him for my math teacher for my full four years. We all loved him and respected him. He was a very strict disciplinarian and during those years there were few real problems. He was a friend to all of the students and expected them to follow the rules.

During these years, Latin and Spanish were offered for the foreign language requirements. Home economics was very popular with the girls. Nearly every girl took a year or two of home economics. The class rooms were in two separate rooms which had formerly been regular class rooms. One was used for cooking classes and the other was the sewing room. I think we had two stoves at that time and about three sewing machines. Ruth Powell was the home

Lois White, 1927

economics teacher. She had just finished at the University the year before she began teaching. Later on, she became the State Supervisor for Home Economics in the schools. I kept in touch with Ruth through the later years and she would laugh and tell me that at the time she was teaching she was just three or four years older than her students, but at that time none of us realized it. We admired her very much. Debate was another class that was popular. Possibly it was called speech class. I am not too sure. Needless to say, I did not take it, but I always enjoyed listening to the debates that were held at night in the auditorium. The town people would come to hear the students debate. Sometimes they would have a prominent person join in on the debate.

During the school year, we would have the annual Class Night Carnival. The different classes would have booths and show their school work. Also, there would be booths selling hamburgers, hot dogs, etc. These booths were set up in the second and third floor halls. Later in the evening, they would have class skits presented in the auditorium. These were more to the ridiculous side than the serious. We worked weeks getting ready for Class Night and it was a real highlight of the school year.

Sports were very popular then as they are now, but on a very different scale. They had football, basketball, and baseball for the boys. I can only remember we had basketball for the girls. The first football field I can remember was located on Highway 62, just one block north of the intersections of Highway 12 and 62. When I entered high school, they had moved the football field to the northeast corner of the intersection of the highways. There were no bleachers or seats of any kind and the spectators stood through the entire game. Needless to say, there were not too many spectators. The cheerleaders were boys and all they had to do was yell through a megaphone and try to get the crowd to yell. There were just two of them as I recall.

The football team wore khaki uniforms, which were rather baggy. They had a conference at that time and played about the same teams they play today. For their non-conference games, they played Watts, Oklahoma, Joplin, Missouri, and Ft. Smith, Arkansas. Probably there were others that I cannot recall. To get to Watts and Ft. Smith, they traveled by train. For other towns nearer, they went in privately owned cars.

The basketball team was not given the importance they are today. They had to play on outdoor courts entirely. They played the teams from the nearby towns. The girls' basketball team also had to play on outdoor courts. I played on the team during my junior and senior years. One year, one of the girls' fathers let us practice upstairs over his business building on south First Street. We had to walk from the school to practice and then back to the school to change our clothes. During those days, we gave little thought to walking where we needed to go. After walking to and from practice, I had to walk a mile to my home. It never seemed to bother me too much for I was used to walking. The girls' uniforms were baggy black bloomers, worn with

white middy blouses that were also baggy. I recall one year when we went to Fayetteville to a conference. One team we had to play wore shorts and blouses. It made the rest of us feel very

Lois Duty, 1954

out of date. The next year, we had new uniforms and were very up to date.

I graduated from high school in 1925 in a class of fifty students. It was the largest class they had ever had and they made quite a to-do out of it. After graduating from Missouri University, I married and raised a family. In 1952, I began teaching in the Rogers junior high, which was in the high school, along with the senior high school classes. The junior high consisted of the seventh and eighth grades. By this time, Mr. Birch Kirksey

Lois Duty, 1960

was the Superintendent of the Rogers school system. He was still the strict disciplinarian that I had remembered from my youthful days, but he was the same sweet, kind man and a friend to all. We admired him very much and felt a great loss when he retired.

Our next Superintendent was Mr. Greer Lingle. Rogers was most fortunate in their selection of a man to fill Mr. Kirksey's place. Mr. Lingle was the Superintendent as long as I taught. I cannot say enough kind words about him. He was close to his teachers and always gave his time to listen to any problem that would arise. He stood behind us one hundred percent.

During my years as a teacher, we had several Principals. Joe Faye Moore was the Principal at the old high school when I started teaching. Next was Mr. Gaines, followed by Mr. Howard Sutton. When the campus-type school was built in 1962, Mr. Sutton was our Principal. The junior high took over the old high school building on Walnut Street.

Following Mr. Sutton as Principal was Mr. Bill Grimes, with John Ford as assistant. I retired in 1973 after teaching 21 years in the Rogers school system. They were years full of happiness, along with gratitude in seeing our school system growing and improving with the times. I was proud of having the privilege of helping teach our young folk. My years were filled with many happy memories and a sense of fulfillment.

Chapter 6

Lois and Jeff—The Honeymoon Years
1927-1934

My parents, Lois and Jeff, both grew up in Rogers. Lois was a tall (5'8") and slender brunette. Her beauty can be attested to by the fact that she was a princess in the Apple Blossom Festival in 1925. Jeff was also tall (6'1") and was robust with a head of curly black hair. While Lois was from a farm family, Jeff was from a well-to-do professional family.

Apparently, even though they had known of each other through school, they were hardly aware of one another until one Sunday in the early summer of 1927 when Jeff beheld a vision of loveliness dressed in white and carrying a bouquet of flowers as she came down the isle of the Methodist

Lois White, 1928

Church. Lois had just finished her sophomore year at the University of Missouri. Jeff had completed his freshman year at the University of Arkansas, in Fayetteville. Although a year and a half older than Lois, he had stretched his high school career to five years in order to play more football. As a result, she started college in 1925, but he didn't get around to it until 1926.

Jeff Duty, 1930

Although they had known each other all of their lives, the spark wasn't struck until that Sunday in June 1927. It had to survive some separation, too. Lois went off almost immediately to work as an advance agent on the Chitaqua Circuit. In fact, it was the very last year of the Chitaquas and the end of an era and tradition. Lois' job was to travel by train around the northern mid-west, arriving in a town ahead of the show to arrange for advertising and ticket sales. So far as I know, she was the first member of the immediate family to reach as far north as Bismarck, North Dakota.

Lois and Jeff corresponded and dated when they could throughout her junior year at the MU and his second year at the UofA. Things must have heated up, though, in the summer of 1928 because they became formally engaged in September, just before Lois returned to Columbia for her senior year. After finishing two years at the University of Arkansas having fun and playing football, Jeff decided to leave school. He spent the fall of 1928 and the spring of 1929 reading law in his father's law office in Rogers. Lois graduated in June 1929 with a Bachelors Degree in Education.

1922 Rogers High School Football Team

1) Penn Jones (LHB), 2) Lance Martin (QB), 3) Ray Hocott (HB), 4) JB Battenfield (Coach), 5) Don Deason (FB), 6) Keith Parsley (RHB), 7) Homer Coleman (Capt), 8) Charles Lester (End), 9) Robert Batjer (RG), 10) Milton Etris (RT), 11) David Long (End), 12) Jeff Duty (LT), 13) Harry Woodruff (RE), 14) Ralph Jackson (LG), 15) Russel Davis (C), 16) Dale Hoover (LT), 17) Preston Bowman (LE)

That summer was the first time that the couple had been able to actually spend much time together. Situations such as this can either make or break a relationship. Apparently it made theirs. In September, Lois headed for Claremore, Oklahoma, where she had been given a job teaching school. Jeff enrolled at Cumberland University Law School in Cumberland, Tennessee. She went to Claremore and he went to Cumberland, but in short order he was on a train to Claremore.

On September 14, 1929, they were secretly married and had a three-day local honeymoon until she had to go back to her teaching job and he had to go back to law school. Unfortunately, it was imperative that the marriage had to be kept under wraps because Lois' teaching contract forbade teachers to be married and Jeff had promised his parents to buckle down to his law studies. They didn't formally announce their marriage until the spring of 1930, after Lois had fulfilled her one-year teaching contract and Jeff had graduated from law school. By that time, she was pregnant and would not again see the inside of a school room from the perspective of a teacher's desk for another 18 years. For Jeff, it was straight into the law office and to work.

Lois, Carolyn, and Jeff Duty, 1932

Their first home was a frame house on south Fourth Street which Jeff's father had obtained in a mortgage foreclosure. It was his wedding gift to them. Jeff joined the family firm, and Lois began to raise their new family. She was not able to resume her teaching career until 1948.

There was one incident in the life of the young Mr. and Mrs. Jeff Duty which provides a picture of them as young, active, fun-loving adults. Lois and her best friend, Elaine Robinson, were out in the woods hunting wildflowers or mushrooms, or perhaps just enjoying nature. Lois stepped on what she thought was a mat of leaves and her foot sank through a depression in the ground. She kicked something hard that clinked. Scooping away the leaves, they found a cache of Mason jars full of

moonshine. This was during the depression.
With many giggles and a real sense of daring,
they scooped up what they could carry and
stowed it away in their car. Back home, Lois and
Jeff secreted their share of the loot beneath the
planks of the partially floored attic. Over a
period of time, the hidden trove was gradually
depleted, but even a year or so later there was still
a sizable jug-full in the hidey hole.

Then the day came when the electric
doorbell ceased to function. Electricians were

Jeff Duty, 1947

duly called, and two young men dutifully appeared and tramped up to the
attic where they could get at the wiring. It seemed strange that it took them
almost three days to complete the job, not to mention the extraordinary
problems which they encountered. Not only did they become quite raucous,
laughing and cutting-up, but they also had a great deal of difficulty
connecting the wiring properly. At one point, the doorbell button turned on
the lights and the light switch rang the door chimes. Finally, though, they
got the job done and departed with their tools.

Several days later, Jeff happened to go up to the attic to check his
remaining moonshine stock, only to find that the jug was as dry as Old
Mother Hubbard's cupboard. Suddenly, all became clear, but it was too late
to do anything about it. In the first place, the Dutys and Robinsons were
technically violating the law by consuming prohibited liquor. In the second
place, Lois and Elaine had stolen the hooch from somebody who just might
not feel kindly disposed toward those who had so cavalierly relieved them of
their White Lightnin'.

The only moral which I can see in this tale is that it behooves one to
take pains to hide your contraband booze well enough so that it won't be
accidentally discovered by children or electricians. It also reflects that Lois
and Jeff were not always as sedate and dignified as they would become in

later life. If this little vignette were to be made a chapter by itself, it would have to be entitled, "A Batch in the Belfry."

Jeff Duty, 1994

Jeff Duty, 1960

Left and above:
Lois and Jeff Duty, 1980s

Lois and Jeff Duty, 60th Wedding
Anniversary, 1989

Duty honored for contributions to law

By HETTA MARTIN
News Staff Writer

BENTONVILLE — "If you don't have Jeff Duty, you don't love the law."

Those were the words spoken by Benton County Circuit Judge Tom Keith and expressed by several others at a dinner honoring Duty Thursday night at the Elks Lodge in Bentonville.

Duty, 86, has been practicing law, primarily in Benton County, since 1930. And although things

have changed in Benton County over the past 63 years, Duty continues to defend clients and win cases.

Benton County Circuit Judge Sid McCollum said of the 100 plus crowd gathered Thursday. "They are here because not only do they honor you, they respect you and they love you."

Duty said the tribute dinner was the highlight of his career and he thanked those who have

❑ See Duty / A3

Nation / Region　　　　Northwest Arkansas Times

Duty

❑ Continued from A1

helped him to continue his career.

"Without the help of four people I never could have gone on," Duty said naming his wife, Lois, his long-time secretary, Marlene Dryden, and Springdale attorneys W.H. Taylor, and Sam Sexton.

Duty was referred to several times Thursday as a "law lawyer." The white-haired man, with his familiar black cane in hand, laughed as Washington County Chancellor Thomas Butt talked about how Duty is notorious for holding case law that no other lawyer has ever heard of.

"He would have you not a new apercu before you even knew he had the book out," Butt said.

J. Wesley Sampier, a retired Benton County attorney, ended his speech with a phrase he said he'd heard many times during his career. "If you done it, get Jeff Duty to defend you."

Duty's main defense is the law. He is known for using the law to convince judges his client should not be convicted.

Keith said once when he was a municipal judge, Duty appeared in his court, with a client whose probation was set to be revoked. Duty told Keith that the law did

not allow him to revoke the client's probation because he did not give the authority to place her on probation.

The next case on the docket was another case in which a woman was to plead guilty to her charge. Duty argued that the judge should put her on probation.

When Keith confronted Duty about the discrepancy in his two arguments, Duty replied, "I object, this was a different case."

"As a trial lawyer, he had few equals and no superiors," Butt said.

Duty has another trademark in the legal profession. "He got more continuances than any dozen lawyers," Keith said.

Taylor referred to a case which was set for trial by then Circuit Judge William Enfield.

Taylor said Duty told Enfield he could not try the case on the day it was set and Enfield replied that the case was set and that's when it would be heard.

Duty informed the judge that if the case went to trial on the date set, "I'll have a stroke and we won't try it."

Taylor said Duty took him under his wing when Taylor was a young lawyer and came to the elder attorney and said, "Jeff, if you don't help me out I'm gonna starve to death."

He, and Duty started handling this case then and the friendship and working relationship started there.

Taylor said one of the best compliments he has received in his law career was when a judge said, "You've been around but damn Jeff Duty too long."

Sampier, who has practiced law alongside Duty since the beginning, talked of the things that have changed since Duty first began.

The courthouse that now sits on the Bentonville town square was the new courthouse during the early days of Duty's career. New county officials say it's much too overcrowded and a new courthouse complex must be built.

Many years ago, Sampier said, hundreds of people would flock to the courthouse to watch trials. Now, there is less public interest, Sampier said.

"I started in the horse and buggy days," Duty said. "And here I am in the auto jet days."

Perhaps one of the reasons Duty is held in such high regard is his charitable heart. Duty agreed to Thursday's dinner on the condition that the proceeds go to provide legal assistance to the poor. The Benton County Bar Association in conjunction with Ozark Legal Services organized the din-

ner in honor of Duty.

Duty has been both a prosecuting and defense attorney in Rogers and in the past has as Benton County prosecuting attorney and as chief assistant the criminal division of the attorney general's office.

A number of local bars and restaurants donated drinks, decorations and for the event.

READ IN TH TIME

Crabtree & Ev

Fine Soaps and T

Melody's C

58 years and counting: Rogers attorney Jeff Duty jokes with a roomful of lawyers and other friends during a surprise party honoring Duty's 58 years as an attorney. Duty went to work as a lawyer in Rogers July 14, 1930. Duty has worked in Rogers most of his career. He worked a few years at the Attorney General's office in Little Rock and four years in Fayetteville. About 40 people attended the party at the law offices of Paul Davidson and Keith Duncan in Bentonville Wednesday afternoon. Duty said he has no plans to retire.

JEFF DAVIS SR. & LOIS WHITE
1906 — 1993

Chapter 7

My Early Years
1934-1940

I began this incarnation in our home at 204 South Fourth Street in Rogers, Arkansas, at approximately 6:00 am on December 20, 1934. At the time, my mother was twenty-six years old and my father was twenty-eight. I was preceded in the family circle by a brother, John William, who was born on March 13, 1931, and by a sister, Carolyn Beth, born on May 11, 1932. On November 10, 1938, I acquired a younger brother, John White Duty. My older brother only lived a few hours, but the rest of us prospered and prosper still (as of the time of this writing).

For the first five years of my life, we lived an idyllic, Garden-of-Eden existence. My father was an Assistant District Attorney and was later elected to the office of District Attorney in his own right. I vividly remember our pet dogs named Sadie and

Toddler Davis, 1935

Grandmother Nonny holding baby Davis

Pepper. I also vividly recall my sister as a little girl. In my mental photo gallery, she will ever remain a gorgeous and delightful child of five years. She dramatically resembled the then-famous Shirley Temple, especially with her crown of golden curls. That is until one fateful day when she got hold of a pair of scissors and began determinably to snip off those self-same curls.

Perhaps it was at that moment that her future shifted from stage and fame to one of academic pursuits and, eventually, marriage and motherhood. But I think it sure did break our mother's heart to see those curls go.

From the outset, John was the cherished baby of the family, but was always his own man. It is hard to believe that the ugly bright red little body which I saw in a crib the day after his birth has become a well-built 220+ pounds, 6'2", craggy-featured husband, father of four, grandfather of two, retired Air Force Lieutenant Colonel, and proprietor of the promising Golden Fried Chicken

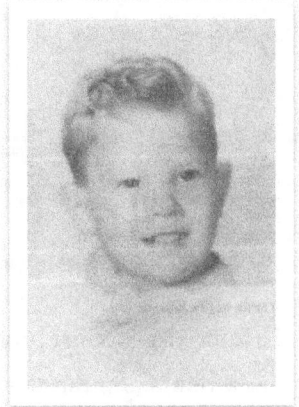

Davis, age 3

Baby brother John

Davis, age 4

franchise in Rogers. But maybe it was all to be expected since as a tiny boy he was independence personified. He could entertain himself for hours with only two pans and a spoon.

When I was about four years old, I distinctly recall my first lesson in morality. I had two best friends, Billy Love and his brother Jerry. Billy's father was a traveling salesman for the Smith Cough Drop Company. He kept his spare supplies stacked

Davis and Carolyn

in cartons in his bedroom. Over a period of time, Billy and I began to help ourselves to more and more of the cough drops until we became true cough drop junkies. Then, one fateful day, Mr. Love caught us with our hands literally in the carton. He delivered a scolding (which in retrospect was probably very mild, but which scared me to death) and I hurried home to sit in despair beneath the

Davis and Billy Love

snowball bush outside my bedroom window until I could screw up enough courage to go in and confess all to my mother. When I did, she promptly bathed me, dressed me in clean clothes, combed my hair, and marched me back across the street to face the music and apologize. I think that I can truthfully say that since that day I have not stolen and have been

Carolyn, Lois, and Davis

extraordinarily aware of the property
rights of others.

Then, in 1939, real life intruded
into the Garden of Eden. About the
week of my fifth birthday, just before
Christmas of 1939, I became very sick.
According to what I have picked up
over the years, I came down with the
mumps, measles, scarlet fever, and
the flu simultaneously. Separately,
or even in combination, these are not

**Carolyn, Lois, Will J.,
Davis, and Nonny**

quite so serious today. However, this occurred just prior to the wartime
antibiotic breakthroughs. The wonder drug of the day was then
Sulfanilamide, which had just been developed by the Germans and was very
scarce. During the course of my illness, I apparently developed an extremely
high fever for a long period of time. For some reason, I experienced
widespread hemorrhaging including the interior of the eyeballs. As a result,
I lost my sight. In desperation my parents took me to Barnes Hospital in St.
Louis. I can still remember my grandfather, Will J. White, carrying me on
board the train and putting me to bed in a compartment. He gave me a
leather coin purse of the old fashioned kind with two snap closures on top,
one for a shallow pocket and the other for a deep pocket. You could keep
your bills in one and your change in the other, or maybe even your chewing
tobacco. I cherished that old fashioned wallet for many years. In any event,
the specialists in St. Louis could do no more for me than Dr. McNeil or Dr.
Hodges in Rogers. They pumped me full of Sulfanilamides, only to later
realize that I was immune to its effect. I did recover from my combination
of illnesses, though, and returned home in fairly good condition. The only
lasting effect was total blindness. This, of course, was a major turning point
in my life.

After convalescence, the biggest problem confronting my parents (and incidentally me) was schooling. Ordinarily, I would have been enrolled in a kindergarten the following September, 1940. However, they were in a quandary as to what to do. On the one hand, they didn't want to leave our family home in Rogers, but on the other, they were made aware of the School for the Blind in Little Rock. They simply could not decide whether to send me away from home for school in Little Rock or some other alternative. So they compromised. My mother and we three children moved to Little Rock and rented a house. My father stayed in Rogers with his law practice, but came to see us on weekends. We even bought a second-hand car for him to drive (brown as I recall).

I went to kindergarten at the School for the Blind for half a year. My parents finally decided that I wasn't learning anything that I couldn't have learned at home and that I was not thriving in the atmosphere then existing at the school, even though I was only a day student. Therefore, we moved back to Rogers, and my parents began to wrestle with the problem of my education. The kindergarten experience at the School for the Blind had convinced my parents that I would not thrive in such an institution, especially on a full-time basis. They also did not want to send me away from home. Of course, none of this affected me much since I just continued to be a little boy doing the same things I had always done

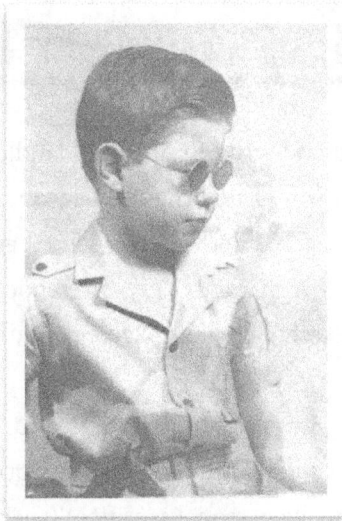

Davis, age 6

before, although learning to do them without vision. For a while, I had to wear pads over my eyes while they healed. Then they tried having me wear sunglasses, but I soon threw them away and just went on being me. But the question of my schooling remained.

In the summer of 1940, my mother began to wonder why I couldn't simply go to public schools. Mr. Birch Kirksey, who was then the Superintendent of the Rogers schools, was an old friend of the family. She sought him out and proposed that I begin regular school. My parents agreed to obtain the special tutoring for me

THURSDAY, DECEMBER 21, 19█

Social and P█

Alyda Greene, Editor—Telephone 8

DAVIS DUTY OBSERVES HOLIDAY BIRTHDATE

Davis Duty, son of Mr. and Mrs. Jeff Duty, celebrated his fifth birthdate Wednesday afternoon when his mother was hostess to a large group of his little friends at a birthdate party in the Duty home, North Fourth street. Mrs. Duty was assisted in entertaining the children by her mother, Mrs. Will J. White.

Games were played both in and out of doors. The house was gala with seasonal decorations, prominent among which was a beautifully lighted tree. At the close of the entertainment hour guests were ushered and seated at long tables in the dining room. Table decorations bore out further evidence of the artistic and original touch of Mrs. Duty's hand. Small chocolate Santas were found at the plate of each young guest as favors.

The guest list included Bill and Jerry Love, George and John Rex, Rex Allen, Patty Carter, Wanda Lee, Marilyn and Marvin Kirby, Montie Howard, Mary and Jerry Lee, Jolinn Duty, Silvia Butt, Laurie Kay Lester, Melba Jo Helmick, Ruth Kelly and Bobbie Burns.

Davis Duty, son of Mr. and Mrs. Jeff Duty, is reported to be slightly improved Tuesday morning after having been critically ill at the Duty home since last Saturday. Davis is suffering from complications of influenza and while he was thought to be a trifle better Tuesday morning, his condition is still considered grave. Carolyn Duty, also ill of influenza, is much improved.

which I would need to learn in order to read and write Braille and handle any other problems that might occur. In other words, nothing special would be asked of the schools. Mr. Kirksey readily agreed and I began school at Central Ward Grade School in Rogers. Apparently my preschool preparation had been adequate, because they started me in the second grade rather than the first.

Before I go any farther, I must, with gratitude and love, give credit where credit is due to my mother. Although she had my father's support every step of the way, plus his willingness to make personal sacrifices (such as living apart from his family for much of 1940), it was my mother who had the determination to keep me at home and conceived of the idea of sending me to public schools. This was no mean achievement, since, to my knowledge, no other blind student had ever done it in Arkansas, especially at the primary school level. She first had the idea, then she had to work out the details and logistics. Finally, she had to convince the school officials.

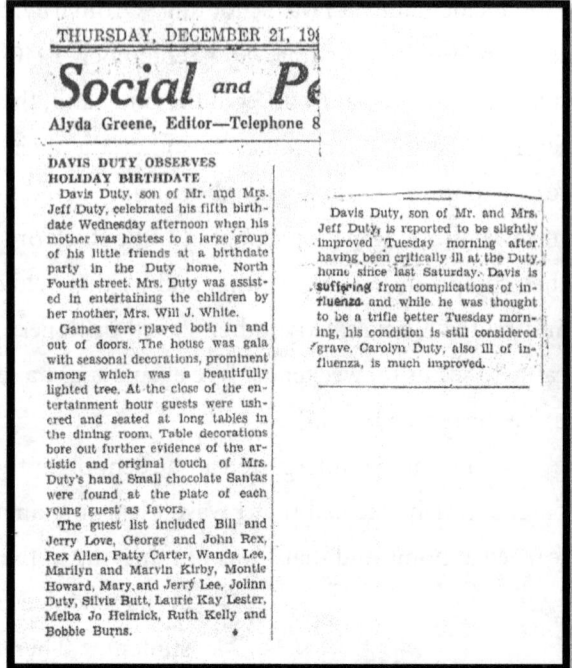

After that, she had to undertake, and did so with all of the grit and determination which is her strength (which she says she got from her father), to encourage, inspire, and sometimes bully me into making the extra effort necessary to compete in the sighted school environment. Without my mother's vision and her iron will, my life would have followed an altogether different road. As a result, my mother and I have shared a special closeness which we both cherish, based upon mutual respect, appreciation, and a common sense of accomplishment. I can truly say that besides being my mother, Lois Duty is also my dearest friend.

For the next four years, my parents hired girls recently graduated from the School for the Blind to tutor me. They would attend school with me for at least half a day and during off periods work on my reading and writing in Braille and help me with my homework. The first of these was Alva Howard of Little Rock and the second was Helen Vargo of Fort Smith. By the time I entered the sixth grade, I no longer needed special tutors, and they were dispensed with. From that point forward, I was on my own. Of course, my mother, who was a certified teacher in her own right, helped me with my homework for the rest of the time I was in school, even reading some of my books on tape when I was later in law school. Apparently, she handled the problem right, because I led my class academically until I left Rogers at the end of the eighth grade.

Above: Alva Howard
Below: Helen Vargo
and Davis

By the time he was four, my brother

John and I had worked out what was for me a
very satisfying relationship. Whenever I was
engaged in one of my endless projects and
needed something which I didn't want to take
the time or was too lazy to get for myself, I
would raise my face to the sky and intone,
"Fairy, Fairy, wherever you are, bring me a
(whatever)." John would promptly retrieve
the desired object and, tiptoeing up, lay it
down in front of me. I found this
arrangement completely acceptable until the
day that he did not respond with the desired

Brother John, age 5

alacrity. I raised my voice in a more peremptory tone for the good Fairy to
get off his posterior and get with it. Whereupon, retaining the anonymity of
his location by stealth, John began throwing rocks at me. Eventually, he did
more rock throwing than errands. I finally countered his assaults by
grabbing whole hands full of rocks and throwing them at him. Some always
hit. After all, I always did know where he was, at least in general, because he
was never as silent as he thought.

I don't want it thought, though, that I was a wholly sedentary child.
Actually, I probably tended more in the other direction. My mother still tells
the story how one morning early in the summer following my illness she
looked out the kitchen window to see me high in the Chinese elm tree which
grew behind sister Carolyn's play house. Concerned that she might frighten
me, she called to me in a very nonchalant voice to be careful and to not stay
up there too long. When I returned to earth safely, she was probably much
relieved, but I supposed I had proved myself, because she never again
remonstrated with me about climbing trees.

Later on, I became a competent roller-skater, employing the
sidewalks in our neighborhood. (I don't remember there being skating rinks
in those days). I also became rather proficient on a bicycle. Of course, I had

enough sense (usually) not to ride alone in the street. Later, when Brother John was six or seven, we worked out a tandem arrangement in which he sat on the seat and steered the bike, while I sat behind and peddled with his feet on top of mine for extra oomph when needed.

Then there were the more organized types of sports. There were endless backyard football games involving anywhere from one to twenty on a team. I never could figure out how to bat in baseball, but I became a fairly capable pitcher. We couldn't always afford baseballs, though. Our favorite substitute was a tin can. After being hit a few times, it would squash into a jogged lump of metal. It made for terrific curve balls, but to get hit by a line drive was to risk life and limb. Another favorite was a cork wrapped in adhesive tape. They were too good, though. When hit, they would usually go out of sight and be lost.

Carolyn, Davis, and John

In the wintertime, we had fewer outdoor activities, although I prided myself on making life-size snowmen. But there was always Jimmy Carter and his sled trains. He was the father of one of my sister's friends, and he was the ultimate outdoorsy type. When the snow was fresh on the ground, he would use his car as a locomotive to tow long strings of coaster sleds. He loved to gun the car around a comer causing a whip-crack effect in the train. If you fell off of your sled, you simply went to the curb and sat down and

waited for the train to come around again.

There were also the more social and less physical activities. Until the custom died out sometime around the beginning of World War II, the advent of spring was celebrated by the children of the town every first day of May with the delivery of May Baskets. These were homemade affairs, usually consisting of cut-down cardboard boxes. Round oatmeal boxes were perfect. The boxes were then sheathed with brightly colored crepe paper. Handles were attached. A few pieces of candy were laid in the bottom and covered to the baskets brim with flowers. The blooms from our snowball bush were my favorites. We would then go from one friend's house to another, stealthily place a basket on the porch, hide in the bushes, and yell as loud as we could, "M a y B a s k e t s!" Custom required that the name of the giver be written on a piece of paper laid in the bottom of the basket. This was sometimes omitted where girlfriends were concerned and we were too shy to admit our crush. Of course, there were also the trick May Baskets. You could tie a string to the May basket and run it to your hiding place. Then when the recipient bent over to pick up the basket, it could be slowly pulled away, leaving him or her grabbing and staggering. Only "bad kids" did this, though. I never actually did it, but there sure were moments of temptation.

I also tried my hand at scouting, but could never quite get into it. As a Cub Scout I became a Wolf, and as a Boy Scout, a Tenderfoot, the lowest earned rank in both. My mother even became a Den Mother when I was a Cub Scout, hoping, I think, to give me a little nudge. The thing I remember best about Cub Scouting, though, was the running and screaming of all of the Cubers at Pack Meetings, causing complete pandemonium, and the wartime paper drive in which our Den participated. Two friends and I pulled a cart all over town collecting old newspapers and magazines. Back at home, we tied the paper into bundles for delivery to the collection center. I found the whole thing dull. I guess I was never cut out for group activities, unless I could be the chief and tell the others what to do.

Chapter 8

The War Years
1940-1947

Like a million other Americans who were children between 1940 and 1946, although life went on, everything was overshadowed by World War II.

I vividly remember the day that Pearl Harbor was bombed, the day that President Roosevelt died, and the climactic aftermath events of the atomic bomb dropped on Hiroshima. All three are memories I could do without.

The most vivid day-to-day memories which I have from those years relate to things warlike. As was true throughout the nation, my whole life was involved with war and soldiers until 1945. We played Soldier. We played with (toy) soldiers. We built airplanes, guns, and tanks, etc. Although metal toys were non-existent because of the war, the stores were full of wooden, papier-mâché, and rubber replicas of military rifles, machine-guns, and cardboard pop-out sets of soldiers to replace the old tin soldiers which were the bread and butter of the toy business pre-1940. I finally learned to make almost anything military, from airplanes to tents, out of cardboard and wrought havoc upon the cardboard inserts from my father's shirts when they came back from the laundry. What I couldn't do with a piece of cardboard, pair of scissors, and pot of flour-water paste!

Other than preoccupation with war, I do not remember a great deal about those years. Perhaps, if the truth be known, I was too young to be interested in much besides my own pursuits, my friends, school, and my ever present radio adventures. Hop Harrigan and Captain Midnight were much more real to me than President Roosevelt or Winston Churchill. Still, I do have some memories of community activities which reflect the spirit and atmosphere of the times.

I remember going with my family to Bingo Evenings held at the high school gym. I did not know any of the details, but I suspect that entrance fees were somehow or other

Davis (far right) with childhood friends

destined for the War Effort. I do know that the prizes were donated by local merchants. The grand prize was usually a blanket, and I remember that the local bakery (Harris Baking Company) baked miniature loaves of their bread, which were the minimum prizes awarded. Whole families attended and the gym would be full of adults sitting in metal chairs at long tables with children running everywhere. I wonder how they managed to keep the noise level sufficiently down to allow for bingo.

I also remember Rogers' introduction to the roller skating fad. Again, I don't know how it was connected with the war effort, although I am sure it was. What I do remember is that the event was held at the National Guard Armory and we attended as families. First there was dinner (and I don't remember whether it was pot luck or paid for), after which the tables were moved back and skating began to the accompaniment of records. Dr. Hollis Buckaloo was the master of ceremonies that first evening. His being there tends to confuse the time factor since he had been a doctor in the Navy and did not return to Rogers to practice until the end of the war. Still, he was there. Perhaps he was on leave. The number one song of the time was "A Pistol Packin' Mama." I think I heard it for the first time that night and it has always been associated in my mind with that evening and roller skating. I also remember that the event was slightly marred by the fact that the floor of the Armory was cement, and the roller skating created clouds of cement dust. In fact, the event was only repeated once or twice more before being discontinued, primarily because of the dust and possible health risks.

I still have a vivid memory, though, of my folks saying their farewells and taking our leave to the strains of those immortal lyrics, "I met her in a cabaret and was she havin' fun, until one night, she shot the light and now I'm on the run. Lay that pistol down, babe, lay that pistol down. Pistol packin' mama, lay that pistol down."

Perhaps events such as those I have described reflected how people were brought together by the war or perhaps it was merely that Rogers was still a small town where everyone knew everyone else and town social events were still possible. Whatever the factors which made such events feasible, though, it is blatantly evident that this phenomena could not be repeated today. Even in small towns, people are far too sophisticated to take part in an evening of bingo or roller skating. I feel that in the passing of that era, we put aside childish things and in the process lost forever that simple, bright, straight forward and, yes, childlike view of life. I am not prepared to say that those were the good old days, but they were simpler, less frenetic and over all less stressful.

On a more personal level, though, it seems that the main focus of my daily life, at least through grade school, was my addiction, along with most other boys my age, to the afternoon adventure serials on radio. There was the Adventures

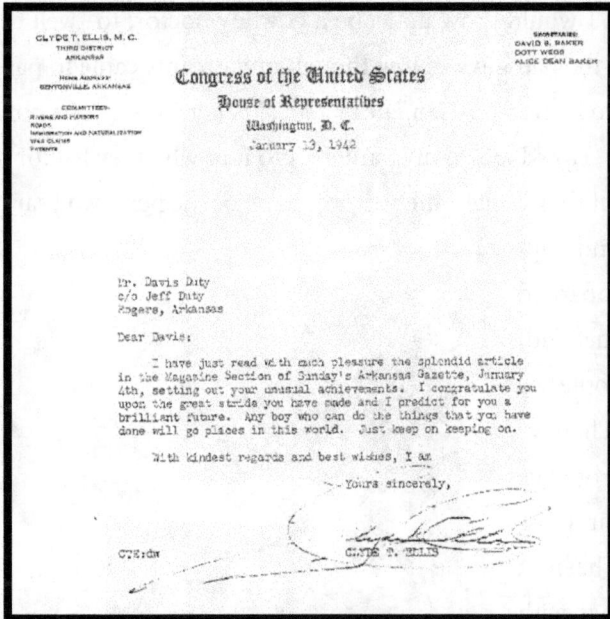

A letter from Davis' future father-in-law when he was eight

of the Sea Hound with Captain Silver; Terry and the Pirates (with the Dragon Lady); Hop Harrigan "Ace of the Airways"; Superman; Buck Rogers; Jack Armstrong "The All American Boy"; Sky King; Tom Mix; but best of all Captain Midnight with his secret codographs and coded messages. I must have eaten tons of various cereals just to obtain the box tops which could be sent off in exchange for marvelous prizes such as plastic arrowheads which glowed in the dark and had a fold out magnifying glass, secret codographs disguised as badges and whistles, cardboard models of wartime aircraft, and on and on. I would sit by my radio each afternoon from 4:30 to 6:00 ruining my supper with peanut butter and crackers (a lifelong favorite) and longing for all of the wonderful and mysterious treasures which I could possess if only I could choke down yet another box of some atrocious breakfast cereal. How simple life was and I didn't even know it.

In 1946, the war was over and I was horse crazy. For years I had been collecting model horses. When I was a very small boy, I was vociferous in my insistence that I would grow up to be a cowboy doctor, to "well the good guys and shoot the bad guys." Now though, my dreams came to pass. One day we came across an advertisement in a local paper for sale of a pony and her colt for $125. How I talked my parents into it or why they fell for it, I will never know. But they bought the pair for me. For the next two years I lived, breathed, ate, and slept horses. At first we boarded Star and her colt Comet with the Mortons, the people we bought them from. Then we moved them into our garage and let them eat our grass which had always been a mowing problem what with our one-fourth of a block of yard.

Davis with Star

Then, in 1947, when I was 12, my parents purely made the grand sacrifice. They rented our house to strangers and rented a small farm for us to live on just outside of town. I call it a farm, although it was just a few acres of pasture with a chicken house. My Granddaddy White gave me baby chicks, from which I raised broilers in the chicken house and later kept some of the pullets for hens to lay eggs. My horses were, I'm sure, much happier with more space and more grass. Of course, it was my job to clean the barn, feed the chickens, etc., etc. I loved every minute of it. I wonder now,

Davis with Comet

though, if carrying those hundred pound bags of oats wasn't subsequently reflected in the back problems which I experienced in later years. If so, I would probably do it again.

During this period, I rode Star, a small mustang type pony, until I outgrew her. Then I broke Comet to the saddle and rode her. I was a charter member of the Rogers Riding Club. We rode in rodeo grand entries, local parades, took overnight trail rides, and I even went on a fox hunt once. Of course, this only amounted to riding out in the dark away from the fire and sitting on your horses listening to the hounds "giving tongue" in the far distance. I loved it, I loved it, I loved it. I even had my first girlfriend. Her name was Helen Cochran. She had a horse named Ribbon and for a year or so we were almost inseparable. By the end, I was even noticing that she was somehow different from the boys I knew. But even this idyll had to come to an end. In 1948, it did.

Chapter 9

From the Pits to the Peaks
1948-Spring, 1952

In the spring of 1948, my father received an appointment as Assistant State Attorney General under Ike Murray, who was then the State Attorney General. He commuted between Little Rock and Rogers on weekends until

Duty Family Home 1948-51
12th Street Pike, Little Rock

Murry Names Jeff Duty as One of Aides

LITTLE ROCK, Dec. 22.—Attorney General-elect Ike Murry today announced the appointment of three more assistants, all of whom are now employed in the attorney general's office.

They are Jeff Duty, of Rogers, Cleveland Holland, of Fort Smith, and Arnold Adams of Batesville.

Murry previously announced the appointment of John Williams of Texarkana as his chief assistant. Two more appointments remain to be made to fill out the attorney general's staff.

Holland joined the department six years ago when Guy E. Williams, the retiring attorney general, took office. Adams was appointed two years ago, and Duty joined the staff in March of this year.

the family was able to move there that summer, horses and all. Because of the livestock, including sister Carolyn's dog, Frankfurter Von Pompom My Petit Cherie, III (a dachshund of course), John's and my collie, Lassie, who had wandered into our lives at the farm in Rogers, a cat and the three equine, Star, Comet, and Star's new colt Ginger my parents bought a house way out in what was then the boonies on Highway 12. It was on a big enough lot that half of it could be fenced off and a small stable built. Prior to the move, brother John had gotten into the horse act with his own pony, Trigger. But he was never very interested and decided to sell her before we went to Little Rock. His only real interest in the 12th Street property was the basketball hoop erected on the end of the stable and the private lake to which we had access. We swam and we fished, and for a while our lives were tranquil.

My mother went to work to supplement the family income, returning to teaching after having been away from it since 1930. She had trained as a secondary school teacher, but took the job where she was most needed as a kindergarten and first grade teacher. Carolyn enrolled in Little Rock High School, which was then probably the best high school in the state. John went to Centenary Grade School and began his schoolboy athletic career playing center field for the Centenary baseball team. But I was the one who found my life the most disrupted.

When I was 13, it was decided that, although I had prospered in public schools in Rogers, since we were in Little Rock we should give the state School for the Blind a try. I was dubious about the idea, but my parents finally talked me into it. I enrolled there for the ninth grade and proceeded to spend the most miserable year of my life. In fact, after almost forty-five years, I still have bad dreams. The problems were two-fold. First, I was an outsider and a day-student. Most of the other students were residential boarders. They resented me and never accepted me. There were several occasions when I was attacked physically, although I never suffered any serious injury.

The second problem was that the school administration didn't want to treat me differently from the others and felt compelled to stuff me into the then-prevailing mold for a blind person. Up until that time, I had never really thought of myself as being blind. During that year, though, I became vividly aware of my blindness. I had never thought that I was any different from anyone else, but now I was taught that I was. I had always managed to get about without any assistance, but now I was forced to learn to use a white cane. Perhaps it was unreasonable on my part, but I felt that this was not unlike the branding of a red letter "A" on the forehead of an adulteress in old

Carolyn, Davis, and John in 1951

Massachusetts. And being stubborn and willful to an unreasonable degree, I resisted. This did not endear me to either my peers or the school authorities.

I don't wish to leave the impression that all of the teachers were unkind or bullying. They were not. There was a Mrs. Wilkes, who taught science, who treated me very nicely. Mrs. Harper, who taught English, made absolutely no distinction and only sought to teach me English. But there were others, including the principal, who I felt went out of their way to make my life miserable.

The main thing I can remember of that year is sitting at the top of the steps up to the driveway every afternoon after 3:30 waiting for my father to pick me up. He seldom got there before 5:00 or 5:30; so I had plenty of time to do my homework and feel sorry for myself. All I really wanted to do was get home and play with and work with my horses. It is ironic that the trend today is to try to put blind students in public schools if at all possible rather than place them in the institutional environment. Unfortunately, it was far different in 1948.

As bad as that school year of 1948-49 turned out to be, it did serve to convince my parents that a change was indicated. Therefore, we went to the superintendent of the Little Rock School System and asked if I could return to the public schools. Virgil Blossom agreed without demur and in the fall of 1949 I enrolled in the tenth grade in Little Rock High School. It is unfortunate that this great school with its wonderful traditions and history has had its image marred by the integration crisis in 1957. For me, however, nothing can take away the wonderful memories that I have of my two years there. I made a myriad of friends who have remained my friends after all of these years. I was elected to the student council. I was tapped for the A Cappella Choir, which I still think was an outright gift since I do not possess a singing voice of any great quality. I was chosen for the National Honor Society. And I was picked as a member of the Key Club, which at the time was considered a valued recognition of leadership and popularity.

It would be meaningless to list all of my friends from those days. However, I will never forget Mrs. Reed, who was my homeroom teacher; Mrs. Lee, who taught me Latin; Mrs. Thompson (known as Miss Pinkie), the choir director; Miss Dowdel, who was a tough, but extremely effective English teacher; and Jesse Matthews, the principal. What a relief to have a principal whom I could respect and who also treated me courteously and with respect and just like all of the other students. For two years I cheered the Tigers, singing, "Hail to the Old Gold, Hail to the Black," and regained all of the self-assurance and self-confidence which had been stripped from me in the ninth grade. I sometimes think I reached my peak in the sense of self-accomplishment and self-pride in the eleventh grade in Little Rock High School. Nothing lasts forever, though, and the Little Rock High School idyll came to an end in the summer of 1951.

At the Capitol

Duty Resigns For Private Law Practice

Assistant Attorney General Jeff Duty has resigned to return to the private practice of law, Attorney General Ike Murray announced yesterday.

Duty is moving to Fayetteville where he will be associated with Rex W. Perkins. He formerly practiced law at Rogers.

Duty attended the University of Arkansas and graduated from the law school of Cumberland University. He served five terms on the Rogers City Council and two terms as prosecuting attorney of the Fourth Judicial District. He has been an assistant in the attorney general's office since March 1, 1948.

Murry said he regretted very much that Duty is leaving state service. "However the advantage and remuneration which have been offered to him are such that I can understand why he could not afford to refuse the offer," he said.

"During his service as assistant attorney general, Mr. Duty has been connected with much of the more important litigation involving the state. I regret very much to lose his services but wish for him every possible success in the private practice."

Duty's resignation is effective June 15. Murray said a successor has been selected and will be announced soon.

That year, Ike Murray was running for governor and my father decided to leave the Attorney General's office and return to private practice. After some soul searching, he decided to return to Fayetteville, not Rogers, although the two are only twenty miles apart and are closely tied with regard to lawyers and the legal system. He went into practice with a prominent attorney, Rex Perkins, who specialized in criminal law. Thus was born my father's still-continuing love affair with criminal law practice.

By this time, I had outgrown my horsey phase. Star was sold to a horse breeder near our 12th Street and Pike home. His son Jimmy was undersized and was dreaming of becoming a jockey. Star was just his size. Comet, with all of my tack, was sold to a black gentleman who recognized her merits. She was not a horse that just anyone could handle. She could be stubborn, affectionate, bullheaded, and irascible. She could also outrun anything of her own size on four feet. I still miss her. We gave Ginger to my Uncle Lee Dean in Rogers, ostensibly for his girls. But, so far as I know, she was never broken to ride and lived out her life in sloth and self-indulgence.

Being free of the encumbrances of livestock, we were able to settle in Fayetteville in a house actually in town. In fact, it was just around the corner from the home of the President of the University of Arkansas, John T. Caldwell and his wife Catherine. Later, we moved up the street to a house directly next door to the Caldwells on Ozark Avenue. University buildings and dormitories now occupy the site, but at that time Ozark Avenue was a block long residential street just off Dickson at the edge of the campus.

It was also during this period that I got my first taste of honest labor. During the summer after my junior year, immediately following our move to Fayetteville, I decided that I wanted a summer job. The problem was, what could I do and who would hire me? The extent of the difficulty can best be measured by the fact that the only job which I was finally able to obtain was snapping off chicken heads on the eviscerating line in Swanson's poultry processing plant. I will hasten to explain, though, that the chickens were already dead. They came down the line hanging head down and it was my job to pop off the already half-severed head.

I almost lost the job during the first hour. The chicken line moved along over a trough of running water. The heads were to be tossed into a barrel. No one told me, though, and I proceeded blithely to drop the heads in the water trough. I managed to stop-up the plumbing system and bring the plant to a complete halt until it could be cleared. I will never know why they let me continue. After they set me straight, though, I had no more problems. To this day, I find it hard to tolerate the smell of raw chicken.

High School Graduate Davis with Granddaddy White and Nonny

Since it took so much of the summer to get a job, I only worked for six weeks. However, I earned enough money to buy a tailor-made blue suit, a pair of tailor-made gray flannel slacks, which were then all the rage, a fur collared, fleece-lined leather jacket at Montgomery Ward's, and a single-action 22 gauge Remington rifle. I am not sure why I wanted the gun, but I still have it and, who knows, someday I may even shoot it!

I enrolled in Fayetteville High School for my senior year. I was shattered to have to leave my beloved Little Rock High School, but the students and faculty in Fayetteville High made me almost forget. I was chosen for a part in the Key Club Minstrel. I was elected President of the Key Club and was selected as a delegate to the District Key Club Convention in Springfield, Missouri. At the end of the year I was elected by the cheerleaders as an Honorary Color Guard for the basketball team. It was also during this year that I became an avid basketball fan and seldom missed a Bulldog game if I could help it. When I graduated from Fayetteville, it was with fond memories of the school and my years spent there. In later years, I came to be considered as a member of the Class of 1952 in Rogers High School, Fayetteville High School, and Little Rock High School. I claim them all and am flattered that they claim me in return.

Davis with the Rogers High School 40th Reunion in 1992
Class of 1952

Chapter 10

Dog Days
Summer, 1952

As I approached the end of my senior year in high school, my parents began to broach the idea of my obtaining a Seeing Eye dog. Personally, I didn't think I needed any assistance. I was able to get around anywhere I wanted on my own. If I was going to go somewhere unfamiliar, I could always go with a sighted friend. On the other hand, they pointed out that with my entry into college I would more and more be traveling in unfamiliar surroundings and might not always want to have to depend upon others. The idea of absolute independence did appeal to me, but it was still with some reluctance that I agreed to apply to the Seeing Eye school in Morristown, New Jersey. Luckily for me, they were experimenting with training younger persons at the time, so I was fortunate enough to be accepted. Right after my high school graduation in June 1952, I boarded the nightly Frisco passenger train in Rogers and began the long journey, not only eastward, but into a whole new lifestyle.

The month I spent at the Seeing Eye is etched indelibly in my memory. Those were the days when training was still done with an iron hand by Martinet instructors. As a result, I am a firm believer in stem discipline, both for one's self and one's dog. The instructor assigned to me was Bob O'Neil, late of the US Army, with service as a Sergeant in the North Africa Campaign. He was a personification of toughness and no-nonsense. There were times when I even thought that he might have served in Rommel's Afrika Korp rather than the US Army. His favorite comment was, "Duty, can't you do a damn thing right?!" By the time I left, I was doing quite a few damn things right.

The dog they picked for me was an eighty pound, black and tan German shepherd female named Binney. She was bright, aggressive, eager and willing, and what is termed a "hard" dog. In other words, she didn't cower and lay down to whimper when reprimanded. She merely bowed her neck and did what she thought was right, whether I liked it or not. At times we engaged in Mexican standoffs.

Davis and Binney

An incident in point occurred a year or so later after I had returned home to Rogers to which my parents had moved in 1953. Binney and I were walking through a residential area. We reached the end of a particular block and, as per the rules, Binney stopped at the down curb. There was no traffic about. I gave her the command "forward." She refused to move. I raised the volume of the command. She stood there as though carved from stone. Finally, I lost both my temper and good sense. I decided to show her who was boss. I dropped the harness, took a tight hold of the leash and stepped off of the curb intending to drag her forward bodily. The step, however, was rather greater than I had anticipated. In fact, it was down into a five-foot hole where workmen had been repairing a storm drain. Even though I still had a hold of her leash, Binney braced her feet and refused to follow. As I climbed to my feet, bruised and bleeding from more than one scratch, there she stood above me and, to add insult to injury, wagging her tail. I never again questioned her judgment to quite the same degree. Ultimately, we

Davis and his Seeing Eye training class (1952)

learned to compromise.

Then as now, the training cycle is fairly standard. Upon being weaned, the dogs are assigned to volunteer "puppy raiser" families in or near New Jersey. These youngsters and their families, who are often 4-H Club members, raise the puppies, not only giving them care and love, but acquainting them with family life and household routines. It is amazing the difference between a dog raised in a home and one in a kennel. (For example, a dog raised in a kennel finds it very difficult to walk on tile or linoleum floors. Climbing steps is practically an impossibility.) Then, at around eighteen months of age, the dogs return to the Seeing Eye and begin three months of training. Those who make it through the training are then assigned to a blind student with whom they train for one month or until they are ready to leave. When that time is judged to be right, the student-dog team (or perhaps one should say the dog-student team) return home to enter upon a life of greater independence, now well prepared to take an equal part in community life. For Binney and me, it meant returning to Fayetteville, Arkansas, to enter college as a freshman at the University of Arkansas.

Soon after my return from the Seeing Eye, I became inspired by the idea of selling my story about receiving my first guide dog. As it turned out, nobody was interested, but it did result in my first literary effort. Reading back over that old manuscript and comparing it with what I have written above reflects a somewhat different perspective. Perhaps it results from the difference in age or the impact of 40 years upon my memory. In any event, I cannot reject either viewpoint and so have elected to offer you, my reader, both.

SEARCH FOR FREEDOM
by Davis Duty

I went to the Seeing Eye along a chain of helping hands. I needed the help because I was blind. But I was resentful of being so dependent upon others. One month later, I returned home no longer needing help and no longer resenting it when given. This change in outlook was attributable to a dog. She was an eighty pound, black and tan German shepherd named Binney.

I was seventeen years old and had been blind since five years of age. My parents had taught me to look upon my blindness as a mere physical feature, rather than a way or life or handicap. They sent me to public schools. They encouraged me to lead a normal life, which included riding a bicycle and horses, swimming, and, later, dating, and active participation in school affairs.

But one factor was unalterable. My physical independence was limited. I could get about alone in familiar surroundings, such as home and school. However, I always needed someone to go with me when venturing into new or strange places. It was a recurrent source of irritation to be dependent upon others. At first, even the idea of procuring a dog guide provoked me. I felt that the added responsibility of caring for a dog would be a further restriction upon my freedom.

But upon graduating from high school, it became apparent that I had reached a decisive point in my life. I could either become a helpless burden upon society or I could assert my independence and take my equal place in the community as a useful citizen.

It had long been my dream to attend college and study law. This would entail leaving home to live in a strange town. I would be on my own. The need for physical independence would be ever present and would increase as time passed. A dog guide seemed to offer the best means of satisfying this need. Thus, I applied for admission to the Seeing Eye school in Morristown, New Jersey.

It is not a simple matter to obtain a professionally trained dog guide. They cannot be obtained primed and ready like ordering from a catalog. On the contrary, the blind person must apply to a dog guide school and, if accepted, live at the school for a specified period and be trained with a dog. The Seeing Eye school investigates applicants thoroughly to insure that candidates are physically and mentally capable of working with a dog and are the sort of individuals who will use their newfound independence in better serving themselves and their communities. It was with great trepidation that I boarded a train one July evening bound for the Seeing Eye and into the unknown.

This trip was one continuous demonstration of good will. Someone was always on hand to help me. Porters took me to the dining car. Redcaps assisted me in changing trains. Literally, I went to the Seeing Eye along a chain of helping hands. The final lap of the journey began in Newark, New Jersey, where I switched from train to bus for the last few miles to the school. I was tired and apprehensive as I neared the end of my trip. That bus ride seemed to last an eternity, but finally the driver braked to a stop and announced the Seeing Eye.

I was met by an athletic young man who extended me a vice-like handshake and introduced himself as my trainer. He would be in charge of the class to which I was assigned. Then, with me holding his arm, we walked up the winding drive to the rambling, two story country house which accommodates the Seeing Eye. This was to be the last time that I would be lead by another person.

The first three days were filled with ceaseless activity. The eight students in my class were kept constantly on the move in the oppressive July heat. We received preliminary instruction in preparation for our dogs. We learned dog training and care, how to use a guide dog harness, and how to properly give commands. At one point, the trainer took each of us for a "Juno" walk. Assuming the role of a dog named Juno by holding a harness at knee level, he guided us on a brief walk. His purpose was to learn our speed in walking, the degree of self-confidence we felt, and our awareness of physical surroundings. This information was needed by him in properly matching the dogs with their new masters.

The trainer prepares a class of dogs for the particular group of students to whom he will be assigned as instructor. But the final pairing of dog and person must be accomplished with the utmost care. The entire process is very intensive and highly specialized. The dog begins his training at fourteen months of age and receives three months of rigorous education before joining his blind partner, with whom another month of training is necessary. The students have been carefully screened. Their every characteristic is known. This information, plus that derived through observing the student from the moment of arrival, assists the trainer in choosing the right dog for the right individual. Until such time as dog and master are actually brought together, however, the student receives no hint of what to expect. I was beside myself with impatience to meet my new companion and begin our training.

After lunch on the third day, the class was assembled. We sensed that the big moment had come. My heart was pounding as the trainer told us one by one the name of our dog and its physical appearance. He was matter of fact, but we were seething with excitement. Next, the members of the class were dispatched to their rooms to await an individual summons. We were poised at the edge of a whole new life.

I sat on the edge of my bed and waited for what seemed to be an eternity. Periodically, the trainer's voice rang out from the common room, calling to one student after another. There would follow the sound of steps along the hall, a brief silence, and then the steps retracing their way down the corridor, but now accompanied by the tattoo of toenails on the wooden floor. At last, my name was called. I had been expecting and waiting for it, but when it came, I jumped as though caught napping.

I made my way to the door of the living room and stood waiting as instructed. There was the sound of movement at the far end of the long room. I could tell by the shuffle of feet and jingling of a chain that the trainer was there with a dog. There came the rattle of a leash being unfastened from a collar.

"Mr. Duty, are you ready?" The trainer was speaking quietly.

"Yes, sir."

"Call her to you. Speak firmly, but keep it gentle. Remember to use the command, 'come.' "

I said a little prayer and called out to the sound of that jingling collar, "Binney, come."

There was no response. I tried again; still nothing, no reaction. Binney was having nothing to do with this total stranger. She ignored me completely.

The trainer laughed and brought her to me. He explained that nothing was lost by the dog refusing to voluntarily go to its new master. But if it had, it might have helped start the relationship on a positive note.

"Binney has a mind of her own, though, and she is a bit stubborn, too," he added. I took the leash in my left hand, as directed, and turned back to my room with Binney walking quietly at my side.

The initial step in the training process is for dog and master to become acquainted. The dogs have become strongly attached to the trainer. It is necessary for the new master to devote all his energies to "winning over" his new companion. The remainder of that day and most of the next were dedicated to this end. We were warned, however, that it might be as long as two weeks before the dogs would begin transferring their affections to us. Binney fulfilled all forewarnings. On the first day, she ignored me. Each time I tried to pet her, I was met by a broad, furry behind, regardless of the direction from which I might approach. I did not even merit passing curiosity.

The change in my life brought about by the acquisition of a dog guide was not spectacular. It did not manifest itself immediately upon my arrival at the school or upon receiving Binney. There was much for me to learn before I would be ready to use my new independence. First, I had to adjust myself to a life in which a dog would play such an important role. Except when at home, Binney and I would always be together. We would seldom be further apart than the length of a leash. She would accompany me to meals; I would take her on her four daily outings. This would indeed be a new way of life for us both.

It was the second day after obtaining our dogs before the trainer decided that we were ready to begin working our guides in harness. The class was divided into two groups of four. One group at a time, we were loaded into the school station wagon and driven the five miles into Morristown. Our training was to be under real life conditions. This town was well suited for such work. It offered a variety of challenges, ranging from rough country roads to bustling, multi-laned city streets.

Our work began-on simple routes with few obstructions. We advanced rapidly, however, to ever more difficult routes. It was intended that we meet and master every type of situation which one might reasonably expect to encounter in the future. We had to learn to deal with situations instinctively. There would seldom be time to stop and ponder what to do. It was necessary that we learn to follow our dogs, give commands properly, and maintain discipline over our guides and ourselves.

The blind master and dog guide constitute a smooth and efficient team. There must be a constant interplay of mutual co-operation and trust. The master must not follow his guide helplessly, but he must have all his senses always alert and be aware of all that occurs about him. The dog can just serve as his eyes. The human component must make the decisions and direct his guide.

A dog guide works from four basic commands: right, left, hop-up, and forward. The master must know when to tell his dog to tum and in which direction. His dog stops at all up and down steps, but the master must listen to determine when it is safe to cross. This is the only time, however, when the dog may use "intelligent disobedience" and refuse to comply with a command to enter the street. If it considers compliance unsafe, the master must not only not argue, but must also praise his dog.

From the outset, our work was hard and exhausting. The trainer was relentless, always driving us toward perfection. The degree of independence which we could achieve would be proportionate to our self-confidence. This could only grow from accomplishment. Thus, from the simple early routes, we moved on quickly to increasingly longer and more difficult courses. Mistakes were expected, but repetition was not.

The reason for this was brought home to me one hot afternoon when the trainer descended upon me for committing some minor error. After roaring at me and insinuating that I could do nothing right, he concluded by saying, "Mr. Duty, some day you may be faced by a situation in which a mistake could cost you your very life. I will not be there to tell you what to do." I settled down to working as I had never worked before.

My goal was complete independence. It was going to take a lot of work and courage. There were times when I felt like quitting. On my very first walk with Binney, my legs began aching unbearably. My walking muscles were unprepared for the fast, steady gait required when walking with a dog. I gradually toughened and overcame this problem, but each day posed new challenges. As each barrier crumbled, the conviction grew in me that I would succeed. Independence was within my grasp.

It was a thrill such as I had never before experienced when I took the handle of Binney's harness and we set out alone. My chin lifted. My chest swelled. I lengthened my stride. Never again would I be limited as to where or when I could go out. I could go anywhere I pleased without asking the help of anyone. It would now be possible for me to take an equal place in my community and nation. As my independence increased, my view of life and the world about me broadened. I was changing in many ways.

By the end of the .second week, Binney and I were improving rapidly in our work. But of more importance, I was winning her over. At first, she worked to please the trainer. Soon, however, she began seeking my approval for a job well done. I first realized the change when I caught her helping herself to a doughnut from a box I had received from home. I scolded her, and she was heartbroken at my reproof. At last, I knew, she belonged to me.

From that moment on, we were a team, inseparable and willing to tackle any challenge together. We enjoyed the final two weeks of our training immensely. Each new obstacle became a moment of high adventure. We learned to maneuver through heavy traffic. A local department store offered us a place to conquer the intricacies of shopping. It was during the store training that Binney first discovered the joys of riding an elevator. To this day, she is convinced that the primary purpose of entering a large store is for her to get her fill of zipping up and down on the lifts.

Every day presents a new challenge, and every new challenge offers new adventure. Our month of training was rapidly approaching its climax.

On the final day of training, we embarked upon a Boy Scout hike. It consisted of a single four-mile walk along country roads. The purpose was to familiarize the student with travelling under conditions where sidewalks and paved streets would be absent. Actually, it proved to be an endurance contest between dog and master. We puffed our way through the distance, almost ready to collapse at the end. But I could have shouted with joy as I covered the last one hundred yards. Binney and I had succeeded. We were ready to go out into the world on our own. True, our work was not perfect. We would be unceasing in our efforts to improve and polish. But we had achieved the first major hurdle in our quest for a life of usefulness. As I boarded the plane for home the following day, I knew that at last I was a whole person, free and self-reliant...thanks to Binney.

THE END

Chapter 11

Oh, Those College Days
Fall, 1952-January, 1956

How can the years which one spends in college be such an important transitional stage and yet be so prosaic? At the time, I felt I was happy, challenged, optimistic, and enthusiastic. Now I look back on those years and wonder how I could have been so immature and shallow. I guess the answer is that it's a time when a person steps out of the nest and begins to search about for new horizons and new interests. At first, those interests involve nearby immediate activities. As one grows and extends, the horizons expand until one reaches maturity. So perhaps it is unfair to minimize the importance of the college years.

I was not thrust into college life with the same degree of separation as many students. We lived in Fayetteville, so I continued to live at home. This made my transition a bit more gradual. Nonetheless, things did not start out well.

My first college-related activity was fraternity Rush. I had finished high school on an up beat, had just obtained my new guide dog, and was at the peak of self-confidence and, perhaps one might even say, youthful arrogance. I was Somebody Special to which nothing bad could happen. I entered Rush already having determined which fraternity I wanted to join, and with some assurance from

Davis, Binney, John, Jeff, and Lois
Christmas, 1952

certain of its members that there would be no problem. In other words, I put all of my eggs in one basket. On the final day, though, when bids were handed out at a convocation in the ballroom of the student union, I was among sixteen young men who received no bid. To say the least, I was shocked and crushed. I think the disappointment and damage to my ego suffered that day has never fully healed. In fact, I still have dreams of the moment. I had fallen from the pinnacle to the pits. There was nothing for it but to pick up the pieces, act as though it didn't matter, and put things back together.

There is a rather poignant footnote to my fraternity debacle. A casual friend of mine from Fayetteville High School, Bob Jenkins, did receive a bid from the fraternity upon which I had had my heart set. Even though we were not close friends, when he learned of what had happened to me, he resigned his pledge and unlike me never did join a fraternity. However, he went on to be elected president of the student body. Ironically, it was me he defeated in the election! The story has a tragic ending, though. Upon graduation from the University, Bob received an ROTC commission to the United States Air Force. He was accepted into pilot school and shortly thereafter was killed in a training accident. Although we had never been really close friends, I felt a strong bond with Bob, and his death grieved me deeply. He had responded with principle to the unfairness done me, but there was absolutely nothing that I could do to soften the greater unfairness done him. One of the hardest letters I ever had to write was the one to his parents. I am sure they found it hard to understand how a mere acquaintance of their son could be affected so deeply by his death.

As far as fraternities went, my rejection at Rush was only a passing disappointment. I was contacted by Phi Delta Theta Fraternity and pledged that spring in Open Rush. As it turned out, this was probably my best choice. The fraternity was new on campus and had several members from both Rogers and Little Rock where my roots were the deepest. I was never sorry that I became a Phi Delt, although I was never really a very strong or active

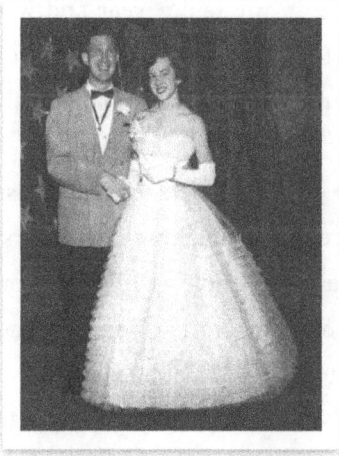

Davis at the 1957 Phi Delta Theta Buccaneers Ball

member. I think my initial disillusionment with fraternities tended to blight my feelings toward fraternities as a whole. I never again saw them as the end-all of college life.

In the meantime, I had finally begun to move away from the bosom of the family and stand on my own two feet. My sister Carolyn had married Warren E. Banks, a law student from Hot Springs, on December 27, 1952. In 1953, my parents, with brother John who was still in high school, returned to Rogers to live. There, my father opened a law office, practicing on his own until1956 when he rejoined his Uncle Claude to restore the family firm of Duty & Duty. My mother had enjoyed a brief respite from teaching, but upon moving back to Rogers, she returned to the school room, first as an English teacher, and later, for many years, as the official study hall teacher. Her firm but fair discipline helped many a student over the rough places. She retired from teaching in 1973 after a distinguished career spanning over twenty years in the Rogers school system alone.

As my parents were reestablishing their lives and careers in Rogers, I was settling into college for the long haul. Academically, I more or less followed in my sister Carolyn's footsteps. She had studied political science and was constantly singing the praises of her professors, including Franklin Bridge, Dr. Alexander, Dr. Jones, etc. Since it was my hope to follow in the family professional tradition and become a lawyer, political science seemed as good as any other for an undergraduate course of study. I did well in my studies and graduated cum laude a semester early in January 1956. Along the way, I was tapped for Omicron Delta Kappa, a leadership fraternity, and Phi Beta Kappa, an academic fraternity, as well as other somewhat less well-known societies. I ran for the Student Senate in my senior year and was elected. Then, my confidence overtook better judgment and I ran for President of the Student Body in my senior year and as previously mentioned was resoundingly defeated.

I was, however, appointed that year to the student court, whose responsibilities were insignificant, but which I enjoyed immensely as my first taste of the legal life. The most memorable case we handled while I was on the court involved a challenged parking ticket. The No Parking sign had fallen over and the ticketee claimed that he could not tell that he was in a No Parking zone. Profound questions were involved. When a No Parking sign is obscured, is it still binding? Does the principle of "Ignorance of the Law (is not an excuse)" still apply? I really don't remember what was decided, but I did get to write the majority opinion for the court. It was the high-point of my legal career to date.

Perhaps my most enjoyable activity during my undergraduate years was as a member of the Touring Choir. Although I lacked a voice of any great quality, I was able to "fake it" well enough to hide myself among a choir of superior and better-trained voices. My interest stemmed from the year I had spent in the A Cappella Choir in Little Rock High School. Therefore, I was very pleased to be accepted into the University Choir in my sophomore year. During this period, we assumed the name of "The Collegiate Singers" and made our first state-wide tour. It was a grueling week-long experience which I will never forget. Binney seemed to enjoy it as much as did I, and she also added a humorous dimension to some of the proceedings. During a concert at the high school in Mount Ida, Arkansas, I had left her on the bus since it is hard to control a dog while standing frozen in the midst of a choir. Apparently, she heard us singing, though, and when the bus driver inadvertently opened the door she was out like a shot and into the school. The first thing I knew was when the audience began to stir and here came Binney walking down the middle isle of the auditorium, up on the stage, and to her accustomed spot below the risers at my feet. From then on, we decided to let her participate. She considered herself a member of the choir, too, and was not about to be left behind.

Then there was my one attempt to make a mark in the world of sports. It seems that ranking in the intramural program was based on a points system in which even loosing participants gained some credit. It was, therefore, suggested that since I was a passive fraternity member at best, I might volunteer to fill one of the hitherto empty slots on the wrestling team. I had never wrestled in my life and had no aspirations to do so, other than in a more amorous setting. However, the suggestion apparently came at a good time because I agreed to give it a try. A friend of mine from little Rock, Henry Moore, who also happened to be on the Razorback football team, agreed to give me a crash course in wrestling technique. First though, he and several other members of the team put me through a brief conditioning program which was badly needed. As a direct result of this, I have maintained a daily schedule of calisthenics clear up to the present. Two incidents during the conditioning stand out in my mind. There was the morning after the first workout when I tried to get out of bed. Literally every muscle in my body hurt. I couldn't sit up, so eventually I had to roll out of bed on the floor, groan to my hands and knees and thence scream to my knees. At that moment, I vowed that I would never let myself get to that shape again.

The second instance was when I challenged Buster Graves to a sparing match. Buster, at 6'4" and about 240 pounds, was the starting right tackle on the football team and the top weightlifter on the squad. He only laughed when I challenged him, but when I launched myself at him physically, he lent down, grabbed me by the ankles, and held me above his head. He made me confess all my sins, take the blame for many of his, and promise him my first born son before he returned me to earth (sorry, John!). I conceded the match, but told him I would get him the next time. Needless to say, there was not a next time.

When the big day came for my first match, I was the hands-down underdog, regardless of who my opponent might be. I also had two physical problems. My bad hip (a minor birth defect) had flared up with a hematoma, which required in intramuscular injection of Vitamin K. It hadn't had time to work, though, and was sore as a boil. Even more telling was the fact that I couldn't eat for twenty-four hours because I was slightly over the weight limit. When I showed up for the match, I was hungry, sore, and weak. The most remarkable part of my one and only match was when the referee (another member of the football team and a friend from Little Rock High School) Eddie Bradford enquired politely if it was my intention to lie there motionless on the mat on my stomach for the entire match. As a matter of fact, that was my *precise* intention. Indeed, it was my strategy! Putting my lightening fast brain to work, I concluded that I would rather loose on points than by being pinned. Since any aggressive action on my part might arouse my opponent's fighting spirit, I chose instead to let him wear himself out trying to turn me over. He won the match, but he was much more tired than me when it was over. Thus, my athletic career did not end in complete ignominy, but with a psychological victory, although the only one aware of it was I.

Davis Duty Graduates from University with Top Honors

By Wayne Taylor

A news story released by the University of Arkansas concerning mid-term graduates stated, "Davis Duty, son of Mr. and Mrs. Jeff Duty of Rogers, was one of ten students graduating from the University of Arkansas Magna Cum Laude."

To the people of Rogers and Northwest Arkansas this was not even half the story—because Davis Duty has been blind since he was four years old. The blindness was the result of a disease which now, with so-called miracle drugs, is not even considered serious. Scarlet fever, which now is very much under control, was the cause of his blindness.

In his fight against the disease, Davis was one of the first patients at Barnes Hospital in St. Louis, Mo., to be given sulfa drugs. Although he didn't win his fight entirely with scarlet fever he is now winning his fight to maintain his place in the world.

Not only did Davis graduate from the University of Arkansas Magna Cum Laude, he finished a normal four-year course in the College of Arts and Sciences with a major in government in three and one-half years. Davis Duty and his seeing-eye dog, Binney, have been a familiar sight on the university campus for the past three years.

Binney and Davis first met at the Pilot Dog School in Morristown, N. J. Davis, although he had gone through high school and elementary school on his own, decided he would need a guide before he could enter and make his way around the unfamiliar University of Arkansas campus at Fayetteville. He went to Morristown and there he met Binney. After intensive schooling for both boy and dog, Davis left to enroll at the University of Arkansas with his ever-present companion. According to Davis's father, Binney probably knows the university campus better than many students who are enrolled in the university.

Davis has always been an honor student ever since he enrolled in his first year of school at Rogers. He attended Little Rock High School for three and one-half years where he was selected to the National Honor Society for high school students. He graduated from high school at Fayetteville in the spring of 1952 and finished as one of the top 10 scholastically in his class.

DAVIS DUTY

After enrolling in the university, he was selected to the ODK national honorary scholarship fraternity for undergraduates. He is also a Phi Beta Kappa. Davis is a member of Phi Delta Theta social fraternity. During his junior year he served as an associate justice of the student court and was a member of the student senate. He also has served as a staff writer on the "Traveler," daily newspaper published by and for the students at the University of Arkansas.

Davis received his bachelor of arts degree from the university of Arkansas with a cumulative grade point average of five-plus. The highest average obtainable is six.

Besides his father and mother, Davis has a sister, Mrs. Warren Banks, living in Washington, D. C., and a brother, John, who is in his senior year at Rogers high school.

Yes, Davis has done all right for a boy with the handicap he has had to cope with, but he isn't through. This week he enrolled in the University of Arkansas School of Law and will follow in the footsteps of his father, Jeff Duty, who is engaged in the practice of law at Rogers.

When Davis completes his studies in law and enters private practice or the teaching profession (he isn't sure as to which he will choose) he will no doubt have collected additional honors to go with those he has amassed over the past years. The Davis Duty story is still being written.

Chapter 12

Taking My Show on the Road
— or —
A Foggy Year in Londontowne
Spring, 1957-Fall, 1958

I enrolled in the University of Arkansas Law School in the spring semester of 1956. Thus began the hardest and most frustrating year and a half of my life. During the first semester, I made the first D that I had ever made in school. The rest were all Cs. Since I had never before made as low as a C, my self-confidence again began to falter. I also had my first love affair during this time, with a girl I met in summer school in 1956. Her name was Carolyn, and from then through the fall semester of that year I was smitten. The relationship did not go smoothly, though, and I found it increasingly difficult to balance a social life with my law studies. I think I came as near to a nervous breakdown during that time as I might ever come. Perhaps, though, it is necessary to sustain a mild infection in order to build up immunities for later in life. I do think the experience strengthened, rather than weakened, me. At the time, though, I was miserable. Also, my grades did not appreciably improve during the next two semesters, although I made no more Ds and did make a B or two in minor subjects.

By the spring of 1957, I knew that I had to take a break. It was at this time that I revived a longstanding interest in a possible scholarship to study overseas. Again, though, things were not simple. I was not eligible to apply for a Rhodes Scholarship because I had no formal athletic credits. I was not eligible for a Rotary Club Scholarship because of my physical disability. But I was eligible for a Fulbright Scholarship. This program had first been made a reality through the efforts of the then junior senator from Arkansas, Bill Fulbright. I wrote to him, and while he did not offer to sponsor me personally, he did encourage me to apply. I did so, and somehow, against all odds, was granted a scholarship to study at the London School of Economics, University of London, for the school year 1957-58. It was not only a tremendous opportunity, but it also afforded me the break which I so desperately needed from law school. With the prospects of a year's vacation from law school and a year abroad before me, I finished the spring semester in 1957 and prepared for a pleasant summer. Then all hell broke loose, and from a quarter which I would never have expected.

Early in July, when I contacted the British Embassy about my trip, I was advised that a six-month quarantine was rigidly imposed on all animals entering the United Kingdom to prevent rabies from entering its shores. In other words, Binney could go with me to England, but she would be in stir for six months. Two problems immediately presented themselves: First, did I want to try to get along for six months without my dog? And second, would I take my dog with me or leave her behind? When appraised of the situation, the Seeing Eye left it entirely up to me. They agreed to keep her in their kennels for the year I would be gone, although they warned me of the problems which might arise. On the other hand, if I took her with me and could somehow or other maintain some resemblance of a training regimen, I would at least have her for the last half of my stay. This is the course I eventually chose.

However, I wasn't to get off quite so easily. Somehow the news media picked up on the story, and before I knew what was happening, I was the center of a world-wide furor of sensationalism. It was just the kind of story that makes for good human interest reading. Since I had always viewed my dog as a means to independence wherein I could participate equally and unobtrusively with others, it was humiliating to me to suddenly be treated as an object of sympathy, but deal with it I must. I did not want to harm either the Fulbright Scholarship program or offend my British hosts.

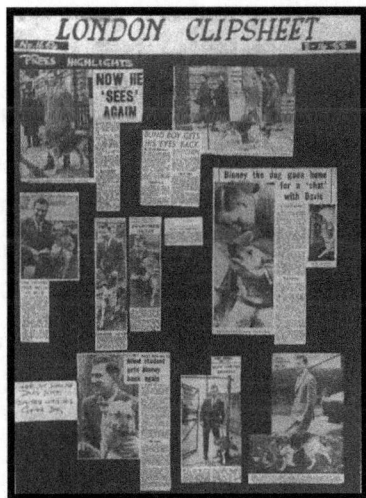

When the long distance calls started coming in from wire services and overseas correspondence of foreign newspapers, all I could do was repeat over and over again that I didn't blame anyone, that I still hoped that some exception could be made, and that I still intended to take up my scholarship at LSE. The clamor didn't abate, though.

My trip to England began on a late summer evening in September, 1957. I elected to travel the first leg by train, not only to save money, but also because it would be fun. I was scheduled to leave on the 9:30 pm northbound Frisco passenger train to St. Louis. The sizable crowd of friends, neighbors, and well wishers who showed up to see me off I put down to my loveable self. However, there was no longer any doubt about my slipping into London anonymously.

When I stepped off the Pullman at Union Station in St. Louis, there was a mass of reporters and photographers blocking the way right at the foot of the train steps. My car porter, Walter, did yeoman service by fending them off until a phalanx of red-

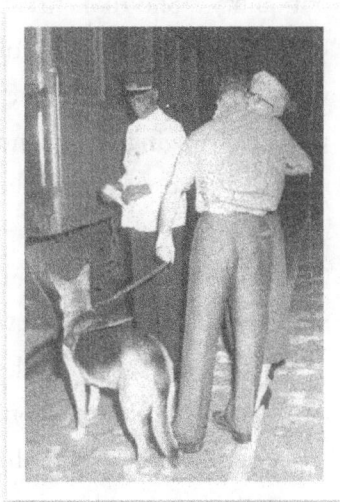

Hugging Lois goodbye

caps could escort my baggage and me to the Penn-Central train to New York. Of course, Walter did all right in the process, since almost every reporter slipped him a tip. I really had nothing to say, though, so their money and efforts were spent in vain.

Davis on board the USS United States en route to London, 1957

Then, when I arrived at the pier in New York City to embark on the USS United States, the press was waiting. Upon boarding, I was immediately escorted to the main salon where a press conference was scheduled. I was questioned again and photographed from every angle. Afterward, though, for the three days of the Atlantic passage, Binney and I had some tranquility. She took to shipboard life like she took to everything else. Unfortunately, there was nothing we could do about the ship's motion, so we developed a very unique technique of walking down narrow corridors with her swinging like a pendulum at the end of her harness. We got pretty good at it and enjoyed the trip considerably. And, unlike my stateroom mate, David Kleinbarger (a fellow Fulbright scholar who was headed for Oxford), Binney and I didn't get seasick, which leads me to believe that motion sickness is as much visual as physical.

At Southampton, the fun time came to an end. Binney was taken into custody and shipped off to a kennel near London. Customs did make an exception, however, to the extent that they did not keep her in the usual quarantine station, but allowed her to be quarantined in a large private kennel within driving distance of where I would be living.

Next, I had to devise a method by which I could keep her in training. This was solved by the members of the Catholic Order of St. Vincent de Paul, plus other volunteers from the general public, who offered to drive me down twice a week to visit and work with Binney. All we could do was walk around a narrow sidewalk skirting a small interior courtyard, but walk around it we did; twenty-five times one way and twenty-five times the other, working on our turns, stops, and other maneuvers. Then, we would go through a very elaborate obedience procedure before I had to pet her and leave for another few days.

Davis training Binney in the kennel yard

She seemed to accept the routine, but I have never seen a dog as happy as Binney on the day that I put on her harness and gave her the command that took us to the door to the outside rather than the door to the courtyard. She had been waiting for that command for six months and almost dragged me to freedom. This event, too, of course, was covered by the mass press. Senator Fulbright, who happened to be in London at the time, held a joint press conference with me to introduce Binney to the British public. Of course, we had to once again explain that we held no grievance against the British Empire, but that I was just glad to have Binney back. Now, even though my first six months had been filled with fun and many experiences, I could begin to really benefit from my scholarship.

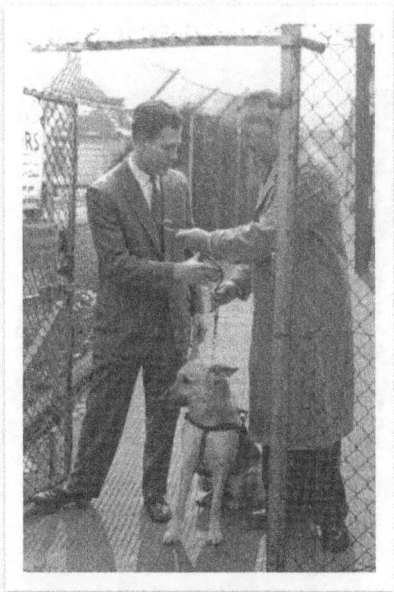

Binney's release

There isn't much that can be said for my academic achievements in England. Ostensibly I was studying international law, and I did faithfully attend lectures. However, I was not required to sit for any examinations since I would only be there for one year and the British system would have called for exams at the end of the second year.

Davis and Senator Fulbright

One academic benefit that I did derive was completion of a course in Conflicts of Law, which is also a course taught in American law schools. When I returned to the University of Arkansas, Dr. Leflar, who taught Conflicts, agreed to let me audit the course without having to take examinations. As a result, I was able to take the course in addition to an already full load. This helped make it possible for me to finish law school with the 1959 summer school session.

During my year in England, I did much more than just study. It was also during this year that I met the second love of my life. Her name was Kate Yannaghas; a British citizen, but the daughter of a Greek family. Her father was the Chief Director of a shipping company and a very proud Greek. Kate and I were all but inseparable during the last few months of my stay in England and we even considered ourselves semi-engaged. Her father took care of that, though. As soon as I was out of the country and back home, he

Binney and Kate

prompted her into a trip to Greece and introductions to a very eligible Greek bachelor who, incidentally, was also a lawyer. In any event, she married George Issaias of Athens, and our short-lived bubble was burst. I have kept up with her over the years, though, and we are still good friends. In fact she later translated a children's story I wrote into Greek and had it privately published in Athens. One of our most fervent hopes is that some day she and George and my wife and I can get together. I know that I would like George and I know that Kate would like Barbara.

Some of the highlights of my stay in England were the following. First there was the television coverage of Binney's release from quarantine. One of the news networks followed me around for a whole day and made a film which was later, after editing, shown on national TV in the States. I have a copy of that film somewhere. Then, I was treated to numerous visits around England. These included Warwick Castle in Warwickshire in central England, Harlech Castle in Wales, concerts at the Royal Albert Hall and the Royal Festival Hall, numerous plays, including Shakespearian dramas at the old Vic, and even an early production of *My Fair Lady* at Covent Garden with the original cast of Rex Harrison, Julie Andrews, and Stanley Holloway.

On a more mundane level, I took up rowing. As with most British colleges and universities, LSE had a rowing club. One of its members invited me to participate. Early each Saturday morning, we would take a train to the rowing club facility on the Thames. There, I would splash away with an oar in the rowing tanks, and occasionally get out in a boat with one of the other novices. I never graduated to even a four, much less an eight, oar team, but I had a lot of fun and got a lot of good exercise. Then there was the comradery and gallons of tea in the club bar before returning to school and the books.

In addition, Kate was generous in playing tour guide. She and I visited Windsor Castle, St. Albin's Church, the Tower, Westminster Abbey, Hampton Court, Canterbury Cathedral, the Houses of Parliament, Buckingham Palace, and even attended the Queen's annual garden party in celebration of her birthday in June 1958. That was when I almost met Sir Winston Churchill. As Kate and I were leaving the party, we were amazed at the courtesy of the crowd as they parted to form an aisle down which we could walk to the exit. It wasn't until we were almost at the gate that suddenly Kate grabbed my arm and whispered, "You'll never guess who is walking right behind us.....Sir Winston Churchill!" Why I didn't turn around and introduce myself, I will never know and I am sure

Jeff Davis Duty, Jr., 22-year-old blind student from Rogers Ark. and his seeing-eye dog, Binney, on their way to realise a Fulbright scholarship in London, Eng. Although British law determines that Binney must spend 6 months in quarantine ample opportunity for visiting will be arranged

he wouldn't have minded. I was so
flustered by the unexpectedness of the
encounter, though, that I missed the
opportunity. Just being so close,
however, was a privilege.

Over the 1957 Christmas
holidays, I got together with Joe Leach,
the son of Dr. and Mrs. Leach, whom I
knew from the Methodist Church in
Rogers. Joe was teaching English for the
overseas extension program of the
University of Maryland,
which provided college
courses for American
service personnel stationed
at overseas bases. He was
teaching at an air base in
France, and he and I met in
Paris to take a two-week
tour of the continent. In his

**Davis in the shadow of the
Matterhorn, Zermott,
Switzerland, Christmas, 1957**

ancient and tiny Opal (this was before Binney came out of quarantine), we
toured Paris, drove to Luxembourg City, and then to Switzerland, where we
spent three days in Zermatt. Neither one of us were skiers, but we got many
pictures of us in ski togs in the shadow of the Matterhorn. Then we went
through the Simplon Tunnel into Italy. In Milan, we attended an opera at
LaScala and toured the local sites, which included DaVinci's painting of the
Last Supper. From there, it was down to Genoa and up the Côte d'Azur to
Monaco and Nice.

In Genoa, Joe and I got a real taste (literally) of Italian friendliness.
We stopped at a waterfront tavern to spend the last of our lira for some
coffee. Not knowing the price and not speaking Italian, we used primitive

sign language to indicate what we wanted and to ask whether the money we offered was sufficient. The patron apparently believed that we were two destitute Americans who only had the price of a cup of coffee. He took pity on us and, on the house, offered to sweeten our coffee with some of the local grape-jack. He tipped the bottle over our cups and said something in Italian which obviously instructed us to say "when." We didn't know the Italian word for "when" and ended up with a lot of grape-jack and very little coffee. The first cup brought tears to our eyes, but the second hardly burned at all.

Neither of us felt any pain as we left Genoa and headed for France. It was a beautiful moonlit night. Much of the road ran right along the beach. There were very few cars out so late. It was like we were traveling through a fairy tale night like one reads about in romantic novels set on the Côte d'Azur. At one point, we stopped to walk on the beach. From all outward appearances, we could have been the last two people in the world. Even with the sound of the surf, the silence was utterly deep and utterly ancient. At such moments, one can sense, at least fleetingly, how small and transient are the lives of individuals when compared to the size and age of the world and the universe.

Reaching France, we found a cheap hotel in Nice and spent two days living the good life, albeit on the cheap side. That was the first time I saw oranges actually growing on trees, and at Christmas time yet. We spent pleasant hours exploring Monaco. I even invested one hundred francs in a slot machine at the Monte Carlo casino (and lost). It made me feel just like James Bond in *Casino Royale*. On Christmas Eve, we stopped at a small town whose name I forget, but which boasted the church where the great Talleyrand was a parishioner. We stayed at a small country inn where we were the only guests. Ordering dinner from a menu which we could not translate, we ended up with scrambled calves' brains. Joe ate both of ours. Then we attended Midnight Mass at Talleyrand's church. It was at this point that I confronted my first kissing opportunity of that vacation. As the Mass ended, Joe leaned over and whispered to me (I was sitting on the aisle) that,

Davis studying (by braille) in Passfield Hall, 1958

when he nudged me, to kiss whatever was before me. I wasn't about to let myself in for that much uncertainty, though, and immediately changed sides with Joe. It turned out that what was to be kissed was the Bishop's ring as he recessed down the aisle. I guess Joe got that blessing in my stead. We then repaired to the local bistro with all of the other mass-goers and partook of wine and escargot. I must confess that, being gastronomically provincial, I had a ham sandwich instead.

My other kissing opportunity was when we toured the Chartres Cathedral. We were given a special tour to the subterranean crypt where their prize reliquary was kept, containing a piece

Above and right: Davis and Binney in St. James Park, 1958

of Christ's robe. Again, I was not prepared for having the reliquary thrust into my face. The custom is to kiss the reliquary, following which miraculous healings have been reported. Although I wasn't there for a healing, the good sisters who are the guardians of the reliquary didn't know this. When the reliquary was thrust into my face, I backed away in horror and made my escape with

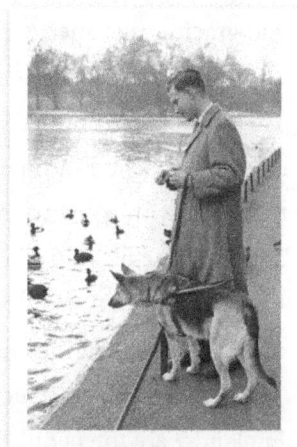

many apologies. I think if I was to go back again now, I might be a bit more diplomatic. Also, who knows, while I don't seek a physical healing of any sort, there are all kinds of spiritual healings which I might well have welcomed.

Another memory which I cherish is that of meeting the Queen Mother and Princess Alexandra. I had the good fortune of being selected as a member of the Goats Club at University College, a sister college to LSE in the University of London. It was sponsored and run by Miss Trevelyan, who was a granddaughter or niece or something of the great English historian, Sir George Trevelyan of the same name. She taught at University College and had formed the Goats Club with members from all the many nations represented at the University of London. We met each week for exotic and cultural programs, but mainly to mingle and get to know persons from other cultures. The climax of the Goats' social year were two receptions. The first that year was for Princess Alexandra who came to have High Tea with us. She was ensconced at a small tea table in the middle of a huge room and the Goats passed by one at a time to be presented. I had Binney by that time, so I was favored with a special invitation to join her for a few minutes and even share a cup of tea. I have no idea what we talked about, but I will always remember her friendliness and gracious manner.

The other big social event was the reception for the Queen Mother. This time I was honored by being included in the presentation line. I was carefully coached in bowing over the Queen Mum's hand and approached the event with some trepidation. It turned out, though, that she was a very down to earth, sweet little lady who showed sincere interest in me and Binney. She put us all completely at our ease and I had another beautiful memory to take home with me.

Probably the most enduringly meaningful rewards of my time in England were the people I met. There was my roommate, Jim Silver, who is

now a successful advertising executive in London. There was Mrs. Williams (whom I later learned was a well known authoress, albeit under a different name), who took me, once a week, down to see Binney during the quarantine months. There was Mrs.

Davis with roommate Jim Silver and Jim's girlfriend Ann

Trevelyan, the mentor of the Goats Club. There were my fellow students, John Stevenson, Cyril Fish, Jeff (who introduced me to rowing), and my fellow American from Atlanta, Preston King.

How could I ever forget the evening that Preston and I came home from one of our rare splurges of eating out (fish and chips) to be confronted by a group of English students who began harassing us. Preston was black and I was white. This was during the time of the Little Rock High School crisis which was heavily reported in the London papers. At first the jibes were good natured, but soon became quite caustic. There was a good deal of racial tension existing even then in England, lurking just beneath the surface. The main thrust of the comments was that I was condescending to be with Preston and that he was Uncle Tom-ing it to be with me. Later, every member of the group would come to me to apologize, but at the time, mob psychology ruled. It was a wee mob, but a mob nonetheless. I don't think that I am a particularly physical of violent type, but eventually I saw red. I was lunging towards my assailants with every intention of beating them senseless (which, of course, wasn't likely), when Preston literally grabbed me by the coat collar and seat of the pants and propelled me up the stairs to our rooms. Being six foot four and weighing about 240 pounds, he had little difficulty; and I will never forget his sage advice at the time to not retaliate in kind when attacked with prejudice. It would only serve to have convinced the crowd that they were right. I guess it is sort of like saying that if you stick yourself with a pin and bleed, it proves that you are only human and are therefore susceptible to being stuck with pins. Oh well!

Many others parade through my memory with whom I have lost contact but who left a bright mark on the slate of my memory. There was Gail Gladstone from New York who was studying at the Royal Academy of Dramatic Arts. I met her on the ship going over. We went out several times and did some of the tourist bits together until our paths eventually drifted apart. There was my fellow Fulbright scholar, Ted Saint Antoine from Michigan. He went with me many places and helped me out with innumerable tasks during the period of Binney's quarantine and after. He introduced me to Bristol Cream Sherry which I still relish. I haven't heard from him in years, but the last I heard he was a professor at some law school in Michigan.

Then there was Dawn Banks. She was the secretary to Bill Gaines, the director of the United States Education Commission office in London. Dawn and I became fast friends, although never romantically (to my everlasting regret). At age 22, English girls, especially those with upper-class accents, turned me on mightily, but also scared me to death. Worship from afar was about all I could manage, except, of course, for Kate. Somehow, I managed to overcome my reticence where she was concerned.

In any event, Dawn and I attended concerts at the Royal Festival Hall. She invited me to parties at her house. One particular evening, she invited me over for dinner. The main course was liver stew. Anyone who knows me is aware that liver is something that God never meant for me to swallow. I have always said that if He intended for us to eat liver, He would have put it right out where we could get at it. On this particular evening, though, I had no choice but to eat liver stew. Then, just as I was congratulating myself on having made it through the bowl with loud exclamations of delight and pleasure, Dawn offered me a refill. I accepted manfully, but I knew that I could never get it down. My only alternative was to resort to subterfuge. I didn't want to hurt Dawn's feelings, but I didn't want to die either. So, I did something which my Seeing Eye trainers would lynch me for. While Dawn was in the powder room, I put that second bowl of stew on the floor and told Binney to get a move on. It was a terrible thing to do as far as Binney's training regimen, but it saved me from liveritis and made Dawn feel like Julia Childs. Mr. Debetaz, can you ever forgive me?

None of the friendships I made have endured so well, though, as my friendship with Frank Burgess. He was the porter at Passfield Hall where I lived. He lived on the premises and spent many hours of each day sitting in his cubicle in the entrance hall. He always waited up to let in errant students who had missed their bus or not missed enough glasses of wine. Frank was everyone's friend. He was always cheerful and always enjoyed a good joke, and he was the handyman's handyman. After knowing him, I can't imagine how American dormitories survive without a resident porter. I did not really get to know Frank, however, until we began our correspondence after I returned to the United States. We have now been writing regularly for close to forty years. I regard him as a big brother or uncle. He is still witty and interested in everything that goes on, from gossip about public figures to international politics. Even in his eighties, he tours about unendingly. His most recent letter described a tour of Buckingham Palace, for which he had to queue up (stand in line) for over an hour. I only hope that I will always retain the same type of enthusiasm for life. Frank Burgess is a kind, intelligent, witty, and gentle man. I sincerely hope that I will be able to take Barbara to England some day so that she can meet him. Frank occupies a special place in my memory and heart.

Finally, my stay in England had to come to an end. I did obtain a three months' extension and was able to stay in England until September, 1958, but the time finally came when I said goodbye to Kate and all of my many other friends and boarded the USS United States for the return voyage.

This time, as it was the United States when we entered, Binney was warmly greeted and passed through customs without slowing down. Having arrived in New York late in the afternoon, I spent the night at the Henry Hudson Hotel and the next day enplaned for home. Another chapter of my life had come to an end.

Chapter 13

From Books to Paychecks
Fall, 1958-February, 1960

And then it was back to law school and back to the grindstone for the home stretch. I had a year and a half of law school to finish, but the year abroad seemed to have wrought wonders. I was rested, more mature, and my mind seemed dearer. While I had struggled for Cs in the first year and a half of law school, the second part went by in a blur and I was able to even get some Bs and an A or two. Indeed, I was on such a roll that I continued on to summer school in 1959 and finished my coursework in August. I would not receive my degree until mid-term graduation in January, 1960, but for all intents and purposes I was out of school.

The next item on my agenda was to find work. From early in my college career, I had been shooting for a job with the Government. I was especially attracted to work in the Foreign Service. However, this was not to be. On borrowed money, I moved to Washington where I camped around with various friends until I finally found a job, primarily through the efforts of my cousin, albeit several times removed, Ollie Collins, with the Justice Department. She was an attorney with the Civil Division in that agency and stood in sufficient regard with the powers that be to convince them to take me on. I should also give credit to the support of my then Congressman Jim Trimble, Senator Fulbright, and my future (although I did not know it at the time) father-in-law Clyde T. Ellis. They all went to bat for me. As a result, I went to work for the Justice Department in October, 1959, as a member of the Special Trial Section of the Anti-Trust Division. At the time, William Rogers was the Attorney General and headed the Justice Department. But soon the Republicans would give way to the Democrats and my overall boss would be Robert F. Kennedy. I only met him once, but I still like to claim that I worked for him.

In due course, I did receive my law degree and in February, 1960, I returned to Arkansas and took the bar exam. By the Grace of God and a lot of luck, I passed. On April 4, 1960, I was sworn in as a member of the Bar by a judge of the United States Tax Court in Washington. I now had the credentials. It was up to me to make a career.

Four Degrees to Go To Rogers' Duty Clan

FAYETTEVILLE, Ark. (AP) — University of Arkansas graduation will be a family affair for the Duty clan of Rogers, Ark.

★   ★   ★

Four members of the family will receive degrees at midyear commencement here Jan. 30.

ONE DIPLOMA WINNER is Davis Duty, a blind student who received international attention in 1957 when British quarantine laws forced him to do without his seeing-eye dog while he was studying there on a Fulbright scholarship.

Davis Duty will receive a law degree. His sister, Mrs. Carolyn Banks, will recieve a bachelor's degree in government. Her husband will get master's degree in business administration. Mrs. Susan Duty, wife of the youngest Duty son, John, will receive a bachelor's degree in education.

JOHN DUTY is a University of Arkansas law student.

The parents are Mr. and Mrs. Jeff Duty of Rogers.

Chapter 14

The Springtime Years
Summer, 1956-March, 1962

Backtracking in my story a little, in the summer of 1956, before law school, I traveled with my parents to Washington, DC, to visit my sister, Carolyn, her husband, Gene Banks, and their two-year-old daughter, Karen. While there, Ollie Collins invited us to the annual picnic sponsored by the Arkansas Club, which consists of Arkansas ex-patriots working in Washington.

At the picnic, I ran into my old friend, Clyde T. Ellis, who had taken special interest in me when he was Congressman for Arkansas' Third District, during the time that my parents were struggling to figure out a way to send me to school and keep me at home at the same time. This 1956 chance meeting with Clyde was of some significance due to the fact that he also had with him his two daughters, Patricia and Mary. I was attracted to both girls and spent the whole afternoon in their company. Most of the time was spent swinging on the playground swings that we found near where the picnic was being held. Following my return to Arkansas, I began a correspondence with them both, although the letters with Pat were only continued for a short period as she was involved in another more serious relationship. I continued writing to

Clyde T. Ellis

Rogers Daily News, Friday, Oct. 9, 1959   Page 3

MISS MARY LYNN ELLIS
... To wed in November

Miss Mary Lynn Ellis, Jeff Davis Duty Jr.
To Pledge Wedding Vows In November

Mary, however, and in the next few years we became close pen pals.

Both girls visited their grandparents in Arkansas in the summer of 1959, and I went out on an actual date with her for the first time. My fraternity brother, Bill Snow, and I (we were both attending summer school in Fayetteville) drove to Garfield where the girls' grandparents lived and took them out on a double date. I was paired with Mary and Bill with Pat. Thus began my first (practical) serious romantic involvement.

Following graduation that fall, when I went to Washington, Mary met me and we became almost inseparable. Very soon, we decided to get married. It had seemed almost foreordained that we would do so, and we did on October 31 (Halloween), 1959. It was a very small wedding in the chapel of the Presbyterian Church in Chevy Chase, Maryland. Only immediate family were present. My parents, plus my brother John and his wife Susan, flew in from Arkansas to attend. And, of course, Mary's family, including her father Clyde, her mother Izella, her sister Pat with

Davis and Mary's wedding: (left-right): Minister, John White Duty, Davis, Mary, Patricia Ellis Marti

**Above (left-right): Lois and Jeff Duty,
Izella and Cyle Ellis (back row unknown)
Bottom Left: Mary's wedding portrait**

husband Bruce, and her Aunt Jane and Uncle Buddy were there.   Another chapter in my life had begun, along with my fledgling legal career.

For two and a half years, Mary and I lived in Adelphi, Maryland, and commuted to Washington to work. She was employed by the Food and Drug Administration's Bureau of Medicine. I worked for the Justice Department, in the special Trial Section of the Antitrust Division. Binney and I were a common sight poking around the streets of downtown Washington near the Capitol, Supreme Court, and Library of Congress. Every lunchtime, we would go for a long walk to explore the nooks and crannies of old Washington. At ten, Binney's health was rapidly deteriorating, but we had many a good stroll together and she got me through yet another crucial period in my life, the transition from student to professional.

Other than the ordinary events of young married life and work on the very bottom rung of the professional ladder, not much happened during that period. It was the era of our country's first baby-steps into space, though, and I was fascinated with science fiction and space exploration. I lived with television as the Mercury astronauts made their historical flights from Alan Shepard's sub-orbital lob to John Glenn's multi-orbital odyssey. In November 1960, John F. Kennedy was elected President. Mary and I were in the stands on Pennsylvania Avenue in front of the Justice Building to watch his inaugural parade on a viciously cold snowy day in January. My most vivid memory of the occasion was our thermos full of hot buttered rum. Without it, we would have perished without a doubt.

Then there were the trips to Monticello, Mt. Vernon, the Gettysburg

Davis, Binney, and Mary

Battlefield, and Williamsburg. On two memorable occasions, we went camping in the Blue Ridge Mountains. The first time, we hiked three or four miles back into the woods carrying huge packs of equipment. Neither Binney nor Mary were cut out for the life, though, and I don't think either of them slept the whole night, in spite of the snug pup-tent and sleeping bags. On the second occasion, we simplified the process and merely pitched our tent in a camping area. Unfortunately, though, we chose a night when it rained. And not only did it rain, but it flooded, and we found our sleeping bags and air-mattresses awash in inches of water. It was a cold bedraggled pair of humans and dog who emerged the next morning, never to try the experiment more.

In the summer of 1961, Binney's health deteriorated to the point where she became too sick to work. I had to make the agonizing decision to have her put to sleep. As long as I live, I will never forget the sense of loss and loneliness and the empty space which her passing left. One always becomes deeply attached to a guide dog, but the first one always holds a special place in one's memory. In fact, I think the standards set by the first dog always make it difficult to fully adjust to the successors. I don't think that I truly got over Binney and accepted my subsequent dogs until my third one, Shane.

Davis and Wyn at the Seeing Eye, 1961

Immediately following Binney's death, I returned to Morristown for three weeks and obtained Wyn. He was a large, black, and very sensitive male German shepherd. Afterward, we returned to Washington to begin the real period of adjustment which follows training, but things were about to change even more dramatically than we anticipated.

Soon after Christmas in 1961, my father's Uncle Claude passed away. Jeff had been sharing a practice in his law practice with Claude for several years. With Claude's passing, the family law firm of Duty & Duty had a vacancy that cried out to be filled. With my mother's urging and Mary's acquiescence (she foresaw the possibilities of a political career in Arkansas), I decided to leave Government service and return to a private law practice in Arkansas. Thus it occurred that on the day of the first circumglobal Mercury Mission by John Glenn Mary and I loaded up her tiny red Rambler American and headed south.

We decided to include a mini-vacation with our move to Arkansas, so our route took us through Virginia, the Carolinas,

Widely-Known Rogers Attorney Claude Duty Dies

and into Northern Florida. We stopped at St. Augustine and toured the historical sites, including Fort San Marcos. While there, we purchased for $10.00 a watercolor painting from a street artist of the site known as the "Old Spanish House. It hung in all of my homes until I passed it on to my daughter, Diana, in whose own home it now hangs. Such is the stuff of continuity and family tradition.

Departing St. Augustine, we drive across Florida, through Alabama, and up through Tennessee and Arkansas to Rogers. This voyage marked the end of the transition from youth and student to responsible husband and father and professional man. I had started in Rogers, then traveling by way of Fayetteville, Little Rock, Morristown, London, and Washington, and returned finally to Rogers to undertake the challenge of adulthood.

Wyn and Mary

Chapter 15

A Time of Ecstasy and Anguish
1962-1974

Mary and I began our new life in Rogers by renting a house on south Fourth Street, exactly eight blocks south of where I was born.[4] Then, having settled in domestically, I embarked upon the private practice of law as a member of the old and respected firm of Duty & Duty, Attorneys at Law.

My father's and my offices were located on the second floor above Ivan Rose's Rogers Pharmacy in the old Golden Rule Building. No one remembers where the Golden Rule name came from, but it can still be dimly seen to this day etched into the facade. The building still stands (as of this writing), much remodeled, on the southeast corner of Walnut and Second Streets.

The first thing I had to do was learn to practice law. For the Justice Department, I had been limited to answering correspondence and sorting evidence. Now I had to learn the nuts and bolts of really being a lawyer, such as writing contracts, wills, and deeds, examining abstracts, filing pleadings, arguing motions, trying cases, etc. My father was patience personified in teaching me the minutiae of the profession. He allowed me to use his own work as forms to follow in preparing documents. He never criticized or attempted to tell me what to do, but he never failed to give good advice and his quiet support. It was always to Jeff that I would go when I hit a rocky spot to cuss and expostulate. Then, with the edge taken off, I could deal with

---

[4] In another coincidence, this same house was later purchased by Mary's aunt Dorothy Ellis Ross, when she moved from her home in Garfield to live closer to her son and daughter-in-law, Bob and Cathy Ross.

the problem rationally. I must remember while I still can to thank him for all he did.

The Siren Song of Politics

Finally, in the fall of 1962, the dream of a political career for me suddenly gained real potential. I decided to run for the job of City Attorney. It was a small beginning, but it was a beginning. I ran against Walter Davidson, also a scion of an old Rogers family, and we just about split the vote. I did manage to get a few more votes, though, and on January 1, 1963, was sworn in to my newly elected position. It was only a part-time job, so I was able to continue with my private practice. That was a good thing too, since the job only paid $25 a month. For the next four years, encompassing two terms, it was my job to advise city officials, attend city council meetings, draft ordinances, and generally try to keep the city's legal affairs in order. I don't think I set any records, but I don't think I left the city's business in a shambles, either. Indeed, I take some pride in the fact that I was able to convince the city fathers to have the town's ordinances, which had accumulated haphazardly since its founding in 1881, formally codified and printed. At long last, one could actually discover what the law was.

Then, in 1968, I made a critical decision. The office of Circuit Judge became vacant due to a re-districting which removed Benton County from the territory served by the incumbent, Mawpin Cummins. I decided to seek the position, although one of the heavy weights of our county bar, Bill Infield, had announced as a candidate. It was a decision which I would in some ways

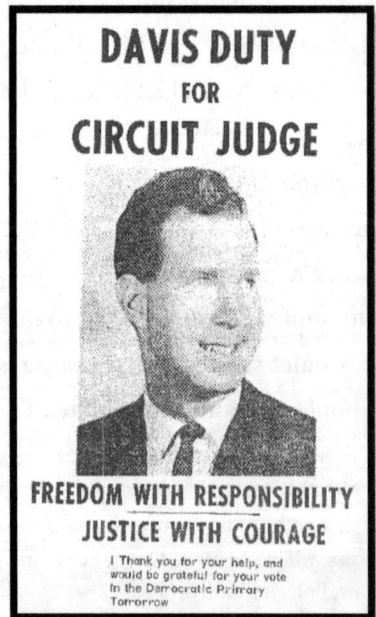

DAVIS DUTY
FOR
CIRCUIT JUDGE

FREEDOM WITH RESPONSIBILITY
JUSTICE WITH COURAGE

I Thank you for your help, and would be grateful for your vote in the Democratic Primary Tomorrow

regret, but in other ways be glad of in view of the new direction it forced upon my life. With my father's help, as he put in countless hours driving me around the three counties of Benton, Madison, and Carroll that comprised the new judicial district, I began six months of almost continuous campaigning. My practice suffered.

I received almost no financial support, but I made many friends and found that I truly enjoyed campaigning. We would drive to a town, I would find a contact, and

Davis and Wyn campaigning for Circuit Judge

with his help I would visit every business I could reach to shake the hands of proprietor and customers. I attended pie suppers. I spoke from a cattle sale barn, standing ankle deep in the manure of the sale ring. And I almost won.

On election night in November, 1968, the returns came in to reveal that I had lost the election by only 600 votes. Perhaps, if I had looked at it positively, I would have seen it as a promise of good prospects in the future. Because of the mental, material, and emotional price I had paid, though, I was at first plunged into severe depression. Soon, this gave way to a growing conviction that I did not really want a political career.

I did give it one more try, though. In 1970, I ran for and was elected to the post of Municipal Judge of Rogers. I served for eighteen months of the two-year term and am satisfied that I did a good job.

During my tenure, I initiated a teen jury program where teenagers guilty of minor offenses were judged by a jury of their peers, who made recommendations to me of appropriate sentences. The sentences were extralegal in that they could involve anything from roadside cleanup to writing themes. However, if the individual accepted the sentence and performed it, the charges against him would be dismissed and he would have no record. I felt that this system worked well, although it was allowed to decline and was eventually disbanded after I left office.

On the downside, though, I fell into a running battle with the Mayor and City Council. The police department was offended because I asserted a totally neutral position and would not accept police reports on their face value without question. Also, I required officers to check their guns with the clerk before entering the courtroom to testify. For this and other reasons, I found myself somewhat isolated in the city government. On the other hand, the court procedures were streamlined and revenues rose. In view of this, I decided, probably unwisely, to invoke state law which required a substantially greater salary for municipal judges than the one being paid by the City of Rogers. The City Council refused and I was forced to file suit.

Judge Infield denied my suit, but I appealed to the Supreme Court and won. It was not wholly unexpected that those who ran the city neither appreciated nor soon forgot. You might say that I had won the battle, but lost the war. Working in this atmosphere of controversy and disapproval, together with the damage suffered by my private practice (everyone seemed to think that I was no longer practicing law, although the Municipal Judgeship was supposedly a part-time job), caused me to eventually decide to resign from the position. I did so with a great sense of relief, but the damage had been done. My practice never really recovered, and I became a pariah among many of the businessmen of the community.

From this, though, I learned two lessons. First, sometimes you can do too good a job. Second, I really didn't want a political career. While I enjoyed campaigning and could win elections, I did not enjoy serving in office and having to make the compromises and trade-offs and engage in the back scratching necessary to perform effectively as an elected functionary. With these realizations, a process began which would dramatically alter my life in the next few years.

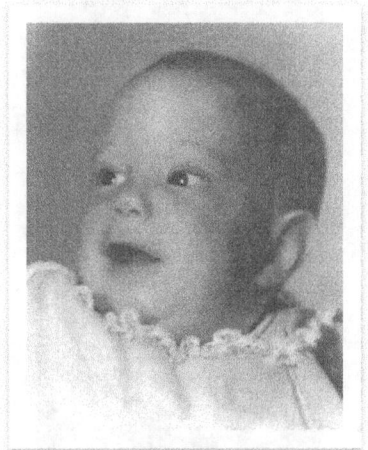

Baby Diana

Life in a Small Town

Other than politically, the 1960s were a time of personal growth. I made many friends. Mary and I had some good years of marriage. After weathering the tragedy of loosing our first baby at birth (a girl, born on August 22, 1963), we went on to have two children, Diana Lynn, born on August 8, 1965, and John Ellis, born on

Lois holding baby John (above)
Davis holding John (below)

Diana not holding John

October 4, 1967. I learned a lot about the profession of law and about myself. Mary began participating in numerous activities outside the home, which ultimately led to active work in Girl Scouting, the League of Women Voters, the Arkansas Art Center, the Arkansas Mental Health Association, and eventually even election to the Rogers City Council.

As a couple, we had many friends and an active social life. We belonged to a local art club where Mary, especially, could demonstrate her not insignificant artistic abilities. Among the members were Sharon and Lanny West. Lanny had been a member of the City Council at the same time as Mary. Although we had not known the Wests very well, they were nonetheless good friends whom we enjoyed very much until Lanny took a job in Fort Smith in 1973. Our paths would not cross again until almost twenty years later; but when they did, it would be in a most significant manner.

Mary and I also participated in a Play Reader's group (a method of acting whereby lines are read instead of memorized) and were fortunate enough to be cast in a number of plays. I even won the Best Actor of the Year award one year for my role as Dracula in the play by the same name. Mary later received the award in her own right.

Not everything which occurred in those years was serious, sober, and sane. There was the occasion when we were told by our young married babysitter, Pauline, that she thought she might be pregnant. The same evening, John came down with German Measles. I became concerned that the babysitter might have been exposed, which because of birth defects related to the disease was something to be taken very seriously. On the spur of the moment, I called Pauline and told her to go to the Municipal Hospital for a rabbit test and to charge it to me. Only later did it occur to my plodding brain that I had probably sown the seeds of delicious gossip! But thank God for both our sakes, the rabbit thrived.

Davis as Dracula for Play Readers

Another time, Mary and I were attending a houseboat party with friends on Beaver Lake. Sometime during the afternoon, a number of the guys hatched a plot. They invited me to join them in a powerboat to go down the lake. Once out of sight of the houseboat, my companions proposed a swim. I was reluctant to join since I had no swimming trunks. They convinced me, however, that I could go swimming in my undershorts since no one could see us. After splashing about for a time, I was persuaded to try my hand at waterskiing. Along with flying a glider and sky diving, this had long been one of my secret ambitions. The catch was that my so-called friends told me how to get up on my skis, but they didn't tell me how to get down and I didn't know enough to ask. Once up and flying along behind the ski-boat, I had no idea what to do but hold on to the rope as tight as possible until the boat stopped. What I didn't know until it was too late was that the boat, with me sailing along behind in my undershorts and nothing more, headed straight back to the houseboat where a movie camera had been set up to record the event. At our next party, the main entertainment was home movies. You can imagine the rest. I had to laugh, but it was kind of strained.

Other events were taking place during the '60s beyond the boundaries of our comfortable small town lives. These years were fraught with momentous happenings, especially on the national and international scene. There was the Cuban Crisis, President Kennedy's assassination, Lyndon Johnson's landslide victory over Barry Goldwater, the Vietnam War and the bitter controversy over it, the election of Richard Nixon to the Presidency, the moon landings, and the beginnings of wildfire inflation, accompanied by ultimately unsuccessful attempts at wage and price controls. Then, of course, there was the Watergate scandal involving President Nixon and his eventual resignation from office.

I was aware of all of these happenings. I was vitally interested in them. However, none of them really affected my life at the time. The possible exceptions were the assassination of President Kennedy and the moon landings. I was of the Camelot generation. John Kennedy stirred within us deep wellsprings of social awareness, patriotism, and a sense of international responsibility. Like so many others, my world seemed to have been dashed from its orbit when on November 22, 1963, the news flashed from Dallas that Kennedy had been shot. I was at the Lakeside Cafe, attending a Friday luncheon of the Kiwanis Club. Everett Bland, the City Clerk, entered the room and called for attention. When conversation was hushed, he announced the assassination. The absolute and

John (whose legs were too chubby to bend) and Diana

total silence that followed was unearthly. It was as though reality had ceased to exist. What we had known and believed in and counted on only moments before was no longer relevant. For the first time I understood the term, "a rudderless ship." The purpose, the hope, and the joy of the nation seemed to have been extinguished. I firmly believe that this was the beginning of a period of depression, both for me and for the nation, which only began to lift in the late '70s. From that moment on I have never again been completely able to believe in a real life dream. Fairy tales should not have bad endings.

The other event which stands out in my mind was the landing of American astronauts on the moon. The phrases, "The Eagle has landed," and "One small step for man; one giant step for mankind," still give me chills. I had long been a devotee of science fiction. I had a ten-year collection of Galaxy Magazine and an additional of Analogues. Star Trek was my favorite TV program of all time. The landing of Neil Armstrong and Buzz Aldrin on the moon seemed almost to lift America and me outside our bubble of concerns and offer us broad new horizons. Unfortunately, though, the party was soon over and we were back to news of Vietnam body counts, Presidential shenanigans, and soaring inflation. I guess we weren't yet quite ready to take the high road.

Truth to tell, like so many others, I was too wrapped up in my own affairs at the time to care much about world news. At first, they were public affairs but, as the years passed, my emphasis began to shift more and more to my private law practice and more especially my family.

As Mary's interest and time spent in the public arena increased, mine diminished. I made fewer public appearances, delivered fewer speeches, was offered and accepted fewer public posts. I spent more and more time working in my office during the day and going home to give the children their dinner, take them for a walk, see to their bath, and put them to bed. Mary spent her evenings doing volunteer work at the library or engaging in her many public activities. It is not unnatural that our lives drifted apart. Indeed, we almost became strangers.

The most vivid recollections which I have from about 1968 to 1975 have to do with my children, my yard, and chess. Almost every evening, after dinner, summer and winter, the children and I would go for a walk. The first time that I took Diana for one, we explored a country road and a grassy field where we had never been before. Always curious, Diana asked me what we were doing. I told her that we were having an adventure. When we returned home, she told her mother proudly that we had been on a "Venture!" From then on, we never took walks, we went on Ventures. This was especially apt since a great deal of new construction was going on in our neighborhood. Old farmsteads were being converted into subdivisions. New houses were sprouting like mushrooms. As soon as a street would be opened, we would explore it. When construction on a house began, we followed it from the foundation up. Times without number, we wandered through half-completed houses letting our imaginations arrange and furnish the rooms.

At first our walks were just that, by foot. Later, though, the children acquired bicycles and my dog and I would trot along behind. The procession was usually led by Diana on her bike with training wheels with me right behind, sometimes holding on to the carriage rack to stay in control of the situation. John would follow behind on his half-bike. We almost always started by taking a road behind our house which led past a pasture owned by the Fairchilds in which they kept their two horses, Honey and Rebel. Our first stop would be to pet Honey and Rebel, who eventually learned the approximate time to expect us. They would be waiting by the fence for us to pass. Then it would be on to some new subdivision to investigate the new changes. Once, when a sidewalk was being poured along Oak Street, from Dixieland to Westside Grade School, I gave the children permission to scratch their names and the date into the wet concrete with a nail. Afterward though, as we walked back home, I regretted my impulse. It might have been neat to go back years later and see their childish inscriptions, but I realized that it was also destruction of public property, which is nothing less than vandalism. I, therefore, had to own up to my error and tell the children I was wrong and why. Then we went back and erased our handiwork. A long time later, I discovered that they both remembered the incident and the lesson we had all learned from it.

My second preoccupation was with my yard. In 1963, we left the house we had rented on south

Fourth Street to a house we bought at 620 South Dixieland Road. This was at the very western edge of the city. Our house was located on the west side of Dixieland Road facing east. Behind us was an unfenced, ten-acre grassy field lying fallow. Beyond that were small farmsteads. Over the next ten years, the city caught up with us and passed us by. Westside School, where both children started the first grade, was not built until about 1970. For the first few years, we enjoyed the grassy expanse behind our house. We came to think of it as our own backyard. But then, about 1967 or '68, the developers struck and a street was cut through just one lot removed behind our house. Seeing the handwriting on the wall, I bought the lot behind us, giving our property a total length of 280 feet from Dixieland Road west. The plot was only 50 feet wide, but we had one huge backyard.

My first move was to extend the chain-link fence to the new property line. Now the children's dog, Lassie-Wyn (named after Lassie of movie fame and my second guide dog) had a place to run, and the children could be safe when they were small, without wandering into the street. Next, I began landscaping the backyard. Before the house was sold in 1975, we had producing walnut trees, Norway spruces, a pecan tree, a Japanese cherry tree, several dwarf fruit trees, a Chinese chestnut tree, and a Dawn redwood tree. For decoration, we had honeysuckle on the fence, trumpet vines, forsythia, lilacs, boxwoods, and gooseberry and blueberry bushes.

For Diana's sixth birthday, I had a pre-fab playhouse placed on a concrete slab, in which her younger brother John placed his footprints to match those of Diana's on our back kidney-shaped porch. We finished the interior with paneling and built-in shelves and her grandmother Lois made pretty curtains for the windows. That was Diana's domain.

My crowning achievement, though, was my grape arbor. I laid out a latticed gazebo twelve feet long and eight feet wide, surrounded by a brick border garden plot. On top of the arbor, we had a running horse weathervane. Inside the arbor, I hung a porch swing. The floor was covered with several inches of sand to double as a sandbox for the children. In the garden strip, I planted tomatoes. With an all-weather light rigged inside, we had a place where the children could play during the day and I could swing at night and play my harmonica or accordion, to, I am certain, the limitless enjoyment of the neighbors. My finishing touch was to plant grapevines, which eventually covered the entire structure with a cool green and almost impenetrable leaf canopy. In the evenings when the children and I weren't out on Ventures, we would sit in the swing making up impromptu rhyming songs to the accompaniment of the swing. I am sure both children will remember the song that goes, "Cows go moo, cows go moo, all the cows go moo, moo, moo, etc." Our poetry may have been limited, but our fun was not.

Diana and John (Diana's playhouse is behind on the left)

John and Diana (the grape arbor is behind to the right)

What with mowing the yard, cultivating my scattered garden plots, transplanting zoysia grass, and stacking firewood, I never lacked for something to do. Eventually, I had a sidewalk poured along the street on the back side of the lot so that the children and their friends would have a place to skate and play without having to get into the street. I rather hoped that the neighbors on either side would follow suit and extend the walk up and

Diana, Davis, and John showing off their tomatoes

down the street. To my knowledge, though, they never did.

The children and my yard left little time for anything else outside the office. My only extracurricular indulgence became my obsession with chess. In the early '70s, as my law practice dwindled, I began inviting friends to come to the office in the afternoons to play chess with me between clients. Eventually, I was playing more chess than practicing law. Most of my chess partners were retired gentlemen who were only too glad to have something to occupy their afternoons. The most faithful of them included Jack Holt, a retired bricklayer; Walter Lane, a retired civil engineer; and Orval Hall, a retired dry cleaner, who also had talent as a Hamm radio operator, amateur magician, and organist. I am sure that my children will remember the Halloweens when we would trick-or-treat the Halls and he would treat us with a magic show accompanied by hot popcorn. He later became known as the Popcorn King of Rogers.

My involvement in chess eventually reached the point where we formed a chess club with members from as far away as Lowell, Bentonville, and Garfield. We worked out a running tournament system based on points and for three years awarded trophies. I won two seconds and a first. In the end, though, I became so preoccupied with chess, probably to distract me from business and domestic worries, that I even dreamed chess. At that point, I

Davis and Shane

began to realize that chess was indeed becoming an obsession and I made a conscious effort to reduce it to its proper place. I continued to enjoy the game, but played it less and less as the years went by. My skill has eroded, but I still have those trophies.

In June 1969, my preoccupation with children, yard work, and chess had to be suspended. My second dog, Wyn, suffered a disintegrated disc in his back. He was only eight years old, but one morning he was unable to get out of his basket. He didn't seem to be in any pain, but his hind quarters were completely paralyzed. There was no alternative but have him put to sleep. Also, there was no alternative but for me to make immediate application to return to The Seeing Eye for a replacement. And her name was Shane; a regal little German shepherd female with boundless enthusiasm and joie de vivre. I don't think that I had ever allowed myself to become totally bonded with Wyn (a classic first dog syndrome), but I fell in love with Shane. I even liked the name. It somehow seemed dashing, especially in light of the recent movie of that name staring Alan Ladd. Shane only had one problem—chronic diarrhea. I had to be forever looking for grassy spots and had to be prepared to take her out at a moment's notice several times a day. She never got over it and it was a constant source of anxiety. In fact, it was indirectly because of the diarrhea that I would later loose her.

I firmly believe, however, that one must accept that life is a never ending series of gains and losses, successes and failures. The degree to which we can adjust to the fact that for every three steps forward we may take two steps backward is the degree to which we achieve maturity. For every beginning, there is an ending; but without endings, there can be no new beginnings.

–Staff Photo

BOSS OF THE YEAR–Mrs. Sally Williams, business education coordinator of the Rogers High School, presents the Boss of the Year award to Davis Duty, Rogers attorney, at a luncheon yesterday for students and their bosses in the Cooperative Office Education program of the school. Each student in the program wrote a theme on her boss. Selection of the award was based on the themes. At left is Marsha Goebel, secretary in Duty's office, who received the Girl Friday award for writing the winning theme. Twenty-five students are in the program.

Chapter 16

Dixieland Road Vignettes
1963-1975

So many little things, brief episodes, occurred during the early years of my adulthood. They primarily relate to the years 1963 to 1975, when we lived in our first family home at 620 South Dixieland Road in Rogers. Many of them I cherish as memories, although they are barely substantial enough to recount. I remember building the top to my grape arbor. I put it together on the patio, but was then unable to move it. I finally solved the problem by enlisting the services of Reverend Charles MacDonald (our Methodist Church pastor) and his five sons, stair-stepped from age 16, to help me lift and carry it to the arbor frame and settle it into place. It was not unlike the spirit board experience where everyone places their fingers on a bridge table and it mysteriously rises off the ground. With all those strong arms and willing hands, my immovable construction verily rose into the air and floated to its resting place. I never appreciated my preacher more.

The grape arbor project was only the first of my woodworking projects. I built a work table in the corner of the carport and worked there summer and winter on one project after another. I designed and built a tiny chair for Diana when she was two years old. I built at least two inlaid chessboards. I built two doll houses; the first was a prototype for Diana and the second was a more elaborate and finished piece as my contribution to the annual Art Club Auction. It was bought by Clyde and Geneva Wyant.

They paid $75 for it and took great pains to fancy it up even more for their grandchildren. For many years, and they may do it yet, they decorated it for Christmas and used it as a centerpiece of their Yuletide decor. They even installed tiny electric lights.

Another memory, also related to my woodworking, involves the very simple and very small box-sled which I built for John and Diana, perhaps in remembrance of my own grand childhood sled rides. When the snows were deep enough, I would harness myself to it with a rope and

–Staff Photo

UNIQUELY UNIQUE . . . That's the best way to describe Davis Duty's accomplishment in designing and constructing this "real-to-life" dollhouse which was sold Tuesday night to the Rogers Lions Club at the second annual FAB fine arts group's auction held at the Bob Wesley workshop barn in Rogers. Duty, who is a blind attorney in Rogers, and his wife, Mary Alice, are members of FAB. Pictured with the couple are their two children, Diana, 4,and John, 2. Diana was willing to let the Lions Club take ownership of the dollhouse, which her mother painted and decorated inside, because her father presented her with a similiar one he made at Christmas.

pull them endlessly around the front yard. The grand finale was always a quick turn upsetting the sled to send them rolling and squealing in the snow.

About 1968, we began to outgrow the house. Rather than move away from my hard-won yard, we decided to add on a wing and a patio. The patio was put in by a client in payment of his fee. It was kidney-shaped to avoid a Mimosa tree which I had grown from a seedling. As mentioned earlier, Diana proudly planted her little three-year-old footsteps in the wet cement by the water faucet as a lasting memento of our happy years there.

The wing was a more ambitious project. It contained a dining room, a spare bedroom, a laundry room, and a library, 26 feet long and 12 feet wide, with a fireplace at the far end. My pride and joy was the woodbox which I designed. It was accessible by an external door through which the wood could be loaded. On the inside, it was a window seat beside the fireplace, and *Voila!* logs were handy for the hearth. When completed, these improvements gave us all of the room and comforts we desired. But it was another story while they were being built. The wing was begun in November and was not heated until it was complete in late January. After the walls were enclosed, it was necessary to open the accessway from the main house, which made it not unlike living with an open door to the North Pole. We hung a

John, Diana, Davis, Mary
with Nonny 1973

plastic sheet over the opening, but we suffered many a goosebump before the new furnace was installed and civilization restored.

The bits and pieces would not be complete without remembering the little red wagon. We bought it for Diana as a Christmas present in 1966 when she was a year old, but it soon began to double as a yard tool. It was amazing how useful it became in hauling sand to the sandpile, dirt to the garden, and firewood and concrete blocks. Every homeowner should have one, whether he has children or not. It is even possible that Diana will remember it as the transportation by which we walked the mile or so each evening to visit her mother and new baby brother in the hospital. We must have made quite a sight as we walked down the edge of the street (there were no sidewalks in that part of town), me working my dog and pulling the wagon with my other hand, and Diana sitting there in the wagon with her Raggedy Ann doll, while carrying on one of our

interminable conversations about the nature of stars, how birds fly, where rain comes from; or she would merely sing to entertain us. These were moments of closeness which a daddy can never forget.

Lest it be thought that I was a complete drudge in those years, limiting myself to practicing law, mowing my lawn, and sharing with my children, my civic activities should also be reported. Although not in chronological order, they included membership on the board of the Friends of the Library, Rogers Museum Commission, Benton County Bar Association for which I was president in 1964, Arkansas Bar Association, American Bar Association, and, of course, Play Readers, The Benton County Chess Club, and the Fine Arts Bunch (FAB). Soon after returning to Rogers, I had joined the Kiwanis Club. This was a family tradition since my grandfather, John R. Duty, had helped found it and in 1924 was the first president of the Rogers Chapter.

I also took part in Scouting, for both boys and girls. For the latter, Mary and I were, for several years, sponsors of a cadet troop, until they all grew up and became more interested in boys than in selling cookies.

I was also an easy mark when it came to making speeches. I spoke to high school assemblies, civic classes, civic club luncheons, and even gave a Commencement Address for Pea Ridge High School. I was asked to help organize the first Career Day program for Rogers High School and was privileged to give the opening address and later to speak to those students interested in the legal profession. On another occasion, I taught a multi-lecture series on farm law as part of the University Extension Program. Once, I was even drafted to teach a simplified course on contracts as part of the Legal Secretaries Certification project.

As a family, we attended the First United Methodist Church where I sang in the choir, taught a Sunday School class, and was a member of the Board of Stewards.

It was also a lot of fun for me to participate in the Community Chorus. Although the chorus only lasted a few years, it was quite good, and

I also had the pleasure of singing again with my old friend Ernie Lawrence. He and I first sang together in the Key Club Quartet at Little Rock High School and in the school choir. Later, at the University, we were both in Phi Delta Theta Fraternity, which won the Fraternity Choral Competition at least two years running. Ernie and I both went to law school at the same time and upon graduation, he set up practice in Bentonville, which was only seven miles away from Rogers. It was inevitable that our paths would frequently cross both professionally and personally. Ernie and his wife Julie were one of the few couples with whom Mary and I actually had a close friendship. On one occasion, our families (children and all: Vicki, Billy, Diana, and John) spent a weekend together in a cabin at War Eagle. Ernie preceded me in 1963 as president of the Benton County Bar Association, and he and I together compiled the prospectus which won for us from the Arkansas Bar Association the annual award for Best Local Bar Association in the State. For a while, we even sang together in the St. Andrew's Episcopal Church Choir in Rogers where Ernie and Julie were members. He conscripted me to help when they were trying to build a choir.

Last, but not least (to be trite), although it took place in 1963, the JCs honored me with the award as Rogers' Young Man of the Year. They took me completely by surprise. They told me that the award was being given to my old friend, Russell Riggs, and I was asked to get him there without his learning what was afoot and then to be prepared to present the trophy and a flowery extollation of his many virtues. It turned out that Russell was getting me to the banquet and doing all of the talking. I was probably never again quite so popular. At least for one night, though, my friends and colleagues

Shane, the Legal-'Beagle'

Shane, a German shepherd seeing-eye dog, leads his master, Jeff Davis Duty Jr., from the Supreme Court building after Duty was admitted to practice before the court. Shane was only the second dog in history permitted inside the court. (UPI Radiophoto)

Supreme Court Admits Duty, Permits His Dog in Chamber

From Gazette Press Services

WASHINGTON — A dog was allowed in the Supreme Court Monday for only the second time in memory.

Shane, a black and tan seeing-eye German shepherd, accompanied his master, Jeff Davis Duty Jr. of Rogers, Ark., for his formal admission to the bar.

The clerk's office said it was only the second time — in modern memory at least — that a dog had been allowed in the Court chambers.

Shane lay at his master's feet for 30 minutes as Chief Justice Warren E. Burger read through a long list of lawyers before coming to Duty's name.

The dog then led Duty to the lectern, where he was sponsored by his father-in-law, Clyde T. Ellis, a local attorney.

Shane appeared a bit nervous when he then had to go and stand for another five minutes until clerk John F. Davis administered the oath to Duty and a group of lawyers.

A Court official could not recall the name of the first man accompanied by his seeing-eye dog, but said permission was granted after he told them his dog "would climb the walls" if he were made to stay outside.

Duty had written in advance to obtain permission for Shane's appearance.

(Duty, who has been blind since he was five, almost had to turn down a Fulbright scholarship in 1957 for a year's study at the University of London because the British government refused to relax its stringent quarantine on dogs.

Senator J. William Fulbright (Dem, Ark.) tried to get the British to allow Duty to bring in his seeing-eye dog, Binney, without subjecting it to a six months' quarantine, but the British refused.

(Duty, then 22, sailed with his dog and accepted an offer of volunteer guide service from University of London students until his dog could be released. He visited the dog daily at the quarantine station near London to keep her in training.)

showered me with affection and appreciation. It is an experience which everyone should have at least once in a lifetime.

In 1970, we traveled to Washington, DC, in order that I could be admitted to the United States Supreme Court. My father-in-law Clyde T. Ellis formally introduced me to the Court which included Chief Justice Burger, and Justices Black, Douglas, Harlan, Brennan, Stewart, White, Blackmun, and Thurgood Marshall. I was the first lawyer ever to be admitted to the Court accompanied by his guide dog. Up until about 1960, all guide dogs were excluded from the Courtroom while the Court was in session. With the support of my Congressman (Judge) Jim Trimble from Berryville and Arkansas Senator Fulbright I was able to persuade the Court to allow guide dogs into the Courtroom with their partners when attending as spectators. Binney became the first Seeing Eye dog to exercise this privilege. Then, almost ten years later, I succeeded and it became Shane's lot to become the first guide dog to actually appear before the Court when Clyde presented us for admission on June 8, 1970. Another barrier down and another milestone passed.

The End of My Springtime

While I was turning inward, Mary was turning outward. Compounding this, my law practice never really recovered from the damage it had suffered while I was serving as Municipal Judge. Too many of my clients had found new attorneys. So, while I struggled at work and immersed myself in yard work and child care, my marriage imperceptibly unraveled.

Later, in a moment of candor and self-analysis, Mary was to explain that when I turned away from public life, I had tacitly violated our agreement. I think she cared for me when we married, but she thought she was hitching her wagon to a star and found that instead she had hitched her wagon to an ordinary horse and not a thoroughbred at that. She was bitterly disappointed and in reaction began to cultivate a public career for herself. The problem, though, was that in our limited environment, she was unable to separate her image from mine. She could never quite shed the identity of Mrs. Davis Duty. In the social context at the time, this was normal, but her need for individual recognition was also understandable, especially since I had deprived her of a chance to participate in more vibrant and meaningful activities.

So, as the early years of the 1970s passed, I struggled financially and more or less insulated myself emotionally and socially. Mary went her own way. Resentment and disappointment between us grew. By 1974, the breach was irreparable.

On the day before our fifteenth wedding anniversary, I packed a bag and moved out. I thought the separation was temporary and would operate to force us to confront our problems. In reality, it was the straw that broke the camel's back. I never again returned to our home on Dixieland Road. For a while, I lived in my office where I had a hot-plate and small refrigerator. This became intolerable, though, and I obtained a nearby apartment in which I lived for several months with only a chair and a bed. For a dresser and bureau I had a cardboard box and a suitcase. I still cooked my meals on my hot-plate at the office.

My biggest problem concerned the children. For years, I had participated equally in their care. Now I only got to see them two or three times a week. In addition, I became so depressed and distraught that my law practice suffered even more. It was with considerable relief then that I was presented with the opportunity for a career change. Some years previously I had learned about job opportunities as an Administrative Law Judge for the Federal Government, particularly Social Security. I filed an application, but it became lost in the bureaucratic shuffle. In early 1975, though, it popped out of the void. Almost like divine intervention, I was offered a position as a Supplemental Security Income hearing examiner. I took it and in a matter of two months closed my practice, traveled to Washington to undergo training and prepared to move to Florence, Alabama, to begin my new job. Another chapter of my life had ended and a new one began.

Chapter 17

A Return to the Womb
of Government Service
1975-1976

It broke my heart to leave my children when I moved to Alabama, but the new job seemed to offer a new beginning, not to mention solutions to my career and financial distress. Also, there was an additional thread which briefly unrolled with the fabric of my life, although in the long run it affected things very little. Just before leaving Rogers, I became involved romantically with a young lady. Her name was Gail Smith and she worked as the office manager for a dentist friend of mine. By this time, Mary had filed for divorce and I know now that I was acting on the rebound. The romance was a whirlwind affair and in Florence, Alabama, on the day that my divorce from Mary was final, April 14, 1975, Gail and I were married. From the very beginning, our marriage was stormy. Matters were complicated by a very young step-daughter, Delane, as well as my own children, not to mention an old boyfriend of Gail's who she could not quite bring herself give up. Within three months, Gail and I were separated.

Other than the birth and death of romance, I only have one other vivid recollection of my time in Florence. It was the visit of Diana and John. Gail had returned to Arkansas, bag and baggage, and I was scheduled to attend a conference in Atlanta, Georgia. There was nothing for it but to take the children with me. I was too strapped financially to be able to afford to go by air, so we took the bus instead. I scheduled the departure for early evening in the hopes that we could sleep through most of the trip. As it turned out, we got very little rest. At one rest-stop, Diana and I got off the bus to get something to drink and emerged from the cafe to find our bus, with young son and little brother John pulling away. We managed to flag it down, though, and I vowed never to let us be separated again. This is one promise I kept.

Early the next morning, we staggered off the bus in Atlanta and, after washing up in the public restrooms, cabbed to our hotel. For the next two days, I shuffled from meeting room to hotel room, trying to entertain the children while attending to business at the same time. At one point, I found the children very upset because they had been expelled from the swimming pool for having no adult companion. We survived, though, and devoted the last day of our trip to a visit to Six Flags over Georgia. By this time, I was woozy with fatigue and spent the whole day drowsing on benches in the sun while John and Diana set out to test every ride in the park. We all three had an unforgettably good time together. Then, it was another night long bus ride back to Florence. The memory is etched into my brain of leading two sleepy children while carrying three suitcases for six blocks from the bus station to my apartment. I suppose, though, that it was a character-building experience. The ironic part is that I now look back on it as one of my fondest memories.

But one trip to an amusement park does not a relationship make or preserve. In the months to come, it became increasingly evident that the child-parent bond must suffer by separation. I did what I could, which was little enough. I wrote to the children once a week and called them every other day, preferably when their mother wasn't at home in order to avoid distractions and conflicts. Still, I became more and more a stranger with each passing month. I did not know their new friends. I was not involved with their activities. They missed me, but their activities began to take precedence over time out for phone chats. It was a wrenching time for us all. It was probably harder on me, though. The children had their friends and activities, but I was mostly alone. Gail had departed in May, and I had no friends and few acquaintances in Florence. It can best be termed as one of those times which have to be endured.

Later that summer of 1975, I had a chance to transfer to Fresno, California. Gail had always wanted to live in California, and we decided to give things another try. In early November 1975, Shane and I headed west with a hired driver in a U-Haul truck, while Gail traveled separately with her daughter by car. We met in Fresno and commenced our second of three abortive attempts to set up housekeeping together. We should have quit while we were ahead. Our marriage was still rocky and the situation was not improved when, two months later, I was offered a promotion to full Administrative Law Judge status with the Social Security Administration. It required that I move to Phoenix, Arizona. I certainly didn't object to that, but the added stress of yet another relocation was just about the last straw for my marriage.

In January 1976, I went to Washington for two weeks additional training as an ALJ and in early February took up residence in Phoenix. Before the month was out, the final breach came in Gail's and my marriage. She and her daughter returned home to Arkansas and I moved into a studio apartment at the corner of Earl and 7th Street near my office. I filed for divorce and in July 1976 I once again found myself single.

To dispose of the unpleasant part first, I must explain that after much agonizing, it became apparent to me that I had no choice but to declare bankruptcy. It went against everything I believed in, but many of Gail's creditors from before we were married had taken the liberty of putting her debts in my name. Although I had not agreed to this, it resulted in my being flooded with claims which I neither could pay nor felt obligated to pay. My credit, though, was in serious jeopardy and this in turn threatened my employment with the Federal Government. I felt that I had no choice but to file bankruptcy, although I later made an effort to pay off most of the debts which were legitimately mine. This took me several years, but I paid off almost everything.

I met Liz on March 9, 1976. This was the day that Gail flew out of Phoenix's Sky Harbor Airport, headed for her home in Arkansas. A psychologist friend of mine was worried that I might be so despondent that I would become a recluse. He, therefore, suggested that like a pilot who has sustained an airplane crash I should go back up immediately. He knew a young lady whose marriage had recently foundered and felt that we would hit it off. He arranged to take us to lunch by way of an introduction. Her name was Joan Elizabeth Peachy.

On that day, we met for lunch at the Playboy Club, which was on the top floor of the building where both his and my offices were located. This is how Liz became part of my life. Ah ha! You caught the discrepancy. First I report her name as Joan and then I call her Liz. This was because I changed her name or rather adopted the abbreviated form of her middle name, Elizabeth. It happened this way. At our lunch at the Playboy Club, we sat and talked for over two hours and made a date to see one another again. The next evening we went out. It was on this occasion that she was transformed into Liz. Still suffering from a mild concussion at Gail's hands (her parting shot with one of my chess trophies), I was totally unable to recall Joan's first name. However, I was never one to be outwitted. I very cleverly asked her middle name and she replied that it was Elizabeth. I thereupon announced jubilantly that I wasn't surprised because she seemed to be more of a Liz than a Joan. Then she told me the story of how her name had actually been confused at birth. Her mother had intended to call her Elizabeth Joan but it had gotten reversed on the birth certificate. In fact, her mother did occasionally call her Elizabeth. In any event, she became and remained Liz from that day on.

Chapter 18

Rising Like the Phoenix
1976-1979

I now lived in Phoenix, Arizona. This seemed appropriate in view of the fact that, like the Phoenix of myth, I was rising from the ashes of my former life. Things were definitely improving. First, my financial situation improved, not only with the salary raise which went along with my appointment as a full ALJ, but also with removal of my ex-wife's debts through bankruptcy. Then my divorce from her became final. In the meantime, Liz and I were developing into a Real Thing.

One of the things which was hardest for me to adjust to was living alone. Living with a family and living as a bachelor are two entirely different kettles of fish. The latter, however can be interesting as demonstrated by my close brush with horror in the best of Steven King tradition.

At the time, I occupied an apartment on the ground floor of a two-story apartment complex. The apartment directly above mine was occupied by a number of young ladies. I cannot prove the exact nature of their activities. I can only relate that as dusk would fall each evening a steady stream of young men would ascend the front stairs while an equal number would depart from the back door of the apartment and descend the back stairs. It is only conjectural what took place between the front and back doors, other than the sounds of lively partying which dearly penetrated my ceiling, especially on weekends.

The incident alluded to above occurred late one Saturday night. I was in bed, almost asleep, when I became aware of a steady drip of liquid falling from my ceiling onto my bedspread. The longer I listened to that rhythmic plop, plop, plop, the more I became convinced that I was in the midst of a horror fantasy. I could clearly visualize the bedroom above mine in which debauchery had led to butchery. Without any doubt, the drops of liquid falling from the ceiling were red and warm. This scenario was strengthened by the uncharacteristically absolute silence from above, in stark contrast to the raucous laughter and music of only a few minutes earlier.

For an eternity, I laid in bed trying to come to grips with monsters from the id. The hardest part was bringing myself to reach my hand from under the covers and touch the wet spot. It was nothing less than utter relief I felt when the moisture proved to be cold and odorless. I couldn't tell what color it was, but its texture was more like ice water than gore. Obviously, a drink, rather than blood, had been spilled upstairs. Instead of confirming that I lived below a nest of homicidal maniacs, the incident only proved that I had very thin and not waterproof ceilings. Still, it was one of the longest few minutes of my life.

When not imagining boogeymen in the dark, events were moving forward and my new life was taking shape. I was becoming a competent, although probably not a great judge, and in the fall of 1976 I gained custody of my children. Mary had decided to go back to school for her master's degree in social work and it seemed best for all concerned that they come to live with me, at least on a temporary basis. Suddenly, from a pseudo- bachelor, I became a single parent.

The children arrived in Phoenix with my mother just before Labor Day, and immediately after Labor Day I enrolled John in Encanto School and Diana in Clarendon Junior High in the

Diana, Davis, and John at
Encanto Park, Summer, 1976

Osborn School District. Diana began the sixth grade and John began the third grade. It became necessary to trade my neat little studio apartment for a three-bedroom model and I began to look around for a house to rent or buy. Soon thereafter, Liz and I decided to get married and set the date for December 29. She was Catholic and I was Methodist. She couldn't get married in a Catholic church because she was divorced. The Methodist church was a bit too Protestant for her comfort at the time. Therefore, we settled on the

Liz at Encanto Park, Summer, 1976

Episcopal service and were married at St. Mary's Church in Phoenix by

Joseph Hart, a real live Episcopal Bishop. Only a few friends and family members were present, and we held the service in a chapel, but Bishop Hart did it up right with all of the flourishes and panoply. This time I really felt married.

Liz and Davis' wedding, 1976

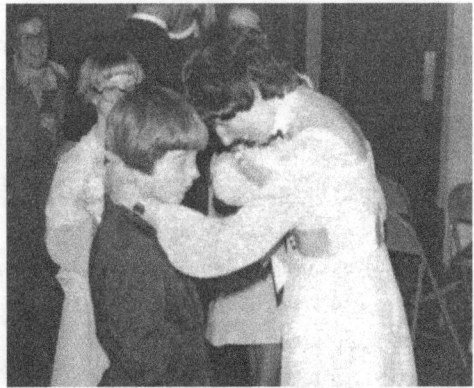

Family portrait, 1977

Dorothy Mitchell, an old friend from Art Club days in Rogers, had moved to Phoenix and we had run into each other by accident. She was at the wedding and volunteered to stay with the children while Liz and I took a short honeymoon. We stayed for three days in a small resort chalet

near Nogales on the Mexican border. As a result of crossing the border and having dinner in Mexico, we both came down with Montezuma's Revenge. It was a happy but pale and somewhat shaky couple who returned to Phoenix to start the new year.

The year 1977 was most notable for when we bought a house and I received my fourth and fifth guide dogs.

Liz and Davis in the Wild West, Rawhide, Arizona, 1977

New homeowners, 1977

Becoming a homeowner didn't take long because we moved in on March 3rd. The new Duty home was at 3307 North 18th Avenue, just two blocks south of Osborn Road. It was a short two mile walk to my office and a half-mile walk to Diana's and John's schools. It was perfect. I immediately began improvements, which resulted in mini grape arbors and fruit trees, especially my figs. The only drawback to house holding in Arizona proved to be black widow spiders. Although we found some and kept on the watch, no one in the family was ever bitten. I finally came to the conclusion that while black widows are deadly, they are not overly aggressive. They don't go looking for trouble.

We also decided that it was time to get the children a dog. In the interest of discipline, I had to discourage Liz and the children from petting Shane. It wasn't fair,

Liz, John, and Heather, 1977

though, so we found ourselves a half black Lab and half German shepherd puppy who joined the family with a vengeance. Ostensibly, Heather was John's dog, at least he was the one who had to go through obedience training; but she was ever the equal opportunity pet. She was one of these animals that craves affection and has no shame in seeking it at any price. Even my dogs, Shane, and later Cinder, couldn't resist her charm.

On July 4th, I lost Shane. I don't know exactly what happened. She was getting old and was almost totally blind, but she continued to work with a will. Her diarrhea was getting worse, though. It had reached the stage where I was having to take her out numerous times each day. Although not an approved practice by the Seeing Eye, I finally resorted to letting her out to run loose in our fenced backyard. Otherwise I would have spent more time in the yard with her than doing anything else. Besides, she and Heather

had fun playing together and I believed that the romping helped Shane dissipate some of the nervous energy which contributed to her intestinal problem.

In any event, I put her out in the backyard on the evening of July 4th. When I went to call her in, though, she was gone. The back gate had been forced inward which meant that someone from the outside had opened it to let her out. Although a sociable creature, Shane was not so friendly that she would have ordinarily left the yard with a stranger. However, two factors came together to achieve a bad result. Shane was terrified of the noise from fireworks and even early in the afternoon of the 4th neighborhood children were exploding firecrackers. This probably made her nervous enough to take advantage of an escape route even from the safety of our isolated back yard. In addition, dogs had been disappearing regularly all over the city. It was later disclosed that a dognapping ring had been operating in the area, collecting animals for resale for laboratory use. Since we never found any trace of Shane, in spite of the fact that she wore a metal collar clearly stamped with the Seeing Eye logo, as well as city vaccination tags and a tattoo on her ear, I strongly suspect that she was a victim of foul play. At least I have the satisfaction, however, of knowing that she could not have lived long enough to be subjected to laboratory experimentation. Although appearing outwardly vigorous and healthy, close inspection would have revealed a delicate older dog who was kept going on medication. Actually, I should have retired her at least a year earlier. Without her medications, she could not have lasted more than a few days. I am still wracked with guilt, though, when I recall what happened.

Fortunately for me, the Seeing Eye was understanding and took Shane's loss in stride. I was immediately enrolled in a new class and once again headed for Morristown. Pairing me with a new dog proved more difficult this time. First, we tried Tara, a gentle German shepherd female who immediately began to develop diarrhea. Before the problem could get bad enough to ruin Tara for someone else, she was exchanged for Jenny, a large powerful outgoing female German shepherd. In the beginning, she looked like the perfect dog. She was energetic, enthusiastic, physically strong, but best of all, tough as a boot. Yet, it was not to be. I had no more than returned home a few days before Jenny, too, began to show signs of the same condition which had afflicted Shane and Tara. I was later to learn that it results from a hypermotile intestinal tract which goes into spasm under stress. Some dogs have it and some don't and there is no really good way to detect it in advance. A dog may do fine through training, but come apart when they have to assume actual responsibility for their human companion. So it was with Jenny. I had no choice but to return her to the Seeing Eye and try again.

Now I was in a real bind. I had taken off almost a month to train with Tara and Jenny. I simply could not take off more time from my job. On the other hand, I needed a dog in order to do my job. Again, the Seeing Eye came through. They had recently had a four-year-old black female Labrador Retriever returned to the school when her master suffered a fatal heart attack. They warned me that she was used to walking with a frail little gentleman and that I would have to resign myself to strolling rather than going at a dead-run as I had always done before. The good news was that because of her maturity and my experience they would be willing to send her out with a trainer to put us through a truncated adjustment program and I would not have to spend any more time at the Seeing Eye proper. Best of all though, I was told that Cinder "shit bricks." I snapped at the offer and in January 1978 Dan Boeke, a senior member of the Seeing Eye training staff, and Cinder flew to Phoenix.

It was just before closing time at my office on a Monday evening when Dan and Cinder were announced. When greetings were over, Mr. Boeke (it is a tradition for Seeing Eye students and instructors to address one another formally) told me to put the harness on Cinder and walk home. When we got outside it was pouring rain, but Mr. Boeke was there to work and Cinder, being a Lab, didn't mind the water at all. The miracle was that

Cinder immediately adjusted to my faster pace and I was never forced to stroll like a little old man. We took to each other like the two pros we were and never looked back. Two miles later, we reached home, more closely resembling drowned rats than two grown men and a dog, but I knew already that my mobility problem had been solved. Three days later, Mr. Boeke flew back to Morristown and Cinder and I began ten years of super teamwork. She lacked the enthusiasm and playfulness of my shepherds. She made up for it, however, in single mindedness when it came to work and had a gentle loving disposition when out of harness. Even with all their enthusiasm, I don't think any of my shepherds enjoyed working as much as did Cinder. She never seemed excitable, but her tail gave her away. She carried it curled up over her back like all good Labs and it wagged continuously and furiously whenever we were working. That tail rhythmically pounding my left leg was a constant reminder that our working relationship was not a job but a joy.

**Caverns Restaurant,
Nogalas, Mexico, 1979**

Chapter 19

Raising a Family—A Drama in 10,000 Acts
1980-1984

Life was good, and the years passed in a blink. I had a new wife, a new dog, and my children back. Diana, and then John, finished Clarendon Junior High and thence went on to high school, Diana to West Side and later Central High and John to Central High for all four years. Both of them did well, albeit in different ways. Diana excelled in the arts, especially languages and literature, and was a member of the marching band. Her musical career reached its peak when she marched with her band in the Fiesta Bowl Parade in January 1983. In the excitement of the moment, however, she left her flute at home and had to march empty handed. It was one of those moments, though, when the spirit of the event was enough.

John became an honor student with his strength in math and lettered in baseball. He wanted to go out for basketball and football, but he was not tall enough for basketball and he will never forgive me for not allowing him to join his friends on the gridiron. I felt that the risks of lifelong injury were too high and did not justify the transitory benefits. While Diana took up French and became a youngest president of the French Club, John took up German and became a member of the German Club. Both of them had more friends than I could count.

John and Heather,
beekeeping, 1977

Diana
candy-
striping and
scooping ice
cream at
Baskin
Robbins

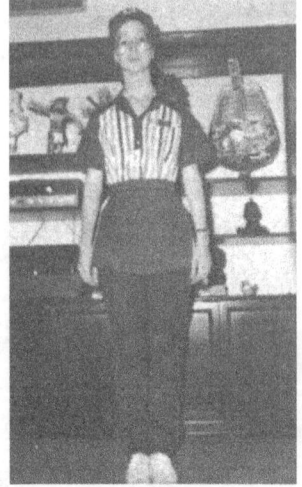

They also had their extracurricular activities. Diana became a candy-striper at St. Joseph's Hospital. Later, she obtained a job at the Baskin-Robbins store near our home where she became a real ice-cream pusher. Sometimes, though, she had to work at night and I was apprehensive about her walking home, even the one block to our house. It became my practice to meet her outside the B&R at 11:00 o'clock each evening. Those walks home, even though brief, were a sort of continuation of our earlier walking Ventures. It gave us a chance to talk without restraint and may well have done a lot to preserve the bond between us.

For his part, John also had his outside interests. During his Cub Scout years, he participated vigorously in the annual selling of Scout-O-Rama tickets. Sales were rewarded with prizes, and over the years, John amassed quite a haul. And, since I did not want a nine and ten-year-old boy out on the streets alone, especially in the evenings, I always stayed near by, as inconspicuously as possible. Our favorite sales spot was on the sidewalk in front of the B&R where Diana worked and the La Piñata Mexican restaurant next door. He would catch the customers as they came out, happy with a tummy full of ice cream or tacos and sell them a ticket, which not only got them in to the Scout-O-Rama, but entitled them to free pizzas. What a deal! I greatly enjoyed those evenings sitting on the bench in front of the B&R and smoking my pipe with my boy hustling tickets out front while my daughter hustled ice cream inside. We always ended the sessions with our own B&R treats. It was a fun time.

John also tried his hand at free enterprise with a stint in a Taco Bell restaurant. He was a good employee, but for a long time he almost gaged at the smell of salsa. Most of his non-school time was divided between baseball practice, racquetball with his best friend John Jacober, and, of course, girls. There were always the girls. It was the era of long hair, tight pants, and bright colors. Thank the Lord he eventually became Mr. Conservative with a military haircut, blazer, and tie. There were times, though, that I despaired, even though the worst was only the growth of a section of hair at the nape of his neck into what was then termed a "tail."

Diana and John were good kids, though, and never caused us any real worry. The only complication was that as Diana moved into her adolescence, the relationship between she and Liz, which had always been shaky at best, proved worse and worse.

During the spring before our marriage, Liz had graduated with her second bachelor's degree, this one in Training and Development from Grand Canyon College in Phoenix. She immediately went to work for the State as a personnel analyst, which was not precisely appropriate for her training. Nonetheless, she continued in that job for three years, but finally decided to quit and look for a more suitable position. Unfortunately, it was a time when women were not as acceptable in training jobs as they may be today. Everywhere, she met with the hackneyed response that she was over-qualified. (In later years, when they were setting out on their career paths, both Diana and John encountered the same type of discrimination.) In fact, Liz never found another job until she later went to work with me. Her failure to find work first led to disappointment and then to a depression which lasted almost five years. It was probably due in large part to this that the problems between her and Diana grew ever more serious. For several years, I found myself caught in the middle, trying to placate a wife I loved and trying to comfort a daughter I loved just as much. It was an agony to me to try to balance on the fence between them. I don't think I handled the situation well, but I dealt with each incident as it arose and did the best I could at the time.

As a result of the friction between Liz and Diana, no mother and daughter relationship ever really took root. Diana, for her part, sought a substitute in a series of surrogate mother figures, usually the mothers of her friends. I watched from afar as she formed close ties with the mothers of Ann and Reggie and later her first real boyfriend, Chris. On the other hand, Liz had no such substitute opportunities. She was the real loser. Indeed, they both were losers to the extent that neither of them got to really know the extraordinary person of the other.

Of course, Liz' depression and the problems with Diana eventually began to affect the marriage. Liz and Diana sought counseling separately and we obtained counseling as a couple. Nothing seemed to work. The situation got so bad that at one point we were even talking divorce. She actually consulted an attorney. Somehow, though, we survived, primarily by simply taking each day as it came and not doing anything desperate or hasty. Ultimately, the marriage survived, but my relationship with my daughter suffered severely. After graduating from high school, Diana enrolled at Northern Arizona University in Flagstaff, but because of a recently diagnosed attention deficit disorder, as well as personal and family problems which besought her from every side, she didn't do too well. Eventually, she dropped out of school after her second year.

At that point, she and I had a falling-out for which we were both to blame and which should never have occurred. I, at least, should have been more mature and understanding of the problems she was confronting. Nonetheless, there was a period of almost a year when we didn't speak or see each other. Son John, though, never gave up on either of us and kept us in tentative touch. Eventually, contact was reestablished and with Liz' gradual surfacing from her depression, the overall relationship improved. Liz even began to refrain from objecting, if not actively supporting, financial help which I would give to Diana from time to time in limited amounts. I feel now, though, that I never helped her as much as I should have. Under the circumstances, however, it may have been as much as possible.

John's path of youth was less hilly. Perhaps it had to do with the fact that there was never any strain between him and Liz. In fact, they developed a close and abiding relationship. I know that he loves his biological mother, but he also loved Liz, perhaps in a different way, but no less.

John became involved in Cub Scouts, then Boy Scouts, and later, somewhere in between, Little League. Liz and I undertook to be leaders of John's Cub Scout Den and later his Webelo Den. For a brief time, I was Pack Leader. I will never forget the Pinewood Derby for which John and I built the "Dragon Wagon" which did just that. It dragged so much that it barely got down the track. Then there was the sailboat race. Each Cub was to build a sailboat and enter

Eagle Scout

John Duty, 13-year-old son of Mary Duty of Fayetteville and Davis Duty of Phoenix, Ariz., has been named an Eagle Scout. Other awards include Arrow of Light, God and Country, and 1981 National Jamboree Bugler.

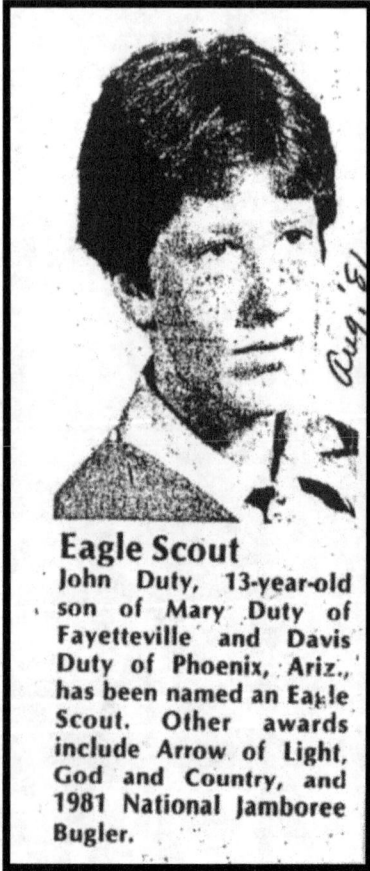

them in races in a neighborhood swimming pool. John and I built a huge monster of a boat with three masts. It sailed alright, but required more wind than gentle Arizona breezes. John was forced to wade after it, blowing and puffing into the sails to keep it moving. He finished dead last, but did finish.

We spent one memorable weekend at a Cub Scout camp in the Arizona mountains. We slept in sleeping bags under tents. We ate from mess-kits. We cooked over open fires. We hiked and we went canoeing. That was the first time since I had had her that Cinder had seen a body of water bigger than her drinking bowl. Her Lab soul could not be restrained, and as we boarded the canoe she went straight over the side into the lake. I think she would have gladly paddled along behind us, but that would have made a mockery of the vaunted Seeing Eye discipline. It was no easy task, though, to haul her back into the boat, soggy and bedraggled, without tipping us all into the lake. But she and all of the Cubs loved it. To add a final rustic touch, it rained the last night and John and I, with packs on our backs, tramped out of the wilderness down a long dirt road, ankle-deep in mud, to the parking lot where Liz and Diana were to meet us. Liz made us rinse off under a water tap before she would let us into the car.

I did not participate quite so actively in John's Boy Scout career, but its success is best illustrated by the fact that he made Eagle rank. He did it at age thirteen, too, which is a real feat.

Then there was Little League. Liz and I became members of the Little League Board and were faithful Little League fans. In fact, I think we were too faithful. I am now certain that John was embarrassed by my constant cheering and encouragement. But he bore up well and made the all-star team at every level, even through Senior League. Then, of course, he went on to high school baseball, where he became the first team third baseman. Every summer for about five years, Liz and I headed for the Clarendon School Little League field several evenings each week. We sat on baking-hot metal grandstands, eating salty popcorn and yelling ourselves hoarse. Liz sometimes helped at the concession stand while I sat behind home plate smoking my pipe and trying to keep Cinder in the shade. It is hard to describe just how dusty and hot a playing field can become in Arizona. For most of the games, Liz and I rode our double bike. When the last out was made, we headed for the nearest ice cream shop. In my mind's eye, it seems to have been a time of soft, warm evenings, family fun, and good friends. We even managed to combine John's scouting with his Little League. As his Eagle project, he organized and pushed through a project to sod and landscape the Little League field. He put a lot of sweat and sunburn into it, but he and his

Diana's 8ᵗʰ grade graduation

friends received a lot of pleasure out of playing on that nice green field under the lights on balmy spring evenings.

I seem to have described more activities which Liz and I shared with John than for Diana. Part of this, of course, was due to her estrangement from Liz. She and Liz were simply not comfortable in one another's presence and it is difficult for a father to participate to any great extent in girl-type activities. Of course, there was the time in Junior High when she entered the Science Fair. I can't remember precisely what her project was, although it involved something to do with shining a light through colored paper to demonstrate the color effect of light waves when impeded. She didn't win any prizes, but we did have a lot of father-daughter fun working together.

Another father-daughter project in which Diana and I took part during this time (1978-80) was a twelve kilometer walk for charity. During the late '70s, it became quite a fad to sponsor such events for charitable causes. There were runs, walks, bicycling, skating, almost anything in fact which could attract cash generating sponsorships. Although the particular charity sponsoring the walk evades recollection, I vividly remember the event itself. It was a very rare and special Venture. We started out, Diana, Cinder, and me, with about a thousand other people at Phoenix College. Our route took us down Thomas to Seventh Street, north on Seventh

Growing tomatoes in Phoenix (with Cinder)

to Northern, I believe, then west to Seventh Avenue, back south to Osborn, west to Fifteenth Avenue and finally south for two blocks to the PC Stadium. We did not stop once and maintained a steady, determined pace. Soon we left behind the plodders. By the time we were half way from Thomas to Northern, it became apparent that the only ones ahead of us were the runners. From that point on, we were virtually alone except when we passed through check-points. We finished thirty-second and were able to sit smugly in the grandstands, eating the box lunch which the sponsoring organization provided and waving at those lesser beings who staggered in after us. We were very pleased with our performance. The button which we received proclaiming "We Did It" is one of my proudest keepsakes. Perhaps it was our finest Venture until our next walk together when I escort her down the aisle as Father of the Bride.

Also, it would not be fair to accuse Liz of total indifference to Diana. They did have one interest in common. Both of them liked to dance. They enrolled together in a ballet class which they both pursued avidly. Eventually, Diana even went on to higher levels and eventually was able to go en pointe. Then she developed foot problems which ended any dancing

John's 8th grade graduation

Cowboys Davis, John, and Jeff

hopes. Liz also continued her dancing until her teacher discontinued classes. Then she took up aerobics and continued to be an avid aerobics fan up until four months before her death. Indeed, this is one aspect of Liz' personality which should be especially commended. She had a tendency to gain weight. Soon after our marriage, she ballooned to over 140 pounds. Horrified at what was happening, she found and went on a diet tailored to her particular body type and kept up with her vigorous exercise program. In short order, she brought her weight down to less than 120 pounds and kept it there. In this respect, she was a good object lesson for us all.

There were also some good times as a family. One thing which we always did together was to go to church. Liz was a good old Italian Catholic. I am of the Methodist persuasion. As a Methodist, being the more flexible, I had no objections to our family worshiping in the Catholic Church. Also, St. Gregory's parish church was only a block and a half from our house, so we could walk to services. I don't think we missed attending Mass at least once a week between the time of our wedding and Liz' death, even while on vacations. While John attended Mass with us, Diana became much more actively involved. She joined the youth group, sang in the choir, and eventually joined the church. I am sure that all of us fondly remember Monsignor Gordon and Father Frank Fernandez. Through good times and less good times, our connection with St. Gregory's was a strengthening theme.

Church-going was not our only family activity, however. Most of our family activities involved planned sightseeing trips. Once we took the kids to the Snow Bowl above Flagstaff and gave them a ski lesson. Both of them immediately took to the sport and still have skis, boots, and sweaters around somewhere. Another time when I was holding hearings in west Los Angeles, the family joined me. While I was holding hearings, they toured a movie studio and when my hearings were done we went down to Anaheim and visited Knotts Berry Farms and Disneyland. Several times, we went to Nogales and visited Mexico.

Our biggest trip, though, was to San Francisco. Again, I was scheduled to hold hearings there so we drove from Phoenix to the coast and north up the Pacific Coast Highway past Carmel, San Simeon, and all of the other sightseeing meccas. In San Francisco, we did the cable cars, Fisherman's Wharf, and some of their marvelous seafood restaurants. We spent a whole afternoon at Golden Gate Park, where we visited the aquarium

Davis and Cinder's elegant traverse over a Japanese bridge

and had tea in the Japanese Tea Garden. There, Cinder and I accepted the challenge of scrambling over an ornamental bridge, which was designed more in the U-shape than the traditional graceful arch. One memorable evening, we dined at a real authentic Indian (from India) restaurant, from which we went away hungry. None of us, even Liz who bragged about her asbestos palate, could handle the curry. We later had hamburgers and doughnuts in a walk-in diner. Then we split up, the girls going to the Opera and John and me to see "Raiders of the Lost Ark." They felt superior with their cultural emersion, but John and I had no doubt whatever that we had made the correct choice. The only drawback was that we had to stand in line on one of San Francisco's infamous hillside streets to get into the movie. I am not sure which stuck in our memory the longest, the waiting line or "Raiders."

**Davis and his hearing
assistants in Las Vegas**

Well fed and well toured, we returned through Yosemite Park and down through Death Valley. We stopped overnight at Las Vegas, where John immediately acquired my taste for gambling. I am satisfied with nickel slot machines, though, and he prefers roulette, craps, and blackjack. Fortunately, both of us are too cheap to squander much on the sport, so it is relatively harmless. Diana and Liz, on the other hand, never seemed to take to the sport. Liz did accompany me to Las Vegas on numerous occasions when I would be up there holding hearings and we would do the casinos at night. She preferred shows, though, and would only play the slots desultorily to keep me company.

One of the most memorable trips we took was to Lake Powell near Paige, Arizona, in the summer of 1984. Due to her extreme estrangement of that time, Diana was not along. We took a friend of John's, Greg Douthitt, and set out to enjoy the pleasures of houseboat recreation. We rented a vessel and headed across the lake to spend the night. Unfortunately, a storm came up and we not only had a rough passage, but only got to the first inlet away from the docks. We were out of sight, though, and proceeded to ground and tie down the boat as directed. From that point on, nothing went right. The rain made everything soggy. The gas stove barely worked and the

John, Liz, and Davis at El Tavor Lodge at the Grand Canyon in Arizona, 1984

food was only partially cooked. The electrical system malfunctioned and the only light we had was from lanterns. And the beds were hard. But the worst part by far was the next morning when we couldn't get the boat off the sandbar. Fortunately, a powerboat was rented with each houseboat, and we were able to use it to return to the docks to obtain a tug to come and pull us off. All in all, we were glad to end that experience. We did enjoy the last part of the trip, though, which consisted of a night spent at the El Tavor Lodge in Grand Canyon National Park. This is one of my favorite places. We went there several times over the years to enjoy the superb meals accompanied by the magnificent view, including one special Thanksgiving dinner with my parents who were visiting from Arkansas. On this one occasion, though, we spent the night and not only had dinner, but breakfast, in the dinning room overlooking the Grand Canyon. It was wet and cold on Lake Powell, but there was a deep snow in the park, so we went from being soggy to being numb with cold. All in all, we weren't at all unhappy to return to the mild climate in Phoenix.

We also enjoyed as a family, and Liz and I by ourselves, many of the cultural benefits of Phoenix. We had the opera, the symphony, the ballet, but best of all, the Phoenix Suns NBA basketball team. I became an avid fan and when I couldn't attend in person, listened to their games on the radio. John shared this enthusiasm with me, and we had good father-son evenings attending games at the coliseum and then walking home past Encanto Park.

Then, of course, there were the annual Scottish games. One March, Liz and I read about them and decided to attend. From then on, we were hooked. We loved the kilted costumes, the bagpipe bands, the dancing, the

Scottish food, and the athletic contests. We even began to acquire tapes of bagpipe music and would drive the children wild playing it on the tape deck in our car as we drove along. To this day, I'll bet both children shudder when they hear the sound of a bagpipe. Liz and I followed this up, though, to become real aficionados. Later, in Fort Smith, we helped to form a Scottish Heritage Society and even went to Dallas once to attend the annual Scottish games at Arlington, Texas. In the course of events, we discovered that the Dutys are descended from the Clan Duthie, who are a subset of the Clan Ross. Liz even discovered that she might well be of Scottish descent on her mother's side, from of all places Poland. Her mother's maiden name was Czakansky. Apparently, during sometime around 1600, many Scotsmen hired out their services on the Continent as mercenary soldiers. A great many of them served the king of Poland. Later some of these, notably the MacCanns, Polacized their names. Cza was an appropriate substitution for Mac. This left only the adding of the decorative "sky" (an indication of nobility, and every Scot considers himself a lord to the manor born) to arrive at Czakansky. After learning this, Liz would proudly say that she thought she was Scottish, but even if not she was definitely of the Clan Wanna-Be.

Finally, I was reminded by Diana that the family reminiscences would not be complete without describing our aluminum can-collecting expeditions. It had its beginning when John's Scout troop began a money raising project which involved the collection and resale of aluminum cans. It is almost fair to say that during that period the streets were practically carpeted with them. The four of us would take our

Davis and Liz on the double bike

bicycles on Sunday afternoon

and scour the streets and
parking lots within a two or
three mile radius of our
home. The first few times
we went together, but later
the children went their way
and we ours; and, naturally,
a contest developed to find
the most cans. We became
so successful that I bought a
wall-mounted can crusher to

John, Davis, and Diana

compact our loot. Every two weeks or so, we would deliver the crushed and
bagged cans either to the Scout collection point or to the recycling plant. It
was not unusual for us to have twenty to twenty-five pounds of cans. When
you add up the number of cans it takes to make a pound, the magnitude of
our collecting prowess can be appreciated. Then too, we got a lot more out
of it than old beer cans. We got exercise, fresh air, and family
companionship which I am only now beginning to appreciate. I had no idea
how much the children, at least Diana, enjoyed it until she insisted that I
relate it.

As for me during these years, I was trying to be a husband, father
and a judge. I don't think I ever
became a great judge, but I do
believe that I was a competent
judge. Our office held hearings in
Phoenix, Prescott, Flagstaff,
Kingman, and Las Vegas. I was
also assigned on numerous
occasions to hold hearings for
other offices. I sat in Sacramento,
San Francisco, San Diego,

Davis dancing with Barbara Dougan
at her daughter's wedding, 1985

Pasadena, Watts, Los Angeles, Detroit, and so on. The job wasn't hard,

Liz and Davis

although it did require precision and concentration. It was rewarding in that by granting benefits to those entitled, we were truly helping people in need. Apparently, I was a reasonably good judge, because those who liked me and those who didn't like me were fairly evenly divided.

What with work and family activities, the years flowed by inexorably. As time passed though, some of my old feeling about practicing law and public service began to gradually revive. By 1983, I was becoming bored with the ivory tower context of being an ALJ and was beginning to crave the rough and tumble of law practice and the real world. More likely, I was merely becoming healed from the damage and scars I had suffered in the early '70s. My mind seemed to turn more and more to what once seemed unthinkable: resigning my job and leaving the government to return to private practice. At first I wasn't sure I could face it and I was certain I could not afford it. After all, it takes at least five years to establish a practice, even for an experienced attorney. But by the summer of 1983, I seemed to have decided, although the precise moment of the decision was never evident, that I was going to take the step and the gamble. The first thing was to obtain financing. On a chance, I filed an application with the Federal Small Business Administration and somehow they granted me a loan of approximately $100,000. I hoped that this would keep my family and my office going for the first year. It was, therefore, with many qualms and not a few palpitations that I submitted my resignation to be effective on Friday, January 4, 1984. My new life would begin on Monday, January 6th. Another of my life segments had come to an end.

Diana and boyfriend Chris
at St. Luke's Ball, 1983

John and girlfriend Jill
at St. Luke's Ball, 1985

Diana's high school
graduation, 1983

John, 1983

Chapter 20

Life in the Real World
1984-1986

I began writing this in May, 1992. In retrospect, the past eight years have been the worst and the best of my life. The early stages prove the old adage that nothing ever comes easy.

Because of lingering self doubts, I wanted someone with me who could help me out when I returned to private practice. It was my plan to use the expertise I had gained as a Social Security Administrative Law Judge to specialize in representing Social Security disability claimants. Associated with this type of work, however, there are a lot of technical matters which must be handled administratively. To take care of this, I employed a young lady who was also leaving the Government at the same time. She had a great deal of experience and I felt she would be a real asset to my new venture.

Unfortunately, though, things did not work out as planned. We did not get along and, because of conflicts which arose between us, I discharged her in May of 1984. She immediately filed suit against me. I eventually won when she withdrew her suit, but it cost me a substantial amount in attorney's fees. The good side of this, though, was that it gave Liz the break she had been waiting for. She had never been able to find work, but now I called upon her in desperation to help me out at the office. I didn't know where to find someone with experience, much less the necessary qualifications. I knew, though, that at least Liz would be loyal, plus having a vested interest in making the business succeed. She proved me right to an extent far beyond my wildest hopes.

She immediately began working on her appearance. She had never worn makeup, but she took a makeup course and began using it with considerable artistry. She bought new business-type clothes and before my eyes the wife who had been withering on the vine for several years began to blossom. She had always kept her weight down and her figure trim, so with attention to her clothes, makeup, and hair, it was only a short step to a brand new image. She was also very capable. She could type well enough to do the job that had to be done and took no time at all to learn the administrative intricacies which I had thought so formidable. That first year of 1984, we only won fifty-seven cases. In 1985, however, we won seventy-four cases. Fees began to come in just as the $100,000 SBA funds ran out. We were able to eat, pay the rent, and pay office expenses. With Liz and a typist, I was succeeding, slowly but surely.

The slow growth of my business was not without its setbacks. The major problem confronting me arose from an inexplicable, at least to me, resentment expressed by my former judicial colleagues. Since I had elected to pursue my profession as a Social Security Advocate in Phoenix, the judges before whom I would practice were those who had shared offices with me when I was a judge. I will never know their thinking, but they held my feet to the fire on every rule and fine point of law.

Monday, July 9, 1984

Alan Thurber

He's no longer riding the bench

Six months ago, Jeff Davis Duty Jr., the former city attorney of Rogers, Ark., walked across the hall here in Phoenix and changed careers. He also hopped the fence and changed horses. After nine years as a judge hearing Social Security cases, he is now representing claimants and presenting their claims.

"I wasn't ready to spend the rest of my life in an ivory tower," he said.

Duty goes by the front name of Davis.

"My father, who is still practicing law back in Rogers at the age of 77, is Jeff," he said. "We weren't named after the Confederate president but after a former governor and senator from Arkansas who was a friend of my grandfather's."

Duty grew up in Rogers and got along fine, right through high school. But when he went off into the world and the University of Arkansas, he got a guide dog.

For Jeff Davis Duty Jr., Phi Beta Kappa, Fulbright scholar, lawyer and judge, has been blind since he was 5.

After terms of city attorney and municipal judge in his hometown, Duty joined the Social Security Administration as a judge, hearing appeals of disability-claim denials.

He spent eight years doing that in Phoenix, most of the time right across the hall from his current office on Central Avenue.

Jeff Davis Duty Jr., pats Cinder, his guide dog.

Pete Peters/Republic

"The claimants are people who, through illness or injury, are no longer able to work," he explained. "They're trying to get their retirement benefits early."

"It's the job of the judge to sort out the facts in relationship to the intricacies of the law. There are very specific legal definitions of disability."

"If you meet the definition of blindness, for example, you are automatically considered disabled and entitled to benefits."

Davis Duty, having paid Social Security since his first job in a chicken plant at the age of 15 — he slew the chickens — would qualify. That doesn't interest him.

— Thurber, B2

Thurber
Continued from B1

But how did he feel hearing a case from a claimant with impaired vision?

"I don't think of myself as a blind person," he said. "To me, blindness is just a physical characteristic, like red hair.

"But I can't superimpose my experience on others. I was probably fortunate in losing my sight so early. It's very traumatic later in life.

"So when I deal with blind people, I have to think in terms of their problems, of how they are affected individually, how they don't all have the same opportunities."

After nine years, Duty switched sides.

"I felt that a lot of people weren't getting the representation they deserved," he said. "It's hard enough for the little guy to fight the government. In these cases, the government had all the cards."

So he now represents claimants and presents the cases he used to hear.

"Not as a lawyer," he is quick to add. "I've been admitted to practice in Arkansas and before the U.S. Supreme Court, but not here. I'm strictly a Social Security representative, or advocate."

At home, he relaxes with his family, plays chess and reads three or four books a week, in Braille. Science fiction, mostly.

And every morning, he and his sixth dog, Cinder, a black lab, walk two miles to work.

He works to represent the little guy who can't.

Favorable decisions were granted grudgingly. They scrutinized my conduct with a microscope to seek improprieties. Even when I did win, they cut my fees ruthlessly. My clientele was growing. My rate of success was increasing, but it was slow and every step was against the tide. The last straw was when one of the judges began commenting in his decision that the claimant was represented by Davis Duty, who had given up the practice of law in Arkansas. The implication, of course, was that I was practicing law without a license. Since no law license is actually required to represent Social Security claimants, this was irrelevant. Still, it so clearly demonstrated the attitude of the judges who held the reins of life and death over my practice that I finally began toying with the idea of moving my practice somewhere else.

By the spring of 1986, I had made up my mind. I decided to sell my practice in Phoenix and relocate, lock, stock, and barrel, back to good old Arkansas. The moment was even more propitious since son John graduated from high school that spring and was off to the University of Arizona. By the grace of God and a lot of hard work, he had received a full-ride scholarship from the Arizona-based Flynn Foundation. As a result, I was relieved of the full brunt of college expenses. This was of real significance since a relocation of my law practice meant another hiatus in fees. This time there would be no SBA loan to tide me over.

As to where we would move in Arkansas, I decided first that, as Thomas Wolfe has said, "You can't go home again." Then, of equal or greater importance, the new Social Security judges before whom I would be practicing maintained their offices in Fort Smith. It would be both more convenient and more efficient to have my office located nearby. Accordingly, after discussing the matter with Francis Mayhue, the Hearings Office Chief Administrative Law Judge in Fort Smith, as well as other attorneys and old friends in that city, Liz and I decided that it would be Fort Smith or bust. Once the process was begun, things moved quickly.

I sold my practice to Sherman Bendilin, a fellow Social Security attorney in Phoenix, and in May Liz and I flew to Fort Smith to scout out the terrain in order to rent an apartment and office space. By the middle of June, we had our household goods and ourselves on the road for Arkansas. On Friday, June 18th, my office equipment was moved in and on Monday the 21st, we opened for business. It has always been my belief that if you are definitely going to do something, do it quickly and do it decisively.

Chapter 21

A Niche in Time
1986-April, 1990

In moving to Fort Smith, I wrought better than I could have dreamed. It wasn't the first time that I experienced the peculiar phenomena of having my life directed by outside forces. Time and again I learned, sometimes the hard way, that when I planted my feet and obstructed the flow, things went badly. When I relaxed and went with the flow of events, things went well. So it was with the move to Arkansas. Everything came together at the same time. It seemed like the right thing to do. I prayed about it and received no negative vibes. Although Liz was prone to be conservative and not much of a risk-taker, she was caught up in the plan with as much enthusiasm as was I. Then, when we got to Arkansas, we were greeted with much courtesy by the local judges. They demonstrated none of the animosity and even hostility which I had experienced from the Administrative Law Judges in Phoenix. Local attorneys whom I met welcomed me warmly. Many of them had been in school with me. It was not unlike a true homecoming. Of course, my family was delighted to have me back home. We found a suitable apartment and office space with no difficulty and everything seemed to be connecting as far as John and Diana were concerned.

John would be off to the University of Arizona in Tucson in September. In the meantime, he got a summer job with a construction company. He is still having back twinges from that experience.

Diana was working as a secretary for a bank and trust company in Phoenix. She was also taking some night courses at Arizona State University. She still had a dream of getting her college degree.

The only fly in the ointment was that we would not be able to sell our house in Phoenix for almost eighteen months. Because of this, we had to remain in an apartment until we had the proceeds from the house sale to use as a down payment on a new house. It taught us to economize and do without, though, and that was a lesson we would need to learn since it would be at least six months before fees began to come in in Fort Smith in any respectable amount.

Liz and I also undertook a new approach to church life. We had been attending her Catholic church throughout our marriage. However, once in Fort Smith, we decided to give equal time to both our churches. I joined the First United Methodist Church and she the Christ the King Catholic Church. We attended services at both churches each weekend and contributed financially to both. We also participated in church activities in both, and at times this could prove tedious. Still, both churches claimed us and it was like having two wonderful warm families. For example, the day I moved my membership to the FUMC, Liz went down front with me for presentation to the congregation, and the minister announced that, although she was a member of another denomination, she would henceforth be treated as an honorary Methodist. In the Catholic Church, while I was unable to take Communion, I was otherwise treated like a full member. Later, I would even be tapped to help with conducting the RCIA program which is designed to introduce the church to persons interested in conversion. After a while, we discovered that both churches were essential to us. I began jokingly referring to myself a Cathodist or Metholic. It would be a real wrench to me today to give up either.

One incident, although minor, which seemed to reflect the rightness of our move occurred the day we opened our office. While visiting Fort Smith in May, I had run across an old friend from my early years of Rogers by the name of Lanny West. He and his wife, Sharon, had moved from Rogers to Fort Smith in the early '70s with their son Brad, and daughters Beth and Kathie. On the morning we opened our office, a potted plant was delivered from the Wests wishing us success in our new venture. We could not have possibly guessed at the long-term significance of this renewal of an old friendship.

Professionally, I began, at long last, to prosper. My television and newspaper advertising campaign bore immediate fruit. The telephone began to ring and clients began to come in. Since I was back in Arkansas and therefore licensed to engage in the general practice of law, I decided to not only specialize in Social Security disability, but also to return to some general law practice. Although even from the outset Social Security disability comprised the major portion of my work, I did soon find myself writing wills and contracts, preparing deeds, and filing divorces. I have never liked the latter, though, and resolved again to withdraw from that aspect of practice as soon as possible.

We only won forty-six cases in 1986, most of those residuals from Arizona, but in 1987 we won eighty-four and have grown proportionally every year since. Also, since I was now able to function as a real lawyer, I began accepting Social Security appeals to Federal District Court. Eventually, this would become a major element of my practice. We did not make a lot of money at first, but the auguries of success were there.

Socially, our lives also took an upward turn. Liz became active in the Welcome Wagon organization, as well as a Christian women's organization which held weekly luncheons. She was elected to the board of the Bonneville House, which is a 19th century dwelling of historical significance owned and maintained by a private organization. She enrolled in a modern dance cum aerobics class where she went to sweat and work out her frustrations twice a week. She even tried her hand briefly at circuit training at a fitness center. She was really working to get herself into good shape.

We bought season tickets to The Little Theater. We joined the Fort Smith Art Center. As I have discussed earlier in these pages, we became charter members of a new Scottish Society. We had many enjoyable hours of meeting with our fellow Scots, listening to bagpipe music, reveling at Burns Night dinners each January, and attending Scottish games.

As for me, I joined the Christian Business Men's Committee after being visited by Charlie Reutzel and Bob Hawkins on the afternoon following the annual Mayor's Prayer Breakfast, which was held shortly after we moved to Fort Smith. I had never heard of the organization, but was attracted to it immediately. For some years, I had been attending a men's Bible study class in Phoenix and CBMC offered a similar opportunity, although its goals are much broader. It is an organization whose mission it is to seek out and bring businessmen to Christ. The committee I joined met on Saturday morning at the Trade Winds Motel. Each Saturday at 6:30 am, Charlie Reutzel would pick me up and we would go to the meetings for breakfast, prayer, Bible study, and a lot of super fellowship. It became a very important element in my life. Similarly, I joined the Methodist Men's Club, which holds a Bible study and breakfast meeting each Friday morning. I was never as faithful in attendance with this group as with CBMC, but I continue be as faithful as time and opportunity permit. One thing is for sure, the breakfast served by the Methodists Men's Club, consisting as it does of eggs, bacon, sausage, biscuits and gravy, and pancakes, is one of the best that can be had anywhere, especially for $3.00.

Add to the above my participation in the Sebastian County Bar Association activities, continuing legal education programs both locally and at the State level, plus my busy work schedule, and I soon found my life both hectic and productive. Life fell into a very satisfying routine. Liz was working with me at the office (indeed, for a while she was my only staff) and happier than she had ever been before during our marriage. I was satisfied, fulfilled, and beginning to see signs of some economic improvement. John did well in school. Diana eventually moved to Maryland where she made her home at first with her mother, and then in apartments in and around Columbia, Maryland.

Liz' and my life slipped into a routine of working hard and enjoying ourselves with our newfound friends and activities. The seasons slipped by almost imperceptibly. You would know when it was spring when the hoopla began for Old Fort Days. Later in the summer, the Junior League would put on the Riverfest with its food, crafts, entertainment, and boat races. Then it would be fall and time for the Arkansas-Oklahoma State Fair. How Liz loved to tramp through those smelly cow barns! I concentrated on Louisiana meat pies and funnel cakes. I had never heard of funnel cakes before moving to Fort Smith. Since then, I have never met a funnel cake I didn't like. Life seemed good and promised to get better.

Storm Clouds

Maybe things were going too well. It sometimes seems that whenever things start to go right, fate steps in to raise obstacles. Perhaps this is the way it has to be, though. If life was one smooth ride with no problems, we wouldn't learn a thing. Perhaps God in his wisdom knows that we can only grow and improve by working through challenges. For some, however, these challenges seem to have to be greater than for others. Possibly those who have it easy this time around get it tough next time.

In any event, in the fall of 1987, clouds began to appear on the horizon which, if I had only known, indicated that the easy ride was over.

The first setback came when Cinder began having old age-type problems. She was fourteen years old and still vigorous, but she began to have trouble with her bowels. She started dropping little pellets all over the place. This could be really embarrassing in a restaurant. Then, too, her concentration seemed to be slipping. She still worked with the same enthusiasm, but she was more easily distracted and she seemed to have more difficulty figuring out problems. By September, I knew that I could wait no longer. I talked to the Seeing Eye and they concurred. It was another of the heartbreaks which a Seeing Eye graduate must endure from time to time when I had to have Cinder put to sleep. She truly had earned her rest, though. Then I began preparing to return to the Seeing Eye for a replacement.

Liz and I combined my return to the Seeing Eye with a visit to her parents on Long Island and a jaunt down to Atlantic City to compare their casinos with those of Las Vegas. We were neither impressed nor amused. They did not provide stools to sit on for the slot players and even hamburgers cost $8.00. One evening was all it took.

Davis, Eddie (playing tug-a-rug), Liz, Jeff, and Lois

We had rented a car to drive down to Atlantic City. Now Liz delivered me right to the Seeing Eye's front door. This was the first time I had not been delivered by public transportation. I was greeted by my new trainer, Chris Verdi, a young lady in her early twenties and the first woman trainer with whom I had worked. I confess that I was apprehensive, but I needn't have been. She selected Eddie for me, the best of my dogs yet. Interestingly, though, I tend to say the same about each dog. I guess the current dog is always the best.

Whether or not Eddie is the best, he is certainly the biggest. At close to one hundred pounds and requiring a size 50 harness (compared to Cinder's size 40), he is far from unobtrusive. On the other hand, with his good nature, exemplary behavior, and quiet demeanor, he is far from obtrusive. I guess he has claimed the perfect middle ground. In fact, he is so affectionate and playful that I have always tended to forget just how big he is. To share a back seat of a car with him, though, is a less than comfortable proposition. I will discuss my various dogs elsewhere. Suffice it to say that after a month, Eddie and I flew back to Arkansas to start our new life together. This is how Edward, Prince of Tails (as he was dubbed by Liz), made his debut into Fort Smith society. And then the other shoe dropped. First, though, I must lay a foundation.

Around the first of 1986, when we were still living in Phoenix, Liz had detected a lump in her breast. A biopsy showed it to be malignant, and she underwent a lumpectomy and follow-up radiation therapy in February, 1986. She felt no adverse effects from the procedures, though, and immediately resumed her aerobics. It certainly did not interfere with our move to Arkansas and there seemed to be no indication of further difficulties.

Around the first of the year in 1988, however, while we were still living in our apartment on south U Street near Central Mall, the malignancy recurred. Again it proved to be virulent, and she underwent a modified radical mastectomy of the left breast. She endured the surgery well. After only a few days in the hospital, she returned home and threw herself into recovering her strength and health. This, in spite of the fact that she underwent six months of stringent chemotherapy. She lost her hair and had to buy a wig. She developed chronic indigestion and for the first time in her life had to restrict her diet. Still, she did manage to get back to her aerobics class. All in all, she weathered this new ordeal with very little complaint and a completely optimistic attitude. The truth was, we just didn't have time to be sick or sorry for ourselves. Eventually, even her hair even grew back and it was thicker and prettier than before. Again, we thought we had dodged the bullet.

Because of Liz' physical problems, we decided that the time had finally come to hire some help at the office. Soon after opening my office, I had hired Gail Githens, who worked as a half-time secretary. When she went on to better things, I hired Linda Threete as a full-time secretary. She and Liz shared all of the clerical duties in the office and Liz handled the books, court briefs, and other specialized work.

Then, when Liz was laid low by her surgery in early 1988, I hire Pat Patterson as a legal assistant. She was a Registered Nurse who had given up nursing because of health problems and later had worked for the local Social Security judges at the Office of Hearings and Appeals. Not only could Pat type, but she had expertise in the medical area as well. She took over the job of reading cases, typing briefs, and accompanying me to hearings.

Just when I thought my staffing problems were settled, Linda gave me notice in July that she and her husband were moving to Texas. Once again, the scramble was on to find help. This was how the sainted Ramona Bailey made her appearance on the stage.

Ramona was a fresh graduate from the American College and a real female Horatio Alger story. She and her husband Terry and little boy Mickey had moved to Fort Smith by way of Oklahoma from Mammoth, Arkansas. She was a small town girl with only a high school education but with a good brain and a lot of determination. After having worked at such jobs as convenience store clerk and other similar occupations, she told Terry (a professional truck driver) that he would have to support her while she went back to school. She enrolled in a business college and graduated first in her class. By the Grace of God, I was the fortunate one who hired her upon graduation. At first she was my only staff, with Liz helping out on the books and Federal Court briefings. Later, when additional staff members were added, she more or less assumed the role of office manager and eventually moved from secretary to legal assistant. Five years later, she has become as much a part of this office as me. Between Eddie, Ramona, and me, we run our office with single-minded dedication. Others may come, and I always hope they won't go, but so long as Ramona is there, I have a sense of well-being which can't be bought with money. We like our work, we're proud of our successes, and we know where we are going.

In March of 1988, we finally sold our house in Phoenix and were able to buy a house in Fort Smith. We settled into our new two-story red brick residence at 919 South 23rd Street as though we had always lived there. We were home at last.

By the time Liz completed her chemotherapy in November of 1988, her health was apparently restored and our lives were pretty much back to normal. By this

Life father, like son: Davis (left) and Jeff asleep in Davis' man cave

time, we had purchased season tickets to Razorback football games in Fayetteville, and our autumn Saturdays were spiced with the beautiful Ozark fall weather, turning foliage, and the excitement of Razorback football. Again, I could sit on the porch and listen to Cardinal baseball games during the summers and after football season, follow Razorback basketball with equal avidity. We broke the routine occasionally by making trips to New York to visit Liz' parents and by attending conferences of the National Organization of Social Security Claimants Representatives in various parts of the country. We attended them in St. Louis, Dallas, Boston, Washington, and New Orleans. Life was good and getting

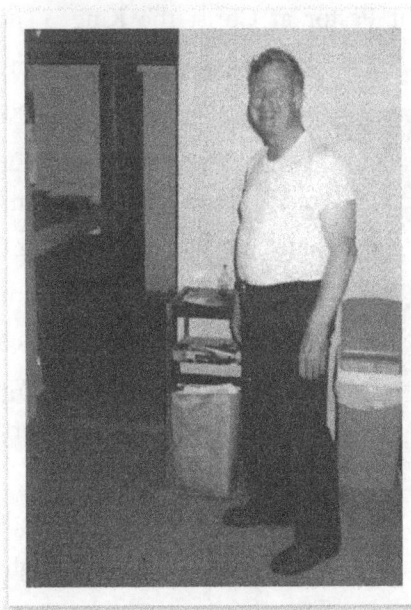

Proud homeowner

better. In 1988, we won ninety-six cases; in 1989, one hundred and four; in 1990, one hundred and eight; in 1991, one hundred twenty-six; in 1992, one hundred and fifty-six; and in 1993, one hundred and fifty-seven.

The crowning event for 1988, though, was when Liz and I got married or rather remarried. Being a good Catholic, she could not feel completely married if the marriage was not sanctioned by the Church. We could not get married in the Church, though, because her first husband Harold was still living and she had married him in the Church. True, they were divorced, but that doesn't carry much weight with the Catholic Church.

For years, Liz had been slogging through the paperwork to get an annulment. It was very depressing work, though, and didn't seem to be progressing. Then, like a bolt out of the blue, we received word that Harold had passed away. It makes a person feel uneasy to benefit directly from the misfortunes of others, but as things turned out, I can only thank Harold for allowing Liz this opportunity to get her life right with God.

We didn't waste any time, either. On September 19, 1988, we were married by Father John, the Assistant Pastor at Christ the King. The wedding was small, only my mother and sister attended, but it took place right there, smack dab in Christ the King Church. I don't think anything ever made Liz happier. She was glowing, almost incandescent, for days. Sometimes things do work out right.

John, Davis, Eddie, Liz, and Diana at Mt. Vernon, Virginia, 1989

Fate was not through with us yet, though. Sometimes life seems to follow inexplicable twists and

Lois and Jeff's 60th Anniversary party, 1989

Brother John, Sister Carolyn, Lois, Jeff, and Davis

Son John, John's girlfriend Melissa, Liz, and Davis

John's girlfriend Melissa Berkowitz and John

turns. Just as things seem to be going really well, a set-back occurs which can change everything. Also, it is never clear why fate rewards one person and betrays another.

After returning from the NOSSCR convention in New Orleans in October, 1989, Liz went to the doctor because of a persistent cold. At the same time, she underwent a periodic check-up for her breast cancer. The results were horrifying. She not only had evidence that the cancer had spread to her sternum, but, even worse, it had invaded her lungs. As long as I live, I will never forget the afternoon that she came to the office after receiving the diagnosis and prognosis from the doctor. In my office, she stood in my arms, her face buried against my chest, and cried. Over and over she kept saying, "Davis, it's going to kill me. Davis, it's going to kill me." To her credit, though, this was the last time she ever demonstrated the slightest sign of defeatism or fear. She immediately elected to undergo the most intensive possible course of chemotherapy.   Overnight, from a healthy, vigorous young woman, suddenly after one chemotherapy treatment she became a semi-invalid.

The evening before the treatment, she attended her regular aerobics class. After the treatment, I had to half-carry her to the car. Fortunately, I had had the foresight to have a friend bring us, so she did not have to drive. Indeed, she drove very little from that point on.

By Christmas, Liz was no longer able to climb the stairs to our bedroom on the second floor and was sleeping permanently in her recliner in the television room. Since I did not want to leave her alone at night, I took up sleeping on the daybed just a few feet away in the next room. I don't think either of us had a good night's sleep for the next four months.

The one thing that Liz wanted above all was to attend John's graduation from college. It was scheduled for May, 1990. That was her goal. It was evident very soon, however, that she was not making progress. Each chemotherapy session seemed to take more out of her and the results never seemed to justify the effort. She did have a brief upsurge when she made contact with a charismatic group in her church which inspired her to seek not only spiritual growth, but a physical healing. The latter did not materialize, but she did make huge strides in the former. More and more, though, our life became circumscribed.

Thank God for Ramona and the others of my office staff. With Liz under treatment, it had become apparent as early as 1988 that I needed help to replace her at the office. It is a tribute to how much she contributed that I had to hire two girls to replace her. First, I hired Pat Paterson to work up my cases and help me with briefs. Then, in July I replaced a part-time receptionist with Ramona as a full-blown secretary. Later, I hired Sheila Smith to handle the books. They were a godsend. At least the work kept getting done. In January, 1990, though, both Pat and Sheila decided to leave. I suspect that part of the reason was the inescapable element of gloom which could not help but dampen my spirits as I watched my wife dying by inches.

Ramona stuck by me, though, and for that and to her I am eternally grateful.

I tried to get to work by noon each day, but it was necessary for me to help Liz get herself up and going and to fix her something to eat. For a while, her lunches were provided by Meals-on-Wheels, but eventually they discovered that she was under fifty and therefore not eligible for the service. Stephen Ministries in the Methodist church assigned a minister to her, but the relationship never really had a chance to develop. The sources of greatest help were the hospice nurses who came by to check on her periodically, but more important were the two Joanns. The first was Joann Ladd. She was a nurse who was on disability leave with whom Liz had become friends in the charismatic group. She began spending each afternoon with Liz, which was a blessing, indeed, both physically and mentally.

The other Joann was Joanne Hill, our next door neighbor. Without being asked, she began to come over each morning to check on Liz. While there, she just happened to clean up the kitchen, wash the dishes, and see that Liz had some lunch. With her toddler, Patty, they were a real bright spot to what must have been a very dreary time for Liz. Directly as a result of Joanne Hill, I was able to resume a more normal office routine. Instead of getting there by noon, I could get there by mid-morning. What a lessening of pressure this was and how can one ever show enough gratitude to the Joannes of the world who appear from nowhere as angels of mercy. Don't ever tell me that there is no one up there who cares.

By March, however, it was evident that Liz' condition was not improving. The cancer was not much worse, but her overall physical state was deteriorating. She simply could not withstand the ravages of both the cancer and the chemotherapy.

The moment of truth finally came in the last week of March, 1990. Liz was having more and more trouble breathing and the doctors told her that she needed to go into the hospital to have her lungs drained. She checked in to St. Edward Hospital on the morning of Monday, March 26th. She underwent the procedure that day and seemed to tolerate it fairly well.

When all seemed to be stabilized that evening, I went home for some sleep.

At 10:00 pm, the doctor called to say that she had taken a turn for the worse and had become critical. I called my friend Lanny West and he came and got me and took me back to the hospital.

I sat by her bed, holding her hand, throughout that night. I am not sure that it was fair to Liz, but I think that my presence and the strength that it gave her kept her here. Also, we were not alone. Around midnight, our Methodist pastor, Joe Taylor, came to the room and prayed with us both for healing and that God's will be done. In addition, the hospice wing maintains a corp of caring volunteers who sit with critical patients. They provide both company and reassurance. In our case, we had Mrs. Chaney. She said very little, but sat on Liz' other side throughout the night, reading her bible and always alert to any need. Mine was the strength of desperation. Hers was the strength of faith.

Liz rallied and by morning seemed to be doing much better. She told me that day that during the night she had seen me dozing in my chair and had decided that I needed her more than she thought. Be that as it may, by Tuesday morning, March 27th, things were looking up. I had been advised, though, to contact the family and tell them of her condition. John and Diana caught the first available flights and were there by that afternoon. Her brother Edward flew in from California, and her parents, in spite of her father's terribly enfeebled condition following a stroke, came down from New York.

The shock to them was unbelievable. We had delayed telling them about Liz' condition, thinking that we had more time. First and foremost, we felt that it would adversely affect her father's recovery. Of equal concern, though, was the fact that her Uncle Eddie, who had shared a house with her parents since World War II, had died of lung cancer only the previous December. We had simply not been able to tell them about Liz. The time never seemed to be right. Then it was too late. So, when the time came, I had to call her brother Andrew and her Aunt Eleanor and it became their burden to break the news to the Albas that their daughter, whom they had no idea was even ill, was near death. I know we could have handled it better, and I wish we had. But circumstances so often dictate the things we do in life. We can only do the best we can as situations present themselves and cannot engage in recriminations later for not having done better when no better path was apparent.

In any event, Diana and John came and Liz' family were on their way. Sharon West spent the afternoon with Liz as I slept and described her as cheerful and optimistic. From the hospital, Sharon went to the airport to pick up Diana and John. At last, Liz and I had the added strength of family bonds. It appeared that, at least for the moment, the crisis had been averted or at least postponed. I even began to wonder whether I had perhaps overreacted in summoning her family, especially in view of the shock to her parents. All we could do, though, was to muddle on and do the best we could. There still seemed to be some hope.

The doctors advised us during the day that the immediate danger was heart failure from mounting fluid pressure. They needed to drain it off. They made it clear to us that this offered only a temporary reprieve of maybe two or three days, but Liz decided that she had nothing to lose. Although I have since come to believe that she had already accepted death, she continued outwardly to demonstrate a will to live. The procedure was scheduled for Wednesday morning, the 28th.

At about 6:00 Tuesday evening, I was rubbing Liz' feet (one of her great pleasures) and she decided that she would take a nap so that she would be rested for the next day's procedure. Before she could do this, however, our pastor, Father Tom Marx from Christ the King Catholic Church came by and administered the Sacrament of Reconciliation. Liz announced fervently that she had a vision of the rest of her life and intended to live it. She was at peace and serene. She had left fear behind.

When Liz finally dozed off, Diana took me to get dinner at a nearby cafeteria while John kept the vigil. After dinner, Diana and I then returned home so that I could take a shower. We hadn't been home but a few minutes when we received a distraught call from John that Liz had died. We rushed back to the hospital and there was nothing more that could be done except to tell Liz goodbye. Then my son and I held each other to share our grief. Diana and Liz had had an opportunity the week before to have a lengthy conversation over the phone and had to some great degree resolved their antipathy toward one another. Still, at least initially, she contained her grief better than John and I did. After the initial shock of grief, though, John was a rock and I was numb.

Although we should have known what was happening, we had still hoped for the impossible and failed to admit the inevitable. We had the satisfaction, however, of knowing that she did not suffer and passed very quickly. Indeed, I believe that, at least subconsciously, she waited until I was gone to take the step. I think that she could not have done it with me there. I would have held her back, even against my own judgment. I will always regret, though, that John was alone when it happened. His first impulse was to rush to the phone to call me because, as he told me later, Dad had always been able to take care of every problem. This was one that I could not take care of. He was very dose to Liz and he may always carry with him the trauma of that moment. After all, she gave a great deal of herself to raise him, and although not his biological mother, she had been his de facto mom since he was eight years old. Worst of all, though, in spite of her best intentions, Liz would not be able to physically attend John's graduation. I have no doubt, though, that she was there.

Liz' brother Edward arrived within minutes of her death. Her parents arrived the next day. I had never appreciated them sufficiently. What strength! In spite of their shock and grief, they comported themselves with dignity and compassion. Indeed, I think we all handled it very well.

The funeral was held at the Christ the King Catholic Church on Thursday, March 29, 1990. Judge Mayhue, who had known Liz both socially and in his capacity as one of the Social Security judges before whom I practice, was gracious enough to serve as one of her pallbearers. She would have liked that. The others included my brother John, her two brothers Edward and Andrew, Lanny West, and son John. She was buried in her favorite red dress, which we felt was appropriate to such a vital spirit. It was tragic that she only lived for forty-five years, but it would have been even more tragic to live longer in a state of physical debility and pain. At last she was free.

I was quite moved when I entered the church to find a very large crowd almost evenly divided between Catholics and Methodists. In fact, the service, while primarily conducted by Father Tom Marx, was shared with Reverend Dorothy Collier from the Methodist church. We sang a combination of Catholic and Methodist hymns. Then, at the Calvary Catholic Cemetery in Fort Smith, she was paid the highest tribute of all. A young man from the Scottish Heritage Society named Jeff had become very fond of Liz over the years. He had been learning to play the bagpipes. The day before the funeral, he called to ask if he could play Amazing Grace at the graveside. It suddenly seemed absolutely the right thing to do. Therefore, following the final words by Father Marx, Jeff, standing some distance off among the tombstones, arrayed in full Scottish regalia and bagpipes, rendered the final tribute. I am sure that Liz approved wholeheartedly. In fact, I have asked to have the same done at my funeral when the time comes. With the conclusion of those haunting and heartrending strains from an instrument almost as old as man himself, Liz was laid to rest. Her epitaph reads, "Joan Elizabeth Duty, born August 8, 1944, died March 27, 1990. Beloved Wife, Best Friend, and Loving Mother." I must relate that "Loving Mother" was added at the specific request of John and Diana. I was moved and gratified that they wanted it. Thus, one chapter ended and another began.

The story would not be complete, though, without describing one of life's poignant coincidences, if that is what it was. On the first night at the hospital, Liz had sunk very low. I was with her and at first was aware of nothing but the two of us. Then, as the crisis receded, I realized that there was someone else there, sitting on her other side. It proved to be an elderly black lady, named Mrs. Chaney. She was a retired practical nurse who volunteered to sit through the nights with hospice patients in their terminal stages. She remained through the night, reading her Bible and helping Liz whenever needed. Her calm assurance and evident compassion kept us from becoming maudlin. She later told me that she arrived only twenty minutes too late the next night to resume her vigil. The coincidence in this is that she was the mother of one of my clients. A month or so after Liz' funeral, when her son came in to thank me for the successful outcome of his case, he concluded the interview by saying that he had a surprise for me. He then left my office to return a moment later with his mother. It was Mrs. Chaney. She and I could only embrace one another in a spontaneous outpouring of feelings born in tragedy, but now transformed in no small part by her gift of faith and love into hope for the future. Three years later, I met her again at the Fort Smith Riverfest, where she joined Barbara and me at a picnic table to share a barbeque dinner. We actually had little to say to one another, beyond trivialities, but the comfortable silence we shared reminded me of her gift and the fundamental experience which we had shared. It is people like her who reassure me about the goodness of man. They are the life rafts to which the rest of us cling in stormy seas.

Chapter 22

A Time for Healing and Renewal
April, 1990-October, 1990

I have heard horror stories about the physical and psychological stress of illness, funerals, and even births and weddings. One has to live through it, though, to truly understand. I have been through five weddings of my own (including the second wedding to Liz in the Catholic Church) and two for my children, and their innervating effects were not significant. I have been through some births, and while they are certainly stressful, the stress is usually balanced by the great relief when it is over and the pleasure of the new child. Of course, as has happened once in my life, the death of a newborn child can cause another kind of stress. In fact, I felt very much the same way after Liz' funeral. Tom Marx kept telling me to get some rest. I knew he was right, but thought that he was being unduly solicitous. Only later did I realize how spaced-out I had been. It turned out that only prolonged rest, including both quiet times while awake and much, much sleep made any difference.

For the last five years, I had been struggling mightily to build up a new law practice and establish myself in Fort Smith. Then we went through the first stages of Liz' illness. It wasn't until the last four months of her final illness, though, that a potentially dangerous stress level was reached. I worried constantly. I didn't sleep well. I didn't eat well. I was trying to continue to work and take care of Liz and see that she was taken care of while I was working. Then there was the sudden bombshell of her death, which came unexpectedly, although in the back of our minds we knew that it was inevitable. I guess death is always a surprise. One is never ready for it whether you are the person dying or a survivor. Then there was the ordeal of the funeral, consoling her family, meeting the public, and trying to exhibit normalcy and such like, ad nauseam.

When the last funeral guest left and I was at last alone, I spent countless hours doing almost nothing. I returned to work immediately and continued to function in that arena, but when I went home at night it was a total flame-out. When I wasn't sleeping, I was sitting on my front porch, dressed in warm-ups, smoking my pipe, listening to the Cardinals, or listening to a taped book. I tried doing this in my study as I had done for years, but even though I didn't want company I needed to be outside where I could have some tenuous touch with other people and other people's lives. The children yelling while they played across the street, the neighbors speaking to me as they walked past, cars rushing up and down the street, all of these kept me in touch. I didn't want intimacy, but I didn't want isolation either.

During these early months, many people made overtures, but I wasn't ready yet for relationships. A very attractive young woman down the street came to visit two or three times and I only think she was being considerate. Still, I didn't want even that. She kept asking me to join her and a male friend for hamburger cookouts in her backyard. Finally, after I had told her no for the hundredth time, she asked me if I would just prefer for her to go away and leave me alone. Without hesitation, I said yes. It certainly ended that friendship, but I wasn't trying to be rude. I really did want to be alone.

By May of 1990, I had begun to surface, although there was a long way to go. John's graduation from college was scheduled in Tucson, and that was the one thing I wouldn't have missed for the world. Liz had focused on attending the graduation as her primary goal. She repeatedly stressed to her doctor that he had to keep her going long enough. As it turned out, I had to attend it for both of us. I must admit that this was on my mind much of the time.

I flew to Tucson and watched with great pride as John graduated.

He had made it through college in spite of many hardships, including our moving to Arkansas, several physical injuries (mostly while playing intermural athletics), a growing problem with his own stress, and finally Liz' death just before finals his senior year. He made it, though, and graduated with honors. It was quite an achievement. I was a proud father. To celebrate, I took John, his future bride-to-be Missy Berkowitz, Diana, and her friend Valerie Borden to Las Vegas for a long weekend. We stayed at the Lady Luck Hotel and did the usual things. We ate voraciously, played the slot machines, and strolled around to watch the sights. Las Vegas is one zoo where the weird creatures are not kept in cages. By Monday, though, the kids had all returned to their various pursuits and I was left alone. I planned to stay in Las Vegas for the whole week. I thought it would be good for me just to be alone, play the slot machines, and vegetate. By Tuesday, I was climbing the walls. Ironically, I had spent hours playing the slot machines alone when Liz and I would go on trips to Las Vegas. However, at least I knew that I had a friend in the vicinity then. This time I was truly alone and it just didn't work. Finally, unable to take it any longer, I changed my plane reservations for Wednesday and went home. It was so good to be back to familiar semi-oblivion.

About the only socializing I did during this time was with my good and true friend Lanny West. He came over every Saturday morning and we would go to breakfast and then do my grocery shopping. This not only kept me in food, but provided me with human contact other than that which occurred during the course of my work. I looked forward to those Saturday jaunts even more than I realized at the time, for when they ended I missed them a great deal.

Other than Lanny's visits and going to church, I slipped easily into the life of almost a recluse. I would have gone on this way for an indefinite period of time, but my mother decided that it was unhealthy. My cousin Jolinn had a cousin named Judy whom I had met as a child and who was now single and raising two almost grown children. She was a school teacher in Noel, Missouri. Somehow it was managed that we would get together. I talked to her on the phone a few times and finally she and her daughter came to Fort Smith to meet me. They spent the weekend and indeed we had a pleasant time. She was an intelligent, talented, and sensitive woman. I think that under other circumstances a relationship probably could have developed between us. As it was, we kept in touch for about two months and she came to Fort Smith one more time. By September, though, it was obvious that the spark was lacking. We let it fizzle out and fade away, still friends but not interested. Truth to tell, whether or not she could have been interested, I wasn't ready yet.

So the world turned and the summer passed. In my memory, it had a vague hot drowsy somnambulant dreamlike quality. It was the best medicine I could have had.

Fate, however, had one more blow in store. On September 29, 1990, six months to the day of Liz' funeral, her father Tony Alba died. He had been partially paralyzed as a result of a stroke for some time, but had appeared to be recovering and adjusting well. I am sure that it was in no small measure the shock of Liz' death that reversed the process. In any event, I was jerked suddenly out of my torpor to grab a plane to New York. Diana also dropped everything and enplaned from Maryland to meet me. Perhaps we were not family, but we were representing Liz at the funeral, and it was right that we were there.

By the fall of 1990, I was beginning to revive. I even went to some Razorback football games up at Fayetteville. I resumed active status in both CBMC and the Methodist Men's Club. Throughout, I had continued to attend both the Catholic and Methodist churches. Since I no longer had a built-in chauffeur, a group of families at Christ the King banded together to provide me with a ride to church every Saturday night. They never missed once, and I was a more faithful attendant at Mass than I had ever been before. It was very revitalizing. At first, it was a way of feeling closer to Liz. Later, as I made a conscious effort to let go and let her pursue her spiritual destiny, it became a source of personal renewal for me. There is no worship experience to compare with the Catholic Mass for spiritual communion. That was exactly what I needed.

On the other hand, I also needed the energizing effect of the Holy Spirit which the Methodist Church gives me. With the Catholic Church I commune. With the Methodist Church I do the Lord's work. It is a good combination. Perhaps it is a measure of my shallowness that I need two churches to give me the depth that I should be able to obtain with one. Be that as it may, I have been fortunate enough to find what I need.

In October 1990, I volunteered to participate in the Stephen Ministry program at the Methodist Church. This is a nationwide, non-denominational project in which churches train groups of lay ministers as care givers for parishioners in need. The task of the Stephen Minister is to listen and to provide strength for those who flag. It is not intended to afford material benefits, but to merely provide someone to share regularly with those who have a continuing need. Typical care receivers are those going through divorces, the terminally ill, and those who have lost spouses. Those who serve as Stephen ministers must go through a six-month training period and must commit themselves for a two year tour of duty. They do not replace the professional church staff, but they provide them with an extended supply of hands, feet, and hearts. Needless to say, I received far more from it than I gave. It was probably the single most meaningful step I took in putting my life back together.

Chapter 23

The Sap Also Rises
October, 1990-December, 1992

During the autumn of 1990, I finally began to look around and take nourishment. Sister Carolyn invited me to Fayetteville to attend a singles group which she belonged to. It didn't take. There was one young lady whom I did find attractive. In fact, she was the reason my sister invited me. However, I phoned her a few days later to test the waters and found out that once more there was no spark. I didn't try again.

John was in law school by now at the University of Arkansas and that was a great comfort. He didn't want to go to Arkansas. In fact, he had been accepted to Georgetown. However, I could never have afforded Georgetown and I truly did need him nearby. I think that he could probably have made it on student loans, but he was sensitive enough to know that I needed him at that point. We got to talk on the phone frequently and he came home as often as he could. If I hadn't been so self-absorbed, I might have recognized what an ordeal it was for John. He was in a strange school in a strange town with no friends and being constantly reminded of Liz' death and my loneliness. It is hard enough as it is to go to law school; one certainly does not need other responsibilities and worries superimposed. In fact, I believe that one year in law school was so traumatic for him that it not only turned him against being a lawyer, but set him back in his career search for two to three years.

Both John and Diana came home to be with me at Christmas. We decorated the house, and we even had a turkey for Christmas dinner with all the trimmings. True, I bought it ready cooked from a cafeteria, but Diana set it out family style with all the flourishes. Unfortunately, I blew that occasion for all of us. It was probably the nostalgia of it being the first Christmas without Liz, or perhaps I was still not back to the level of equanimity which I think is my norm. Whatever the reason, Diana and I managed to have a dispute just before dinner time and I went upstairs to sulk. She and John ate dinner alone. I regret my pettishness and lack of consideration.   However, sometimes one has to do what one has to do. One of the great secrets of life is that you cannot expect to control your every action, but instead

**Diana, John, and Davis
Christmas, 1990**

can expect to make many mistakes along the way. The solution is to admit your mistakes and move ahead, trying not to repeat them. Accordingly, we all made an effort to put the incident behind us and ended up having a pleasant Christmas holiday together. Thank God for loving and forgiving children.

Then came 1991. The healing period was apparently over, as subsequent events would reveal. I was pretty much back to normal. I was once again noticing the opposite sex. The field looked sparse, though. Then, about the middle of January, my niece Karen Banks decided to take a hand. She worked with a state agency that services blind children who can be mainstreamed in the public schools. Her office was in Little Rock. She had a friend, Barbara Raines, who was a mobility specialist with the same organization. It seems that some group or other was selling t-shirts with a Braille logo across the chest. Although I don't ever remember my niece sending me a birthday present before and it was a month after my birthday,

Karen called me to say that she had a birthday present for me, but was having trouble getting it to me. She said that her friend Barbara traveled the western part of the state and occasionally came to Fort Smith. Would it be all right if she sent the present with Barbara? I was very touched by the gesture and, being the gentleman that I am, I said I would be delighted and perhaps I could take her friend out to dinner or for a drink. Little did I know that I was playing into the hands of fate, not to mention Karen Banks. Karen and I made the arrangements. I never talked to Barbara beforehand. She was to be in Fort Smith on the 21st of January, which was a Wednesday night. She would bring me the t-shirt and I would take her out to dinner. Blessed be all ye conniving nieces.

Davis, Eddie, and Barbara, 1991

Barbara called me that afternoon and asked if I would mind going over to meet some of her friends. It seems that several of the girls working out of her office just happened to be in Fort Smith that evening and would be having drinks during happy hour at the Fifth Season Motor Inn. She said I didn't have to if I didn't want to, but that the girls would like to meet me. I was smart enough to realize that what she was saying was that they wanted to look me over and vote. I agreed. Little did I know, however, that when Barbara rang my doorbell at 6:00 that evening it was signaling a whole new life.

Barbara drove us to the Fifth Season, where I found four of her female friends and one male colleague ensconced in a booth by the indoor swimming pool. I decided to get ahead while I could, so when I was introduced I told them that I understood that I was there so that they could vote on whether to let Barbara go out with me or not. They laughed good-naturedly, but I could tell that I had hit the nail on the head. Apparently, though, the vote was in the affirmative because when I suggested that we should leave if we were going to make it on time for our reservation at Taliano's Restaurant, Barbara got up without hesitation.

The evening went well. Barbara swears that she decided to marry me during dinner, but I think it was simply that I provided her with a filet of which she is inordinately fond and a bottle of good wine. Afterward, we went to my house where we made a pot of tea and talked until almost midnight. I found her very comfortable and was attracted to her physically. We didn't even touch, though, except to shake hands. I have learned some self-restraint over the years. We did make a date, however, to go out again the next time she was in Fort Smith. By some coincidence, that turned out to be Valentine's Day. Wouldn't you know it! Fate had the bit in her teeth.

Little did I know that St. Valentine's Day, 1991, would be the beginning of the beginning. We went to dinner again. We enjoyed it again. We got a little friendlier that evening. Barbara was easy to talk to. She had a good sense of humor. She was very bright, although she expressed humility about her intelligence, in spite of having a Master's Degree and being well on the way to a Doctorate. She was successful in her career and she was affectionate. In other words, she was just what I needed. That second evening we both decided that we wanted a relationship. From that point on, events seemed to take on a life of their own.

Barbara began coming to Fort Smith almost every weekend, even without the excuse of work. In fact, it soon began to be a real strain for her. She lived in Sheridan, which is thirty miles south of Little Rock. It meant that she was only home during the week when she wasn't on the road, and she began to have more and more difficulty keeping all of the threads together. Her daughter Snow was entering into a serious relationship with

her future husband, Jim
Brunson. Barbara didn't have
to worry too much about this
since Jim was in the Navy.
Still, he seemed to manage
enough leave to court Snow.
Barbara had irons in so many
fires she was beginning to

New Caddy

show stress. At the same time, I was beginning to enjoy life like never before.

In evidence of my coming out of my shell, I even bought a new car. I had still been using the Buick which I had bought as a business car when I left the Government in 1984. It was a good car, but it was beginning to show its age. The only problem was I didn't drive. For some time, I had been experiencing back problems. I had tried to sweep them under the rug due to Liz' illnesses, but after her death my back began to bother me more and more. One of the worst aspects of this problem was that riding in the car became very uncomfortable. For some reason, the Buick was particularly aggravating to my back. At the same time, Barbara's car died. She had been driving a little Hyundai that she had originally bought for Snow, but, when her previous car gave up the ghost, she commandeered it for her work. When it reached 90,000 miles, it decided one day to throw in the towel. The poor little beast was never designed for a business car and was probably just looking for an excuse to retire. In any event, it expired, and Barbara was in a real quandary. This gave me just the excuse I needed. I lent her my Buick and bought myself a late model used car. It was a 1989 Cadillac DeVille. It had several features which I had been coveting for a long time. It had leather seats, which didn't catch the dog hair so badly from Eddie, and could be cleaned easily. It looked good. The front passenger's seat had a myriad of adjustments that made it possible for me to minimize my back discomfort. Everyone loved to drive it.

I had wanted to buy a pink Lincoln Continental with lots of chrome and wire wheels that I found at a used car lot, but Barbara showed her first sign of stubbornness. She told me flat out that it was a pimp-mobile and that if I bought it she would never be caught dead in it. That settled that right there.

So now I had a Cadillac, Barbara was driving the Buick, and we were seeing each other almost constantly. Indeed, the day finally came when Barbara sat me down and said that even though we had only been going together a comparatively short time, we were either going to have to get serious or she was going to have to quit spending so much time in Fort Smith. It was not only wearing her out, but a neighbor of mine had caught her out in the yard one day and questioned her very closely as to whether she was my secretary or just what. Barbara has a bit of a Puritan streak in her, and it was beginning to bother her that our regular weekends together weren't really the right thing to do. Sometime in April, therefore, I finally decided that although we were probably rushing things some, I wasn't going to find a better mate than Barbara and I sure didn't want to lose her. So, I took her out to dinner again at Taliano's and proposed. She didn't hesitate more than three seconds. We set the wedding date for Sunday, May 26. In the meantime, though, I had a bunch to do.

In 1987, Diana had moved to Maryland. I think she mainly wanted a change of scene and a chance to start fresh. Also, her mother lived there and she wanted the chance to get to know her better. They had never really had an opportunity to develop a mother-daughter relationship. Upon arrival, Diana found a good secretarial job and, after the inspiration of John's graduation, she enrolled in the Howard County Community College. She had two years'

Houdini and Barbara, best buddies

Mary, Diana, and Davis
Diana's Associate's Degree
graduation

accumulated   credits   from
Northern Arizona University and
was able to re-enter school as a
sophomore. In May, 1991, she
graduated Summa Cum Laude
with an Associates degree. It was
a   magnificent   achievement.
Somewhere along the way she had
discovered that she had been
diagnosed as having Attention Deficit
Disorder,
which
contributed to her difficulty in studying. Here
was a girl with a magnificent brain and all of the
personality and charm of a Miss America, but
who found it difficult to concentrate and thus
experienced extraordinary stress in a college
environment. The completion of her two-year
college degree was proof to the world, but
especially to Diana, that she had what it took to
get a college education. I think that somewhere
along the line she made up her mind that she
wasn't going to be the only member of our
family to not have a degree. Of course, there
was no question that I would attend her
graduation. There was nothing in God's world
that would have kept me away. But fate sure
tried.

The first thing that intervened was that
Barbara's daughter Snow surprised us all in May
by announcing her marriage to Jim. Barbara

Mr. and Mrs. Jim Brunson

Snow Raines and Jim Brunson are married in Virginia

Snow Raines, daughter of Barbara Wilkinson Raines of Sheridan and Sam L. Raines of Little Rock, and Jim Brunson, son of Rosemary West of California and Jim and Janice Brunson of Sheridan, were married Friday, May 10, at 7:30 p.m. in a double-ring ceremony in Norfolk, Va. The ceremony was performed by G. Dewey Simmen, Jr., Justice of the peace.

Mrs. Lois Wilkinson of Sheridan is a grandmother of the bride.

Pam Purifoy served as maid of honor. Jeff Price was best man.

After the ceremony a reception was held at the home of the best man.

Both bride and groom are graduates of Sheridan High School.

The bridegroom is a Petty Officer 3 in the U. S. Navy.

was delighted with her choice of a husband, but she was upset by the sudden decision. I think at first she felt that Snow had rushed into marriage because she felt that her mother was abandoning her by marrying me. I don't think this was the case at all, and time and circumstances have proven that Snow knew what she was doing and was exactly right. Still, it was a distraction.

More seriously, my back problems were intensifying. Before my trip to Arizona for John's graduation in May, 1990, I had gone into the hospital for what is called a twenty-four hour epidural infusion. Under some circumstances, this can give relief if the back pain is due to irritated and swollen nerve tissue. I did receive some temporary relief, but in a few days the pain came back with a vengeance. At least it got me through the trip to Arizona and Las Vegas. By the spring of 1991, my back condition was many times worse. I was, therefore, scheduled for a second epidural infusion in early May, 1991. I hoped that this would get me through what I had to do in the next few months. It didn't work worth a damn. Soon after getting out of the hospital, I began to feel sickly. Soon I was running a low-grade fever and feeling absolutely rotten. I believe that I somehow or other contracted a low-grade infection from the surgical procedure. Be that as it may, by the time I was enplaned for Maryland for Diana's graduation, I was a sick puppy. I was running a constant fever of 100-101° and I really didn't care whether the school kept or not. Somehow or other I made it to Maryland and I made it through the graduation. Of course, I have never been so proud as I was that evening when Diana's name was called and she walked across the stage to receive her diploma. What a grand achievement that was and what a magnificent moment it was for the whole family. If I had only felt better. Showing even minimal interest and enthusiasm was a major effort. I hope I was able to convey to Diana how proud I was, but I can remember very little of what happened.

Somehow, though, I did make it back to Fort Smith on the morning of Sunday, May 26th. Diana and John came with me and Snow had flown in from Norfolk, Virginia. That afternoon at 5:30, the pastor of the First United

Methodist Church, Joe
Taylor, with Father Marx
present as a guest and for
spiritual support, married
Barbara and me in
Roebuck Chapel at the
comer of North 15th and
C Streets. Afterwards, we
went to the Plaza Holiday
Inn for a wedding dinner.
It was small. It was
intimate. It was lovely.
Perhaps our wedding was
slightly precipitous, but
like Snow's I believe that

**Barbara and Davis' wedding
(Left-right): Diana, Snow, Barbara,
Davis, and John**

it was intended by fate and it was right. I have never regretted it one moment
and I don't think Barbara has either.

The first thing we did after being married was to leave on our
honeymoon. With all our children in tow we went to Eureka Springs for two
days. I was still sick and spent almost the entire time in bed, in a semiconscious condition. I think the others were bored to death and I know Barbara was disappointed, but I was simply too sick to play my usual role of pointman. Somehow, though,

**Barbara and Davis' honeymoon
(Left-right): Snow, Davis, Barbara,
John, and Diana**

everyone muddled through. It is a tribute to us all that we managed to live through it and to return home friends. That was probably the best we could have hoped for. Someday maybe I can give Barbara a real honeymoon.

Being sick on our honeymoon was only the beginning. The next few months weren't much fun either. My back condition was growing progressively worse. By early September, I could barely walk. Tests showed that I had severe lumbar stenosis. As a result, very little blood was getting through to the nerves in my lower extremities. Not only did my back hurt, but I could walk only a few feet before my legs went to sleep. I would then have to stop and bend over to allow the blood supply to renew. This was really no way to live.

Still, there was some backing and filling before surgery was scheduled. One doctor erroneously read a cardiogram and told me that I had had a heart attack. Then on the day when surgery was scheduled, like the fool that I am, I ate a Rolaid while waiting to be taken to the OR. When the doctor found out, he refused to operate. Apparently it created a risk of lung problems. So I had to stay in the hospital overnight and go into surgery the next day. Finally, on September 21, I underwent a four-level lumbar decompression laminectomy. The first thing I recall when coming to was somebody trying to put something over my face. Apparently it was an oxygen mask. However, I have been experiencing claustrophobic tendencies for a number of years. As the mask was put in place, I heard a doctor say, "That's a waste of time, he's going to knock it off," and sure enough, my hand was already on its way to the target. Evidently, I had been fighting having something put over my face even while under anesthesia. Then a little later, my doctor, Albert MacDade, told me that he was going to do some tests. I was still groggy, but he explained that it was routine after back surgery to do pin-prick tests on the genitals. He advised me that this might hurt a little, to which I replied that it damn well better. I don't know what I would have done if I hadn't felt it. Still, it wasn't a prospect that I relished. Fortunately, though, it did hurt.

I spent five days in the hospital. The first two were in Intensive Care, which I remember best for the time the orderlies decided to turn me over. They used a technique called "log rolling" which involved picking me up in a sheet and flipping me. It hurt so badly that I managed to turn myself over from then on before they could get to me.

One memorable moment was when Eddie finally got to come in. They allowed him even in the ICU, although he didn't get in until the second day. The minute he spied me in the bed, he made a lunge, but my yell of terror stopped him and apparently he immediately realized that something was wrong because he treated me like fragile china for the rest of my stay. When I finally got to a private room, he was allowed to stay with me full-time. He stayed behind the bed, though, and remained quiet as a mouse. I think he was convinced that if he was noticed he would be evicted. For me, though, it was reassuring to have him with me.

On the third day, they got me up to walk and I decided right then and there that I wasn't going to become a post-back surgery cripple. Even though it hurt like hell, I forced myself to take normal strides and walk as fast as I could manage. I think it was because of that intention that I very quickly overcame the pain and was able to resume normal activity. Since that day, I have experienced a few back twinges, but the chronic pain and numbness are completely gone and I can walk normally again. At long last, Barbara found out that she had married a middle-aged man, not an old geezer.

I stayed home for two weeks after the surgery, but I didn't stay idle. My Girl Friday, Ramona, came to the house and we read cases, made notes, dictated briefs, and generally managed to do a fairly full schedule of work. It kept my mind off of the pain and it also helped keep the bills paid. It was a while before I could walk the full mile and a half to work, but within two weeks I was back at the office.

I was still moving about gingerly, though, and even attended a few hearings in a wheelchair. I thought maybe that I could play on the mercy of the court by appearing in a wheelchair with my Seeing Eye dog trotting along beside me, but no special benefits came my way. I guess I just didn't look pathetic enough. This only lasted for a few days, and then Barbara and I left in the last week of October to drive to Saint Simon's Island, Georgia, for the annual convention of the Christian Legal Society. At the hospital, I had been provided with what is called an egg crate pad to lie on. It offers a particularly resilient surface suitable for back patients. Since I had paid for it, I took it home. With this forming an extra cushion, I climbed into the Cadillac with Eddie and Barbara and we headed south. The traveling part of the trip was not particularly enjoyable, at least for me. It probably didn't do much for my healing process either. Still, we made it to Georgia and I was able to participate in the convention. Afterward, we drove down to St. Augustine, Florida, and toured the sights. I had been through them thirty years before when Mary and I left Washington to drive to Arkansas in the big move west. Now, three decades later, I saw them again, older, wiser, and with both a different dog and a different wife.

Both on the west and east coasts of Florida, Barbara and I spent time on the beach where I found that my swamp bunny from Sheridan was really a beach bunny. It also turned out that my New Jersey-born German shepherd was a beach hound. He didn't particularly want to get his feet wet as he has always been allergic to water, but he thought it was great fun to play tag with the waves. At first, I tried keeping him on a leash, but Barbara was busy running up and down the strand and Eddie was barely able to contain himself. At long last, I let him off the leash and sat in the sand while he and Barbara romped. He would chase her for about fifty feet and then stop and look back at me to see if it was all right. Then he would come dashing back. A few times he got caught by waves and eventually was covered with saltwater and sand. He didn't particularly enjoy the bath I gave him back at the motel, but I had no doubt both he and Barbara would do it again, which was proved to be correct just over two years later.

Recently, Snow and Jim moved to Mobile, Alabama, which is within driving distance, so I think Barbara and Eddie will have an added excuse to go seaside. So, once again, the gods have smiled. Barbara can see her daughter and granddaughter, as well as the ocean, almost any time she desires.

Back in Arkansas it was already time for Barbara and me to start making plans for Christmas. It was our first one together and we decided to make it a family Christmas. Snow and Jim couldn't come and Barbara's mother didn't feel like coming, but nothing would deter my family. Jeff and Lois came, John and Missy came, and Diana was there. It was one memorable event. Barbara put on a full-blown Christmas dinner. The culmination of the event, though, was the videotape which John made. We will all of us cherish it. It showed each of us at our best and our worst. It was priceless. We tried to do it again the next year, but the result was a poor imitation and fortunately was accidentally erased. Thomas Wolfe said you can't go home again, and I think it is possible that you can't repeat truly good spontaneous happenings.

Probably the most exciting event of that Christmas, although we didn't realize it at the time, was that Diana met Brad. Many, many pages ago I described how when Liz and I moved to Fort Smith we rediscovered Lanny and Sharon West, old friends of mine from Rogers. Since I had seen them last in Rogers in the early '70s, their son Brad had not only grown up, but had graduated from college and was working for a high-powered aerospace concern in California while working on his Master's degree.

As a favor to me, after Diana's trip to Fort Smith for Liz' death and funeral the previous year, Sharon was driving Diana back to the airport and made the fateful remark to me (as Diana sat blushing in the back seat) that she "...was just so impressed with Diana and knew she was going to make a good wife for some lucky boy some day." She had even brought her camera with her and took a snapshot of Diana while she checked her bags. Evidently, Brad must have liked what he saw. In October, he wrote her a very nice four-page letter and an ardent pen-pal relationship began. A month later, Diana took the bull by the horns and called him. After that, it seemed to them like Christmas couldn't arrive soon enough. Needless to say, they both planned to come back to Fort Smith (to visit their beloved families, of course). Diana arrived on my birthday (December 20th), and Brad flew into town the next day. After greeting his parents, he immediately came over to our house to meet my daughter. When I look back on it, that took real intestinal fortitude. I am not sure they were overly impressed with one another at first sight, but they spent the next ten days together, and by the end of the holidays there was no doubt that they were interested. Brad, too, was on the Duty Family Christmas tape. We wanted to record him early so that he couldn't claim anonymity.

Therefore, when 1992 began, we had a budding romance on our hands. Brad and Diana did most of their courting by phone, although he did visit Washington a time or two. Fortunately, his company had an office there and he managed to find business reasons to travel. They became engaged on Diana's birthday while she was in California visiting Brad. It looked like we had a live one on our hands.

In the meantime, John was in Miami, Florida. After his first year in law school, he decided that he didn't want to be a lawyer. He had spent the first few months in Maryland with his mother and sister. Then he went to Florida and spent the next year looking for work and deciding what he wanted to do with his life. In the meantime, Missy had gone from being a top-notch photocopier salesperson to a national sales representative for a men's formal wear concern. To understate it, this was not a good time for John, but he needed the time and space to align his goals.

For Barbara and me, the year was one of working and watching our children start their lives. Snow became pregnant and Barbara and her mother went to visit her in Norfolk, Virginia, in April. The baby was due in October, so the next few months were fraught with anticipation. Finally, at the end of September, Barbara went east to be there when the baby was born. Nicole Lea finally decided to make her appearance on October 13. By that time, both her parents and both grandmothers were ready. She was a beautiful little girl with everything in place and plenty of personality. Everyone was completely satisfied with the results. I was beginning to wonder, though, if I still had a wife as the days and then weeks passed. Finally, on the 16th of October when Jim's mother came to visit, Barbara decided that it was time for her to come home. She didn't commit until she had a promise from Snow that when Jim went to sea the following January she would bring Nicole home to Arkansas to visit Grandma. I never thought that I would be a grandfather.

It wasn't until February of 1994, however, that Nicole became much more than an abstraction. Jim went to sea again and Snow and Nicole came to stay with us for a month. Nicole and I became great friends. She was seldom cranky and was always on the verge of laughter. All I had to do was sing the Mickey Mouse theme inserting Nicky for Mickey, and she would be thrilled; of course, part of my attraction was Eddie. Still, I knew that I had a granddaughter on the evening that she came into my study where I was smoking my pipe in my recliner and listening to a ball game. Without warning, there was a little girl struggling with mite and main to climb up into my chair. She only stayed on my lap for about ten seconds before reversing the process, which, to her, was not unlike climbing and descending Mount Everest. I took what she did to be a sign of acceptance. From that moment on, we were pals.

To return to 1992, though, Carolyn invited the family to her house to celebrate Thanksgiving, and at Christmas wedding plans were thick in the air. Diana had been spending months getting ready. She had bought her wedding dress the previous June but, to my amazement, there were many, many more things to be taken care of than merely buying a wedding dress. Both she and Brad again came to Fort Smith for Christmas and we were at long last able to have an engagement party. To double the joy and excitement, John and Missy became engaged just before leaving Miami for Arkansas. Therefore, we had an engagement party for Diana and Brad one night and an engagement party for John and Missy the next night. The former was at Hardscrabble Country Club in Fort Smith, the latter at Mary Maestri's Restaurant (one of my personal favorites) in Tontitown. The participants were slightly different, but the principles were the same. I was a happy dad with the choices in life-mates which my children had made. I couldn't have done a better job of picking them if I had done it myself.

Diana and Brad's engagement

Duty-West

Diana Duty
...to wed Bradley Alan West

Mr. and Mrs. Davis Duty of Fort Smith and Mary Ellis Duty of Columbia, Md., announce the engagement of their daughter, Diana Lynn Duty of Ellicott City, Md., to Bradley Alan West of Redondo Beach, Calif., son of Lanbert and Sharon West of Fort Smith.

The couple plan a 10:30 a.m. wedding May 8 at First United Methodist Church.

Ms. Duty is the granddaughter of Mr. and Mrs. Jeff Duty of Rogers and Ms. Izella B. Ellis of Columbia. She is a graduate of Howard Community College and is an industrial psychology student at the University of Maryland, Baltimore County.

Mr. West received a bachelor's of science degree in computer science from the University of Tulsa and a master's degree in computer science from the University of Southern California. He is employed by The Aerospace Corp. in El Segundo, Calif.

Chapter 24

A Time for Flowering
January, 1993-December, 1993

It is an interesting phenomenon of life that events can drift along, like a stew simmering on the back burner, for months and even years. Then, like flowers blooming in the spring, many threads come together in a limited period of time and life seems to step up to a higher level of intensity. Thus was the year 1993.

In January, Snow and Nicole came to visit. It had been a long time since I had had a tiny baby in the house. Fortunately Nicole was as unobtrusive a guest as a baby can be. Eddie would have given anything to take charge of her, but we tried to keep him at bay. He did manage to sneak in for an occasional lick, though.

During this time, Barbara and I celebrated our second anniversary of our meeting. How women do like anniversaries, of anything. Then it was Valentine's Day and we were celebrating the second anniversary of our mutual but undisclosed decisions to get married. Then it was April, and Diana was packing up her apartment in Maryland preparatory to moving to California. John went up from Miami to help. I am sure it was a wrench to her mother for both kids to have moved away, but these things happen. I, myself, had gone through it years before. It hurts, but life goes on, and there are compensations. No matter how much you love your children, if you only get to see them periodically you come to cherish your time together all the more. Quality time is often worth much more than a quantity of time.

Diana's and Brad's wedding was scheduled for May 8. They arrived in town separately and the last minute preparations leapt ahead, gaining speed and momentum with each day that passed. Of course there were

Biggest Venture,
walking Diana down the aisle

Mr. and Mrs. Brad West

setbacks. The wrong tuxes were delivered and had to be replaced. The florist got sick and we had to find a new one. Still all in all things went very smoothly. Diana, with almost no help except what she could get long distance from Sharon and Barbara, had planned every detail of an elegant but simple wedding. In an attempt to save me as much money as they could, Diana and Brad handmade many of the decorations and gifts. It still would cost a bundle, but by all rights, it should have cost at least twice what it did. Nonetheless, it took a year of determination, study, and frustration to work out the details. What a job they did and what a magnificent result they achieved!

The formal festivities began on Friday night, May 7, with the wedding rehearsal at the First United Methodist Church. Rose Bethel and Mickey Jamell represented the church. They supervised the affair with velvet gloves, but military precision. Indeed, there were some rather unique aspects to be considered. For one thing, we were not at all sure that we could fit the three of us, Diana and her big dress, Eddie, and me into the aisle for the processional. But, by "healing" Eddie ahead of me, the technique employed for boarding public transportation, we finally worked out a configuration which would fit the available space. I think that it was about that time with this last hurdle

overcome that Diana finally
realized that it was really going to
happen. Maybe, though, I am
speaking for myself.

After the rehearsal, the
Wests hosted a truly unique
rehearsal dinner. The guests
boarded the historic downtown
trolley for the two block run to
the Old Fort Museum. There we
rode up in the elevator to the top
floor where we emerged into a

Diana, Davis, and Barbara

huge loft, decorated to resemble an outdoor cafe under the stars. The dinner
was organized as a lottery. Each plate, cup, glass, utensil, and food item were
represented merely by numbers. One had to pick the numbers in the order
they wanted to receive them. As a result you might end up with a glass of
water for dessert and a salad with no fork. It was fun, though, and certainly
helped to break the pre-wedding tension.

Then dawned Diana's wedding day, May 8, 1993. Diana, her
mother, John and Missy, and Diana's friend Valerie Borden, who had flown
in from Tucson to be her maid of honor, were staying at the Holiday Plaza.
They managed to make their way to the church separately. Jeff and Lois were
coming down with John and Susan, so instead of being overwhelmed with
family, Barbara and I found ourselves making our way alone to the church.
I think it helped us to retain our poise. We arrived early to help arrange the
flowers and take part in wedding pictures. Then the wedding began.

With the first chords from the organ, the frantic activity and tension
were miraculously transformed into a ceremony of beauty and serenity,
made up in equal parts of religious devotion and love. My part in the
proceedings, of course, was all but incidental. I only had to walk down the
aisle and to the minister's query of "Who gives this woman in holy
matrimony?" I need only reply, "Her family and I do." Still, it was a truly

moving moment for me when my daughter took my arm and we started that very short but interminable stroll. I managed to whisper to her that this was our biggest "Venture" of all. She smiled in spite of her nerves, and we were off.

Eddie was a trooper. He only once looked aside when he glanced into the pew where Barbara was seated. I guess he either thought we would stop there or she would join us. But then we went on down front where, once in place, he proceeded to lie down on the carpet and feign sleep, or boredom.

From that point on things seemed to me to move like lightening, yet in slow motion. Suddenly, Brad was there taking Diana from my arm. Then I was moving back to sit beside Barbara. Diana and Brad were mounting the steps to the altar. They were taking their vows. The minister, Dorothy Collier, was reading the scripture selections and leading my daughter and her bridegroom through the responses. I wasn't euphoric. I didn't feel like crying. But I was deeply moved and aware to the very core of my being of the importance of this step. Despite all the successes and all the setbacks, my daughter had reached her maturity and was entering upon the rest of her life. I was the happiest father who ever lived.

As memorable as the wedding was, though, it will always be the reception which remains the most vivid in my memory. Shortly before the

Lanny, Brad, and Sharon West
Parents of the groom

wedding, Barbara and I had applied for membership in Fort Smith's grand old Hardscrabble Country Club, because that was the only place in town we could find that was really suitable for the event. The wedding was at 10:30 am and by 11:30 the church was cleared and everyone was heading for Hardscrabble. The reception consisted essentially of a grand gourmet brunch with champagne toasts and a three-tiered wedding cake. The top of the cake was adorned by the wedding piece which Lanny and Sharon had used at their wedding. Diana had planned everything with absolutely perfect taste and propriety. It was elegant but simple, tasteful, and appropriate. It was truly a lovely and delightful affair, and by doing as much as possible herself, she kept the expenses at a minimum, which in turn kept my blood pressure within safe bounds.

Barbara and I sat with Reverend Collier, her husband King and Lois and Jeff. Diana and Brad were graciousness personified, circulating through the crowd, speaking to all of the guests, and even sitting down at each table to chat. I am not sure that they even got anything to eat, but everyone else did. Ramona said that her husband Terry went back for ham three times. The denouement, however, was the grand exit. We had rented a horse and carriage which picked the couple up at the front door of the club and whisked them off to a recently opened and very Victorian Bed and Breakfast establishment. We even had something to throw at them as they left. It wasn't rice, though (which apparently kills birds), but rose petals that Diana had

Mr. and Mrs. Bradley A. West
...formerly Diana Duty

West-Duty

.Diana Lynn Duty and Bradley Alan West, both of Redondo Beach, Calif., were married May 8, 1993, at First United Methodist Church by the Rev. Dorothy Collier. A reception at Hardscrabble Country Club followed the 10:30 p.m. ceremony.

The bride is the daugher of Mr. and Mrs. Davis Duty of Fort Smith and Ms. Mary Ellis Duty of Columbia, Md. Parents of the bridegroom are Mr. and Mrs. Lanbert West of Fort Smith.

The bride was given in marriage by her father and his seeing-eye dog, Eddie. She wore a gown of candlelight brocade fashioned with a scalloped sweetheart neckline edged in pearls, a basque bodice and renaissance sleeves. The full skirt extended into a chapel-length train. She carried a traditional bouquet of cream roses.

Maid of honor was Valerie Borden of Phoenix. Rod Knowlton of Tulsa, Okla., served as best man. Bridesmaids were Kathie Thompson of Fort Smith, Beth Shumate of Plano, Texas, and Melissa Berkowitz of Miami. Sean Cox of Flower Mound, Texas, Robert Myers of Westland, Mich., and John Duty of Miami were groomsmen. Danny Thompson served as candlelighter.

After a wedding trip to Sweden, the couple live in Ellicott City, Md. The bride is a student at the University of Maryland, Baltimore County, and the bridegroom is a computer scientist.

laboriously tied up by hand in little net bags. It is too bad that now that she has become such a wedding authority she can't turn the knowledge to good use and become a bridal consultant. That is probably true, though, of all brides.

In any event, Diana and Brad's wedding is a memory which I will always cherish. It wasn't exactly cheap, although it could have cost much more than it did had it not been for their efforts above and beyond the call of duty (no pun intended), but it was well worth every penny. This is the place where I am supposed to say that I wish I could have done more. Truth to tell, though, I think we all did all we could and it was a tremendous success. Rose Bethel, who had been the prime mover in orchestrating the wedding through the church, told me on several occasions later that it was one of the loveliest weddings she had ever attended. Since she is practically a professional at the business, I believed her and was much flattered.

Brad and Diana flew off to Sweden on a honeymoon to visit the family with whom he had spent a year as an exchange student during high school. What a perfect climax to a super happening. Barbara, John, and I were not to be outdone, though. We immediately took off for Las Vegas to recover, physically and spiritually, if not financially. We spent almost a week out there, staying at my favorite haunt, the Lady Luck Hotel and Casino.

Barbara and Davis in Vegas, 1983

Barbara took the opportunity to catch up on her sleep and John and I took the opportunity to stay up most of every night playing the quarter keno machines. I think he and I sat there for hours, hunched over our machines, talking little but concentrating deeply. For us, it was a form of togetherness, perhaps in mindlessness, but enjoyable nonetheless. We would play until we all but fell off our stools, then we would head for the all night discount food specials. One night it was an omelet, another it was steak. Then about 3:00 or 4:00 o'clock in the morning, we would stagger up to our rooms, take a hot shower, and crash until noon. I am not sure how much fun Barbara had, but John and I had a ball. Also, it was a terrific way to break the tension which had been building up around the whole family for several months. When the week was over, we were all ready to get back to normality and our regular daily routines. We were poorer and no wiser, but certainly a lot looser.

The next item on the agenda was John's future. He had applied at the University of Maryland and Northwestern University to go to graduate school to work on a Master's degree in public relations. I was never completely sure what it was all about, but it was an interest which he had developed while working as a proofreader for a public relations agency in Miami. As it turned out, he was accepted by Northwestern, which was his first choice. Their advanced degree in public relations is what a Harvard MBA is to business. They only accept twenty-five applicants a year for the graduate studies, and low and behold, John was one of them. Was I ever proud!

Now came the rush to get him outfitted for the northern climes and off to Northwestern, which is located Evanston, Illinois, just outside of Chicago. I had to do some harm to the old bankbook, but we managed.

Also during this time, Snow and Jim (and Nicole, of course) came to visit. They had been moved by the Navy from Norfolk, Virginia, to Mobile, Alabama. In August Barbara went down to visit Snow while Jim was off at a training course.

Before she went, though, I lost my head and went car shopping. The seed of the process was planted when I heard that because Jim's work was several miles from their apartment, Snow either had to bundle herself and the baby up to take him to work so that she would have transportation or she was left without wheels. I did not like this idea with a small baby involved. Therefore, it occurred to me that the old LeSabre which I had bought as a business car in 1984 was just what she needed. Barbara had been driving it since 1990, and it had proved a real god-send to her. Still, by this time it had almost 130,000 miles on it. Although it was still running well, it was obvious that it should be subjected to a less demanding lifestyle. Therefore, I made up my mind to let Barbara take the Buick down to Snow when she went in August and to give Barbara my car which she had helped me pick out before we were married. It was a 1989 Cadillac DeVille and I loved it dearly. Still, when I thought of how many miles Barbara drives a year and how much time she spends on the open highway, I realized that she means too much to me to run any risks. If anyone needed a safe, dependable car, it was she.

I, therefore, went shopping for a new car for myself. Also, I decided that it wasn't fair that the driver of my car be the only one to be protected by an inflatable safety bag. I wanted a car with a safety bag on the passenger's side. That's where I ride. I also wanted a car with one of the newly developed lumbar supports in the seat which would ease my back considerably on long trips. Over the years, it had become increasingly painful for me to travel any distance at all. Even after my surgery, my back would only take it for an hour or so before I had to stop and get out to walk around. The new lumbar supports offered some measure of relief in this department. However, only the more expensive cars have such devices. After much soul searching and flip-flopping between a Lincoln Towncar, a Lincoln Mark VIII, and several models of Cadillac, I finally settled on a 1993 Cadillac Seville. I was also encouraged to make the move by a special interest rate which Barbara was able to get on financing through her credit union. When I look back, it seems as though it was almost pre-ordained that I buy a new car when I did. Then, when I started looking at the later model DeVilles, I realized that the DeVille which I was giving Barbara had over 60,000 miles on it and was, itself, beginning to get older. I did some more jockeying about and maneuvering and finally ended up trading it for a 1992 DeVille for Barbara. The end result was that I bought two new cars, both white and both Cadillacs.

This was a far cry from my first family car, a two-door 1958

American Rambler which Mary owned when we got married. Apropos to nothing, I did some arithmetic and found that I have bought fifteen cars in my lifetime. This is a real achievement for someone who doesn't drive. Then, too, I think there is a broader truth hidden in the foregoing recital. Given enough time and thought, a person can rationalize and justify almost anything he wants to do.

These new acquisitions also started another chain of events. It is painfully obvious that it is not sensible to allow such expensive new cars to sit out in the weather. The one thing that we were unable to get when I bought the house in Fort Smith was a carport. Now, I have decided to change all that. After much discussion with architects and builders, and contemplation with my bankbook, I decided that the best and cheapest solution would be to tear down my old garage in the backyard and build a carport there with an entry off the back alley. This, of course, meant that my raspberry patch and three trees had to be moved. It would also mean that I would lose about half of my backyard. Still, I have finally reached the point in life where, although I love my grass and trees, I have been forced to leave the mowing and trimming to my next door neighbor's twelve-year-old son. Only my dog really enjoys the grass. There will be some greenery left and my cars will be both safe and protected. I suppose this is an example of one of life's less dramatic compromises. Now if I can just avoid a hail storm until the project is completed. As of this writing, the three trees and raspberry bushes have been transplanted. My next door neighbor is attempting to get a variance for me from the city planning commission. Then I must contract out the building of the facility itself. Maybe I can delay that until after the first of the year to put off the expenditure as long as possible.

At long last, after one of the hottest summers which Fort Smith had seen for many a year, September finally arrived. It brought with it not only the official beginning of autumn but more importantly football fever. As we have done for several years, my brother John and I again bought season tickets for the University of Arkansas Razorback football games which would be played in Fayetteville. There would only be three in 1993, but we were ready. Then, too, with the advent of big-time Arkansas Razorback basketball a new arena was under construction. It was to be known as the Walton Arena, being named after Bud Walton (the brother of Sam Walton who founded the Wal-Mart department store empire) who had donated $15,000,000. Brother John and I decided that this was a good time to try to get some basketball season tickets as well. We applied for four but eventually only got two and they are situated somewhere near outer space. Still, all the seats in Walton Arena are good and we are delighted to have them. We will be especially delighted to have them if we are afforded the luxury of following a team on its way to a national championship. As basketball fortunes have risen, though, Arkansas' football fortunes have declined. We still go to football games and enjoy the brisk, and sometimes more than brisk, fall weather, but we have little to cheer about.

The amazing thing is that our mother Lois also still attends. Jeff has finally given it up and stays at Sister Carolyn's to watch the games on TV or listen to them on the radio. Lois still goes although she is 86 years old. She says she still enjoys them. It may be that she is mainly enjoying being with her boys, but we would have to say the same thing in return. How many sons nearing 60 can pal around with their mom attending football games? Not many.

Also, with the 1993 season, John and I and our wives have began a new and very pleasant custom. After each ball game, we go out to some place nice to eat. After the first game we drove over to Eureka Springs ("Little Switzerland") and ate at the Bavarian Inn. After the second game, we ate at a lodge outside Garfield near Beaver Dam. After the third game we talked Sister Carolyn into joining us and dined at a Mexican restaurant in Rogers. This was a particularly a memorable occasion because of the pouring rain. First we sat through a drenching downpour during the football game, swathed in plastic ponchos and feeling very stoic. It helped that the Razorbacks won, only their fourth victory in 1993. Then we drove the twenty miles to Rogers in a blinding rainstorm and had to dash from the car to the restaurant through sleeting rain and virtual rivers in the street. Once again, the cheap plastic ponchos saved us from being altogether soaked. Eddie was not so lucky. I doubt that he will remember the evening as being quite so delightful as the rest of us. There is something about inclement weather which seems to replace the usual concerns and proprieties with the simpler, almost carefree, exuberance of childhood. There is nothing like being half frozen from snow or soaked by rain to bring people together, simply, without pretense, as themselves. Maybe we should all go stand under the shower with our clothes on occasionally to help us to really see and appreciate life around us.

As the final months of 1993 wind down, events seem to move faster and become more hectic. In October, Barbara and I spent the last ten days of the month out west. We flew to San Francisco so that I could attend the annual convention of the National Organization of Social Security Claims Representatives. It lasted three days. Over the following weekend, Brad and Diana flew up from Los Angeles to join us in doing a real tourist number on the city. We ate all the Chinese food and seafood we could find and hit as many tourist attractions within reach. We visited the cable car museum, we went out on a cruise on the bay, and we toured the maritime museum. It was also on this occasion while touring the shops on Pier 39 that we came across a shop featuring imports from the British Isles. One of its offerings was a computerized family tree reference source. The information I had on the Dutys was confirmed, and I once again decided to try to take the family tree back to our Duthie precursors. To my amazement, the computer printed out a summary on the Dubhacht family (one of the early versions of Duthie which I had previously discovered) and took the family back from Scotland to its Irish antecedents. I ordered an embroidered copy of the Dubhacht crest to sew on a blazer, a picture of which I have included in the preface to this book, and deemed the San Francisco trip a whopping success.

Diana and Brad are a charming couple and delightful as tourist companions. The Wests and the Dutys have much to be proud of. I even believe that it is safe to look forward to the next generation with much anticipation.

Diana and Brad were in the process of being moved by his job to Maryland where Diana would also be able to return to school and finish her university degree. Therefore, they were not free to join Barbara and me on the next leg of our odyssey. We flew from San Francisco to Las Vegas where we spent an additional three days doing the town. Without John to keep me in line, Barbara had to pick up the slack, but I think she enjoyed it. We saw a George Carlen show, which was memorable only for the number of imaginative ways in which the "F" word was employed. I was not overly amused after the first five minutes. I was, however, interested in his diatribe against the anti-abortion movement. He observed that the movement has embraced a love affair with the fetus, but shows no compassion for children after birth or young helpless mothers. He had a point.

As usual, we ate a gourmet dinner at Hugo's where Barbara received her rose and we dined like royalty. This time we stayed at the Golden Nugget where the rooms are nicer, but the atmosphere is not quite as congenial as at my good old Lady Luck. Then, we finally had to go home. It was only two days later however, that we were off to Fayetteville for the second Razorback football game. It was the cold one. In memory, I can distinguish the 1993 games by the weather in which they were played. The first was sunny with a pleasant autumn chill to the air. A jacket felt good, but was not really necessary. The second game was bitterly cold. I wore my sheepskin jacket, sheepskin helmet, fur-lined gloves, and two pairs of pants. Still, my feet were numb by the time the game ended. The third game, as I described above, was played in a flood.

Attending sporting events has not been the total extent of our social life during 1993. We have attended plays at the Little Theater and have regularly enjoyed our membership at Hardscrabble. We only go there to eat, and in fact, we only have a social membership.

It offers a pleasant change, though, from the usual fare of Chinese and Mexican restaurants, Western Sizzlin' steaks, and cafeterias. I have already mentioned that in the spring we attended a formal dinner dance in support of the Heart Association. In October, we attended a semi-formal

**Davis and Barbara at the Art
Center Gala, 1993**

reception climaxing the local Cancer Drive. Barbara is a member of the Cancer Board, so it was a must that we attend. I wouldn't have missed it, though, under any circumstances, because Nolan Richardson, coach of the Razorback basketball team, was the guest of honor. I even got to shake his hand.

Also in October, Barbara and I attended a formal dinner dance, again to raise money, for the Fort Smith Art Center. Another pleasant evening was when we joined Linda and Judge Mayhue (the Chief of the Administrative Law Judges before whom I hold Social Security hearings in Fort Smith) to drive to Tulsa for dinner and to attend a revival stage performance of *Oklahoma*.

November and December, 1993, were a blur of activity. On the 19th of November, I attended a Social Security conference with the Arkansas Trial Lawyers Association in Little Rock. Afterward, Barbara and I rushed home so that she could head off to Alabama to spend a few days with Snow and Nicole. Again, Jim was away on duty. On the way back, she stopped to spend Thanksgiving with her mother in Sheridan, just south of Little Rock. The day before Thanksgiving, Diana and Brad arrived on stage in Brad's new 1993 Saab 900

**Davis and Barbara at the
Symphony Dinner, 1993**

on their cross-country move from California to Maryland. I joined them for Thanksgiving dinner with Brad's parents.

Then it was suddenly December. The final month of 1993 got off to a running start with Barbara and me attending the annual St. Edward Hospital charity ball held at a local country club. All of the sudden, I seemed to be trotting about town on a fairly regular basis wearing a tuxedo. In fact, formal occasions were becoming so frequent that I decided to buy a tux rather than to continue spending rather sizeable sums on rentals.

Then suddenly it was time for the jaunt to join the Mayhues in Tulsa for the John Denver Christmas concert. This had special poignancy for me. I once before saw John Denver in concert. It was at Gammage Auditorium at Arizona State University about 1980. I was living in Arizona. I was still a Federal Administrative Law judge. The children were still at home and in junior high school. Liz was still alive and both she and the children attended the concert with me, as did Eddie's predecessor Cinder. I still have the John Denver tapes I bought in the auditorium lobby after the concert. Now I saw John Denver again. He was fifteen years older, but just as entertaining. This time, though, I live in

John and Missy

Arkansas. I am no longer a judge. The children are grown, gone, and married. Liz is dead and I am married to my beloved Barbara. What a contrast! Life does seem to proceed no matter what. Even if you want to get off, you can't, for the act of getting off simply channels life into new directions.

In the meantime, John's wedding plans moved on apace. Of course, Missy was doing most of the work. John managed to get out of Miami just in time. He was deeply engrossed in his new studies in Evanston and it was not surprising that he fractured his foot while trying to break-up a midnight

fight between some friends and some high school bully boys. John has always thrown himself into life with verve and abandon. I wasn't too surprised when I found out that he had once again become a casualty. It is just the way he is and I wouldn't change a thing. As soon as the term was over in December, he flew to Miami to help out as much as time would permit. From talking by phone with both Missy and John, it was evident that they were tired of their recent separation and ready to make a permanent life together. Such nice people, my son and daughter-in-law!

The final and big event in December was, of course, John's and Missy's wedding. It is hard to say when we started getting ready. Barbara had been shopping for the right clothes for months. Having gone through

Above: Brad, Missy, John, and Diana
Below: Barbara, John, and Davis

the same process, though, with Diana's wedding in May, I was by now becoming inured.   In fact, for Barbara's Christmas present, I bought her a gold necklace and bracelet to complement the dress she wore to the wedding. It is a wise husband who can combine projects and get two for the price of one.

Although it had seemed an eternity away when the wedding plans were first made, with plenty of time to do everything all too soon the day was upon us. On December 14th, we flew to Orlando where we met Diana and spent two days touring Epcot Center at Disney World. Then we rented a car and drove to Miami to meet Brad and throw ourselves directly into the wedding festivities.

From the very beginning, we were surrounded by a host of new friends and relatives. Missy's family went far beyond the call of duty (no pun intended, really) to make us feel welcome and comfortable. Their friends adopted us as friends. Everything had been thought of, from baskets of fruit in our rooms at the Inter-Continental hotel to transportation from event to event. On Thursday night, December 16th, the men held a bachelor's party for John and the girls held a bachelorette's party for Missy. I only know vaguely what happened at the latter, and I only know half of what happened at the former. After dinner, we old guys were gently pointed in the direction of home and bed, while the young crazy ones went on to the exploits of great manhood that are required as part of the rites of preparing for marriage. They drank strange drinks, smoked powerful cigars, told ever more funny stories, and viewed various examples of publicly displayed female anatomy. I think it was a mercy that they sent me off to bed early. As Missy's mother Sandy Berkowitz' cousin Carl observed when offered a private dance lesson by a go-go dancer, "Young lady, does your mother know where you are?"

Friday night, December 17th, Barbara and I hosted what began as a rehearsal dinner and later turned into what is termed an "out-of-towners" dinner. There were upwards of a hundred people present. Of course, most of them were friends of the Berkowitzes, but from the outset, their friends became our friends. It was held in the ballroom of an old seaside hotel. Drinks and canapés were enjoyed on the patio, then we adjourned inside for what proved to be a very lively and joyous dinner. Toasts were offered, tales were told (some in and some out of school), and Missy and John began what would turn into two days of table hopping, hand shaking, and making everyone feel welcome and appreciated.

Finally came the big day. I decided to do it the hard way and woke up sick with a chest cold that had begun at Epcot. By Saturday, I was hoping for death. But, it was not to be. We kicked off the proceedings at 4:00 pm with wedding pictures. At 7:45, the wedding itself got underway. It was conducted in a room adjacent to the hotel's grand ballroom with live music and a traditional Jewish wedding canopy. Rabbi Goldstein blessed the event both in English and Hebrew. Missy was beautiful in a white satin wedding gown. I know this because the minute John laid eyes on her at the front of the improvised chapel, he was transformed into a man possessed. His mother and I were escorting him down the aisle, and when we reached the front, he was to kiss her on the cheek, shake my hand, and escort us to our seats. When the wedding party in the procession ahead of us parted, though, revealing Missy in all of her glory, forgotten was the kiss, forgotten was the handshake, and forgotten was the escort service. Other than that, John and Missy were the picture of self-possession. They spoke clearly, precisely, and with feeling. Between them and the Rabbi, they produced a meaningful and sacred ceremony. I truly feel that their union was blessed. Afterward, it was well toasted.

We repaired to an anteroom for hors d'oeuvres to restore our strength. Then we sat down to a sumptuous feast in the grand ballroom, followed by dancing and conviviality until after 1:00 in the morning. In spite of my near terminal cold, I managed to eat dinner, drink some of Marshall's 62-year-old cognac, and do a credible rock and roll number with Missy, Barbara, and Diana. I tried to include Sandy, Missy's mother, but she managed to hide at just the right moments. Both Diana and Missy were astonished that I could do such lively gyrations on the dance floor. Diana remarked that she didn't know I could dance "like that" and Missy told me that I was "almost as good as John," which was high praise indeed since John is the family's Fred Astaire. Finally, I had to explain to both girls that I had had a whole life before they were born and that I had been dancing with notable abandon forty years before. I also explained to Missy that John's dancing had not come about by chance. It is part of the Duty genetic code. Finally, it was with joy in my heart and fever on my brow that I led Barbara off to our room in the wee hours.

The only thing left was to attend a brunch given for out-of-town guests at a yacht club by Missy's godmother Phyllis. Once again replete with food and fellowship, we said our farewells and Diana, Brad, Barbara, and I headed our car down Alligator Alley to Sanibel Island near Fort Myers, on Florida's west coast. We spent two days there in a condo at the Sanibel Harbour Club soaking up sunshine and fresh sea air. Sanibel Island is noted for its seashells so, of course, we spent one evening just before sunset scampering about the beach picking up shells. Even Eddie had fun. As I had done once before when visiting the beach, I removed his harness and let him off the leash. He wouldn't go more than fifty feet away from me, but it could be in any direction, and this gave him plenty of latitude for leaping, bounding, jumping, chasing, and being chased. We ended that day by sitting on the beach watching one of Sanibel Island's beautiful sunsets. This happened on December 20th, which, as the world knows, is my birthday. As is my custom, I called my mother to wish her a happy birthday. It has always been my conviction that the child should fate its mother on birthdays, since it is the mother who did all the work. On this occasion, however, all Lois got was a croak. I started loosing my voice at Epcot, and by Sanibel, there wasn't even a reasonable facsimile of a voice left. Still, I think I got across to her my love and appreciation. By the way, in order to settle all raging disputes, this was my 59th birthday.

Everything has to come to an end, though. On December 21st, we took a plane back to Fort Smith where we arrived in the very middle of the night to fall into bed in total exhaustion. Diana and Brad toddled off to the West's because Snow and Jim (but mainly Nicole) arrived on the 22nd to spend two days with us before Christmas. Nicole won a place in my heart by showing the good taste of wanting to hold Eddie and be held by me. Also, when we exchanged Christmas presents, she liked my present best (a Mickey Mouse Santa Claus).

Above: Nicole at 16 months
Below: Nicole loves Granddaddy's Mickey Mouse

From that point on, the year unwound with less drama. Against all my dire predictions, the Arkansas Razorback basketball team had, for only the second time in its history, achieved the number one ranking in the polls, so all us good Arkies were almost too preoccupied with tall boys in floppy shorts throwing big round balls through hoops. Brad and Diana did join us for Christmas Eve dinner at Emmy's German restaurant, but then there was no game scheduled for that night. On Christmas, the four of us had brunch at the Holiday Inn (the only brunch in town on Christmas), then Barbara headed for Heber to pick up Snow and Nicole so that they could spend the evening with Barbara's mom. Diana and Brad and I headed north to Fayetteville to forgather with the Duty clan for a Christmas exchange. Of necessity, it was short because we had to get back before dark. I could not but give thanks for having both my parents for yet another Christmas. Jeff was still grieving the loss of his dog and long-time best friend and Doberman Pinscher Penny and I who have shared several such losses could certainly empathize. Still it was a Christmas filled with the meaning of Christmas.

The year ended with Brad and Diana flying back to Washington. Inexplicably, they felt they needed to get back to work and school instead of spending weeks on end entertaining their elderly parents. Barbara and I were able to soften the blow by attending a New Year's Day reception to which we had been invited at the Hardscrabble Country Club. Thus did 1993 end and 1994 begin.

Each moment of one's life is a vantage point from which we view and interpret the world and our lives. Meanings and relative importance may wax and wane, but over the long-haul patterns and purposes become apparent. I sometimes wonder just how much control we have over this larger picture. In any event, I stand at this moment in my life at the end the year 1993 and at the beginning of my 59th year of life. There is no way that I can foretell what lies ahead, nor would I want to. Surprises, both pleasant and otherwise, provide much of life's leaven. Yet, in light of all that has gone before, I can only look ahead with great anticipation. I have a prospering law practice and social life in Fort Smith. I am blessed with numerous friends. My spiritual growth continues with influences from both Catholic and Methodist churches. I am blessed with two fabulous children who, despite everything, are well launched on exceptional marriages and promising careers. Closer to home, and most directly entwined with my personal happiness, I have Eddie the wonder dog and I have my beloved

Barbara. Without her, my joy would be so much less. With her at my side, I can stride forward to meet the future with eagerness, confidence, and enthusiasm. I am, indeed, most fortunate among men.

(To be continued...)

NOTE TO THE READER

The balance of this work, Chapters 25 through 34, will consist of my thoughts on a number of unrelated subjects. While it does contain some biographical material, its primary purpose is to make the reader not only acquainted with my views on various subjects (which in itself is of minimal consequence), but also to help the reader to become acquainted with me as a person. It is the real purpose of this book to introduce myself to my posterity and there is a lot more to knowing a person than the chronological facts of daily living. So, pick and choose as you will...

Chapter 25

The Pink Bunny Legend

When my sister and I were quite young, we occasionally found ourselves taking car rides with our parents. If the rides lasted for more than an hour or two, we, like any children, became restless. At some point whose origins are lost in the mists of time, our mother began telling us animal stories to stave off our boredom.

The protagonist of these stories was a pink rabbit named Pink Bunny. Later, when I was slightly older and my little brother John was of the proper age, I took over the bard's role and became the spinner of Pink Bunny tales. I don't remember how long this continued, although I do remember telling them to my brother and to my cousin Thomas Melton and his little sisters Sarah Jane and Mary Elizabeth. It was probably around the age of ten or eleven that we all grew out of such childish things. But, the seeds were planted.

Years later, while I was working for the Justice Department (about 1960, '61, or '62), I had a lot of time on my hands. They really couldn't find suitable work to keep me busy. I sat down at the typewriter and began to bang out Pink Bunny stories. Over the years I wrote about thirty. Mary and

I revised them, and her sister, Patricia Marti, illustrated four of them, *Pink Bunny's First Birthday Party*, *Pink Bunny in the Snow Storm*, *A Pink Bunny Christmas*, and *The Haunted Cave*. We submitted the manuscript for publication along with the sample illustrations, but there were not takers. Vanguard Press did agree to publish it at my expense, but I was looking for someone to publish it at *their* expense.

Eventually, the manuscript and pictures came to rest in the family archives. They gathered dust until about 1970 when I was the beneficiary of someone else's stroke of genius. The tiny village located at the crossing of the War Eagle River about twelve miles east of Rogers started holding an annual crafts fair. It caught on and soon was drawing huge crowds. Both locals and professionals rented space under huge tents to sell their primitive wares. It occurred to me that I could have the Pink Bunny stories privately published and sell them at the fair. I filled out the proper copyright forms and had *Pink Bunny in the Snow Storm* and *A Pink Bunny Christmas* printed in booklet form by the Shofner Printing Company in Rogers. Then we rented space at War Eagle and set up a bridge table to exhibit my books. We priced them at 50¢ a piece and waited. I had several thousand copies printed and ended up selling about a hundred.

To say the least, my dreams of authorship and fame were scotched. At least though, I

could say that I had two books published. Later, when FAB (Fine Arts Bunch) had one of its annual auctions, I donated copies of the two books, duly autographed and dated, and was surprised when they elicited some brisk bidding. Our friend, Bob Haynes, bought them and his pleasure made my day.

Not long after that, I had the bright idea of going international. Over the years I had kept up a desultory correspondence with my old flame Kate from my years in England. By the early '70s, she was married and living with her family in Greece. I sent her a copy of *A Pink Bunny Christmas*, and she liked it so well that she decided to translate it into Greek. The translation and printing went well enough, but she had same luck as me in finding a market. Eventually, while I was living in Phoenix, about 1985, she sent me the entire supply of her Greek edition. I kept them around the house for a while and then donated the bulk of them to the local Greek festival which had a crafts booths for raising money for their parochial school. I never heard whether they were able to sell any or not. I hope they had better luck than Kate and me. In the end, I still remain the proud possessor of far too many pristine copies of two English and one Greek Pink Bunny books. I also have a manuscript with twenty-eight other stories, but I think that in all probability they will remain unpublished.

The best way to introduce the reader to the spirit of Pink Bunny and to Pink Bunny himself is to provide one of the stories as a sample. Diana and I searched through the manuscript, reading one story after another (many of which I had almost forgotten). We finally settled upon the following stories about Pink Bunny and Rufus going boating and Horace and the haunted cave. Fortunately, *The Hooting Cave* was among those which Patricia Marti had partially illustrated and by a stroke of luck we still had the original illustrations which are included. May I wish you good reading and I hope you love Pink Bunny as much as my generation did.

Pink Bunny Goes Boating
by Davis Duty

Pink Bunny had always liked water. Sometimes he almost wished that he were a fish or a turtle so that he could go swimming. Rabbits do not swim and this made Pink Bunny quite mad. He had tried to swim once when he was a baby rabbit, but Father Rabbit had had to pull him out spluttering and coughing. He had sunk straight to the bottom.

Since then Pink Bunny had not tried to go swimming. Still, he liked water and often lay on the creek bank in the shade of a big tree and dreamed dreams about having a beautiful boat all his own in which he could sail up and down the creek just as he pleased.

One fine sunny day, Pink Bunny and his friend Rufus the Bear were lying thus beneath the tree on the creek bank. Pink Bunny was telling Rufus about the boat he dreamed of owning, and what he would do if he just had such a boat.

"Could I go for a ride in your boat, if you had one?" begged Rufus. Bears do not ordinarily swim either, and Rufus, too, had always wished that he could have a boat to paddle around in.

Pink Bunny thought this question over carefully.

"Well," he said, "I might let you ride in my boat if you would promise to sit very still. You are such a big bear, Rufus, that if you got excited and moved about in my boat it might turn over and then what would we do?"

Rufus promised that he would sit quite still.

The two friends were having a lot of fun dreaming about going boating. All of a sudden, Pink Bunny had a big idea. He jumped right up in the air and landed on his feet, and danced all around under the tree.

"Rufus!" shouted Pink Bunny. "Why don't we build a boat?"

"Pink Bunny, are you crazy?" Rufus looked very worried about his friend. How in the world could Pink Bunny think they could build a boat? After all, they were only animals.

"I mean it!" said Pink Bunny, looking very serious. "It would not be so hard, either. You see that big wooden box over yonder on the bank?"

He pointed to an old box on the creek bank which some picnickers had left a long time before. It was very old. The paint had all peeled off, and the bottom had caved in.

Rufus went over to the box and turned it over with his big paw.

"We could never make a boat out of this," he said. "It is big enough, all right, but there is a big hole in the bottom. It would sink the minute we put it in the water."

"We can patch the hole," answered Pink Bunny. "Then our boat would be as good as any boat. We could go anywhere we wanted to on the creek. Just think how all the other animals will wish they had a boat like ours!"

Pink Bunny then set to work to figure out a way to patch the hole. He searched through the forest for something to use. Finally, he settled on the bark of the birch tree. It peeled off in big sheets and water would not run through it.

Next, he had to find a way to fasten the birch bark to the bottom of the box so that it would cover the hole and keep the water out. He and Rufus sat beside their new boat and thought very hard about this problem. Rufus wrinkled up his nose. Pink Bunny wrinkled up his nose. Rufus scratched his ear. Pink Bunny scratched his ear.

"What we need," said Pink Bunny, "is some glue to stick the birch bark to the bottom of our boat. But where are we going to find anything sticky enough to do that?"

He was almost ready to give up, when Rufus let out a whoop.

"Pink Bunny, I know what we can use! It is the stickiest thing I know of!"

"What, what?" demanded Pink Bunny. Now he forgot all about giving up.

"I'll show you," said Rufus, feeling very smart and important. Off he lumbered into the forest to get whatever it was that he was talking about.

Pink Bunny waited impatiently for him to return. He was very restless and excited, and could barely wait for the boat to be finished and get out on the creek. It seemed to take hours for Rufus to get his secret sticky whatever-it-was, but actually, Rufus was gone only a few minutes. Finally, he came clumping back out of the forest carrying a big jar in one paw.

Pink Bunny dashed up to Rufus and peered over the rim of the big jar. "I know what that is," he said, clapping his paws together. "It's honey!"

"That's right," Rufus grumbled. "It is a shame to use it to glue birch bark over a hole in the bottom of a boat. I guess I can always find more honey, though, but I won't always have a chance to take a boat ride."

Rufus loved honey. All bears like it, but Rufus liked it even better than most bears do. He just loved it! Every chance he got, he would sneak up to a bee tree and reach his big paw right inside and grab all the honey he could before the bees stung him so much that he had to run away. He had just found a new bee tree the day before, and the honey he had found there was the sweetest and stickiest he had ever eaten. He certainly did not like to waste it, but maybe using it to build a boat was not wasting it after all.

Rufus stuck his paw into the jar and pulled it out covered with honey. Licking his paw as though it were a big popsicle, he said, "Alright, Pink Bunny, let's get started fixing our boat."

They turned the old wooden box upside down. There in the bottom of the box was the hole which they planned to patch. It was at least six inches across. Pink Bunny stood on one side of the big box, and Rufus stood on the other.

"You hold up the sheets of birch bark," said Rufus, "and I will smear honey all over them." (He wanted to put the honey on so that none of it would be wasted.)

Pink Bunny picked up a big sheet of birch bark and held it high over his head. Rufus stuck his paw into the jar of honey and then rubbed it round and round on the bark until the sheet was completely covered with sticky honey.

When the birch bark was ready, Pink Bunny slapped it over the hole in the bottom of the box. It stuck tight. Pink Bunny and Rufus were very pleased with themselves.

Two more sheets of birch bark were smeared with honey and stuck on top of the first one. Pink Bunny decided that that should be enough to keep the water out. Rufus was glad he did not have to use any more of his precious honey to fix boats. He pushed his big black nose into the jar and ate the rest of the honey with one great gulp.

"Ummmmmm, that was good!" He licked his lips. "Let's try out our boat, Pink Bunny."

Together they carried and pushed the box to the edge of the creek. When it was in the water, Rufus very carefully climbed into it and sat in the middle so that he would not turn it over. Then Pink Bunny hopped aboard and, with a big push, sent the boat gliding out into the very middle of the stream.

"Whoopee, we're sailing!" cried Pink Bunny with glee.

His dream had come true. He was actually out on the creek in his own boat. Pink Bunny and Rufus each took one of the big leaves which they had brought along to use as paddles and began rowing.

Swish, swish, swish, they went. The boat rocked along just like a boat ought to do. They were having more fun than they ever had had before in their lives.

"I'm a pirate!" roared Rufus, waving his leaf in the air.

"I'm the captain!" shouted Pink Bunny. "Look out for Captain Bunny and Pirate Bear!"

"What is that thing that just floated past?" asked Rufus, looking at something in the water beside the boat. Pink Bunny looked closer.

"It looks like a sheet of birch bark," he said. "My feet feel wet," announced Rufus.

"Uh, oh!" groaned Pink Bunny, "Our birch bark patch is washing off. The boat is sinking!"

Sure enough, one at a time, the three sheets of birch bark came loose and floated away. You see, honey is very sticky, but it does not fasten things tightly together like glue. In fact, when water touches honey, it dissolves and washes away just like jelly washes off your face when you rub a wet wash rag over it.

All at once, there was no patch on the bottom of the box-boat at all. The water rushed in with a great whoosh.

"What are we going to do?" moaned Rufus.

"Abandon ship!" cried Pink Bunny. He was still playing that he was the captain of a pirate ship. But he was a very wet captain now.

The two friends jumped overboard just in time. Glug-glug went their box-boat, and it sank out of sight.

Pink Bunny spluttered and floundered in the deep water. Rufus could not swim much better. He, too, was coughing and shouting for help. They were way out in the middle of the creek and there was nothing that they could do.

"Help, help, help!" yelled Pink Bunny and Rufus.

No one answered. Things looked very bad indeed, when suddenly a voice right behind them asked, "What is going on here?"

It was Thomas the Turtle. He was a good friend of Pink Bunny's with whom Pink Bunny had had many long talks while he lay beneath his tree on the creek bank dreaming of boats.

"Help us!" begged the two bedraggled friends. "We can't swim and our boat has sunk."

Thomas thought he had never seen such a funny sight in his whole life, but he also knew that Pink Bunny and Rufus were in bad trouble and needed help.

"Climb on my back," he told Pink Bunny. "Rufus, you grab hold of my tail."

When they had done as he instructed, he paddled slowly toward the bank. Rufus was very heavy and so soaked with water that he was like a big rock, and Thomas had to pull with all his might to drag him along. He huffed and puffed, but at last he reached the bank.

Pink Bunny hopped onto dry land and reached down to help Rufus crawl out of the water. With Pink Bunny pulling and Thomas pushing, they got the big bear onto the bank where he and Pink Bunny flopped down on the grass and panted for air.

When his friends were safe, Thomas could not hold back the laughter any longer.

"'Ha, ha, ha, ha!" he chuckled. "You two sure make a funny looking sight. Next time you decide to go boating, you had better use a proper boat and not an old box full of holes. Ha, ha, ha!"

"You know," said Pink Bunny, when he was at last able to get his breath, "I don't think I will go boating any more. It is silly to take such chances. From now on, I am going to stay on dry land where I belong and leave the water to those who belong in it."

Rufus thought that his friend had a very good idea.

The Haunted Cave
By Davis Duty

Pink Bunny caught sight of Rufus ambling down the forest trail ahead of him.

"Wait for me!" he called, and hopped faster to catch up with his friend.

Rufus began slowing down a little bit at a time and finally came to a complete stop in the middle of the trail. He stood there a minute waiting for Pink Bunny, but his memory was not very good and suddenly he forgot why he had stopped in the first place. He decided that he would not have stopped unless he was tired. If he was tired, he probably had stopped to take a nap.

"I am glad I remember why I stopped," he yawned to himself and plunked down on the green grass.

Pink Bunny was only a short distance behind the bear when he called him, but before he could catch him, Rufus was already asleep and snoring loudly.

It was a warm summer afternoon. Pink Bunny felt a bit sleepy himself. When he first saw Rufus lying there sound asleep, he thought of tickling his nose to wake him. But the more he thought about how sleepy he felt and what a nice afternoon it was for a nap, the more he realized that Rufus had a good idea after all.

Pink Bunny looked up at the sun to see how high it was in the sky. This is the way animals tell time. It was not quite straight above as it would be at noon, but still it was not very far down in the west.

Next, Pink Bunny looked at the shadows cast by the

trees. This is another way of telling time. As it grew later in the day, the sun would go down in the west. And the farther down in the west that the sun went, the longer the shadows grew. Pink Bunny did not know why this happened, but he did know that it happened every day and that it was a very good way to tell time. He saw that the shadows were not too long, probably not more than five times the length of one of his ears. That meant that it was still early in the afternoon, so he stretched out beside Rufus in the middle of the trail and fell into a deep sleep.

The two friends slept and slept and slept. The afternoon followed the sun away into the west. Dusk settled over the forest. Heavy black clouds appeared. Night was coming, and if Rufus had been awake, he would have felt an aching in his bones and would have announced that a rain storm was on its way. But Rufus was not awake and Pink Bunny was not awake. They slept straight through the afternoon and into the night.

All the other animals had gone to bed long before. The forest grew still. Not a sound could be heard anywhere. Occasionally, a bright flash of lightening streaked across the sky, lighting up the forest as bright as day.

Pink Bunny and Rufus did not see the lightening, though. They were very fast asleep. Then suddenly a patter of rain drops began sprinkling down. With a splat, one of them landed right on Pink Bunny's nose. He woke with a start. He tried to snuggle back down into the warm grass, but it was no longer warm. Something cold and wet was running down his face, too. Finally, he opened his eyes and looked about.

"My goodness!" cried Pink Bunny. "We have slept the whole afternoon away. Rufus, wake up!" He yanked on his friend's ear until the bear opened one eye and peered up at him.

"Rufus, get up!" insisted Pink Bunny. "It is night and it's beginning to rain. We are a long way from home. Wake up, we must find shelter before we get soaking wet."

Rufus scrambled to his feet and began shaking water off of his shaggy fur.

"Stop that!" sputtered Pink Bunny, who had been practically swamped by the shower from the bear's coat.

Rufus quit shaking and looked at Pink Bunny mournfully. Water was streaming down his face and into his eyes.

"It's raining harder," he grumbled. "Where can we go to keep dry?"

"Follow me!" he cried over a loud clap of thunder, dashing off through the rain with Rufus puffing along behind. Pink Bunny kept looking over his shoulder to see if his friend was still there, and it was a good thing he did, too, because twice Pink Bunny ran faster than Rufus and twice he lost the bear and had to go back to find him.

Pink Bunny was heading for the big hill in the center of the forest. It was not too far away and he thought that he remembered Franklin the fox having once told him about a little cave somewhere in the hill. Suddenly a dark shape loomed up before the two animals as they hurried through the rain.

"Here is Bath Rock Hill," shouted Rufus.

"There is supposed to be a cave in the hillside," called Pink Bunny. "Rufus, you go to the right and look and I will hunt for it on the left."

Off went the friends in different directions to search for the cave. Pink Bunny had gone only a few steps when he spied a round dark hole in the rocks.

"Here it is!" he shouted, as he raced for the cave entrance and hopped inside.

It did not take Rufus long to follow, because if there is

one thing which bears do not like, it is getting wet.

The two friends were so happy to be out of the rain that for a few minutes they just sat there and enjoyed the dryness. At last, however, their eyes grew accustomed to the dark and they could look about. They were seated on a deep bed of dry leaves which covered the floor of a tiny room. The walls and ceiling were made of stone. It was indeed a cave. At that moment, it looked almost as good to Pink Bunny as his own burrow.

Behind them was the mouth of the cave, which was closed now by a curtain of swishing rain. Before them, the animals saw another opening which seemed to lead into a tunnel.

"Where do you think that goes to?" asked Rufus.

"I guess I don't know," answered Pink Bunny, peering

into the tunnel.

"Almost anything could be in there," said Rufus.   He edged a bit closer to the mouth of the cave.

"Aw, Rufus!" scolded Pink Bunny.   "You are supposed to be the biggest and bravest animal in the forest."

But Rufus was not at all sure that he really was the bravest animal in the forest, at least not at that very moment.

"I think we should go exploring," announced Pink Bunny. "Come on! We can't go back out into the rain, and we don't want to just sit here. It might not stop raining until morning. Let's see what we can find down this tunnel."

He inched his way down the narrow passage, with his paw stretched out in front of him to feel the way.   Rufus followed his friend, but he did not move quite as fast as did the rabbit.

"See! There is nothing at all to be afraid of," whispered Pink Bunny over his shoulder.

"Why are you whispering, then?" Rufus whispered back.

"I am not whispering," said Pink Bunny, aloud this time. "What's that?"

They both stopped in their tracks and strained their ears to listen. From far back in the cave had come a weird sound.

""Whooo, whoooo, whooooo," it came again.

"Let me out of here!" cried Rufus. "This cave is haunted." He turned around and began running back down the tunnel.

"Where are you going?" called Pink Bunny. "Rufus, come back here. This cave can't be haunted. There are no such things as ghosts."

"Maybe not," answered the bear from the entrance of the cave, "but I would rather get wet outside than stay in here to find out!"

"Well, wait for me, then!" Pink Bunny shouted and

scampered after his friend. Once again, they heard the strange sound floating after them as they dashed out of the cave.

"Whooo, whooo, whooooo."

With a great bound, they were through the cave mouth and outside once more. They both knew better than to be afraid of something just because they did not know what it was, and they both certainly did not believe in ghosts. Still, it was much easier to say this once they were out of that dark spooky cave!

When they got outside again, Pink Bunny and Rufus were surprised to find that the rain had stopped, the dark clouds were gone, and the heavens were filled with twinkling stars. They ran a short distance and then began slowing down until they stopped altogether. The two friends looked at one another and suddenly began to laugh.

"What were we so afraid of?" giggled the rabbit.

""I'm sure I don't know," rumbled Rufus. "I was not scared, anyway," he added. "It was just dark in the cave, and I couldn't see, and, well, it is getting late and all."

"Where is the forest trail?" asked Pink Bunny, looking about. "I have lost my way with all this running and rain and everything."

Rufus scratched his ear thoughtfully and then got to his feet and began lumbering off into the night.

"Come on, Pink Bunny," he called. "I think we have somehow gotten way on the other side of Bath Rock Hill. We must walk around it to find the trail."

Pink Bunny jumped to his feet and hurried after the bear. He was not afraid any more, but he did not want Rufus to get out of sight.

They walked around the base of the hill, and finally came to the old split pine tree which marked the trail. At the same time, both of them heaved a big sigh of relief. They knew they had not been scared, but it was nice to be back in familiar surroundings.

Just at that moment, when Rufus and Pink Bunny were about to forget how frightened they had been in the cave, they heard that same sound again.

"Whooo, whoooo, whooooo."

It was much nearer, but it was outside and not in a hollow cave, so it did not sound so strange. They did almost jump out of their skins when they heard it, but then all at once, Pink Bunny and Rufus burst out laughing.

"That sounded like our ghost, but it's only Horace the owl!" sputtered Pink Bunny.

"Whooo, whoooo, whooooo?" came the voice again. It was right above them in the pine tree.

"It is Pink Bunny and Rufus," they answered together. "We thought you were the ghost."

"Oooh, hellooo," called down Horace. "I am glad it is you, Pink Bunny and Rufus. I was a bit scared when I heard strange voices down there at this time of night. But where are you? It is so dark beneath the tree that I can't see."

Pink Bunny hopped around the big tree trunk and up the hillside so that he could be higher. He knew that Horace could not see very well. Most owls cannot see well in the daytime, but can see much better at night. But this was not true of Horace. He could not see very well at any time. Pink Bunny thought that if he could climb up the hillside and get on the same level with Horace's tree limb, the owl might be able to see him more clearly.

All at once, Pink Bunny stopped in surprise.

"What is this?" he asked. Right before him there

appeared to be the entrance to another cave. It looked just like the one out of which he and Rufus had scampered only a few minutes ago.

"What is what?" inquired Horace. He could see Pink Bunny now and stared down at him with big round eyes from his perch in the tree.

"What is this hole in the hillside?" Pink Bunny said.

"Oh, that is my hooting cave," replied Horace. "It has a very nice echo, and I go in there sometimes to hoot and listen to the beautiful sound it makes."

"Oh,!" cried Pink Bunny. "Rufus, we have found our ghost! Horace, tell me something. Does this cave have two entrances?"

"Indeed it does," answered the owl. "The cave runs all the way through the hill and comes out on the other side. But Pink Bunny, what does all this have to do with my hooting cave? I don't understand." Horace, who usually looked so wise, was looking very puzzled and bewildered just now.

Suddenly, Rufus understood what Pink Bunny meant and had to cover his face with his huge paws to hide the red which was creeping up his neck and over his face. It was so bright that it showed right through all that heavy fur.

"Well, Horace, some day I will explain it to you," said Pink Bunny, as he climbed back down the hillside and slipped into the shadows beneath the tree so the owl could not see that his pink face was a shade pinker, too.

"I will tell you this much, though," added Pink Bunny when he was out of sight. "Horace, your hooting cave sent Rufus and me scooting tonight. But I think we have learned one thing which is very important: it is much better to try and find out about things which are frightening than to get scared and run away!"

Chapter 26

You Gotta Start Someplace

The entire exercise of writing this autobiography is a testament to my conviction that communication skills are humankind's ultimate talent. It is what distinguishes them from the lower animals. I would not want it thought, however, that I entered upon this project without preparation or experience. As shown in the previous chapter, I had already tried my hand at children's stories, which brought me no literary recognition whatsoever. Even before that, though, I had attempted to fictionalize my first trip to the Seeing Eye. This, too, I was unable to sell. Perhaps even then I should have assessed my literary talent more realistically, for I had put my hand to the pen at an even earlier age. Two examples follow, and I will let you judge their merit.

The Seashore

by Davis Duty (Age 7)

Dictated in 1941
(Transcribed verbatim, without correction)

Once upon a time there was along the seashore. That was where the jay birds lived in America. There was one little jay bird that always said things wrong. His mother named him Witty.

One day Witty was out flying around when he met Jay Bird. They were talking about how they liked to live there and Jay Bird said, "I want to be a hippomatous.

So Witty said, "How can you be a hippomatous when "there

is nobody around to turn you to a hippomatous?"

Jay Bird replied, "Yes, there is somebody to turn me to a hippo. The lady that lives on down the seashore. She can turn anybody to what they want to be," said Jay Bird.

Witty said, "Let's go on down and see her now. Maybe then I will decide I want to be something."

"Let's go now." said Jay Bird.

So they started out. It took them all day to get there, but get tired or not they were determined to go. Witty decided he wanted to be an elephant, so they tapped on the door of the lady's cave and they heard some jolly music that was played on a shell piano that came out of the sea.

The lady came to the door and said, "What would you two like to be?"

They said, first Jay Bird said, "I would like to be a hippo."

And then Witty said, "I would like to be an elephant."

She said, "Alright." So she got her shell and tapped on it and said, "Grumpy. Grumpy, come to the top. See what I wish to say."

So Grumpy came up scolding her, "I've been up to the top three times today. I'm getting tired coming to the top."

"Grumpy, Grumpy, bring me an elephant pillett and when you bring that one up bring another one with it, and this other kind, let it be a hippo pillett."

So down went Grumpy and brought up a hippo pillett and an elephant pillett. So they started out they wondered if their throats would be too big to take the pilletts. They carried them under their wings for awhile.

They stopped under a nice shady tree when they said, "I think it's about time to take out pills now," said Jay Bird.

They both said, "Here goes," and they took their pilletts

but they caught in their throats. Their voices weren't alike because their throats were stopped up.

They said, "Let's go take a drink of water at this spring nearby and maybe they will go down."

So they went and took a nice cold drink of water and they both went down. Their feet turned in no longer the Jay Bird's feet and he turned to a ropy tail and so he turned to a hippo all over.

Witty began to take a drink of cool water and his feet were no longer a jay bird's feet. They were elephant's feet. He had a flat tail that looked like rope and his ears turned to great big flat ears and he had a long trunk and he turned to an elephant all over.

About this time two people came along and saw a hippo and an elephant. They wanted to be a Jay Bird again — they thought they were foolish turning themselves into an elephant and a hippo.

So they said, "Let's go back to the lady along the seashore and have her turn us back into jaybirds again."

So back they started and when they got there she said, "Grumpy is too tired. I can't ask him to come up any more. I fixed a stick and this string here, two of them, for Witty and Jay Bird. You can turn back to a Jay Bird now. I have put them on your tail. Now swing them three times."

And soon they had their wings and feathers. They flew back to that shady tree. Witty said he would talk right from now on and have a new name and Jay Bird said he would not be foolish. Both said they would not be foolish and turn themselves into anything again. So they flew home and lived happily ever after.

Davis Duty's Experiences at the Circus
by Davis Duty (Age 7)
Dictated in 1941
(Transcribed verbatim, without correction)

First I came in and you know you can sit down free after you've already given them a ticket the day before, then you can sit down free. I went in behind the stage first. They showed me how to turn on the lights and then they had the seals and I saw a horn that the seals blew. They blew music too. I saw a ball that they put up on their nose and made it go around. Then I saw a steel ball that the men stand on and roll. I stood on one. Then I saw an elephant. After I saw an elephant I saw a pony. I rode the pony and then I saw the tables that you jump on. The clown was going to give me a picture — I have it at Little Rock. The clown was wearing a big piece of material with a lot of stuff stuffed and that was his billy club. Then he had .a hat, a policeman's hat, and it had a badge on it. He had a thing with buttons all down the front of it and then he had a fox's tail on. I bought a fox's tail just like he had on. They sold them and I have it at Little Rock.

After a while I went downstairs. First I went into a little room. I saw a lion — it was a tame lion they just petted it and do it like they do a dog. A little lion about three months old and it would play with you and it had harness on like a dog and dogs take care of it. The thing tried to play with me. Then they had a real lion upstairs and this was one of the mother lion's babies. They took it way from the mother so it wouldn't know it had a mother and wouldn't get growly. It had a father and a mother and another mother upstairs. When I was upstairs, I couldn't see a lion because they were too wild but one of them was asleep and a man went up to it and reached over and caught a hold of the lion's tail. The lion was asleep and I got a hold of the lion's tail. The thing woke up and I was just there when it woke up holding its tail. I let go.

When I was downstairs I saw seals and they weren't seals they were sea lions. Then I saw their dogs too. In the circus, they bought some wings. And they had a little sausage grinder and a stove. So they took this box with the dog in it and put it down in the sausage grinder and played like they grinded the dog into sausage and then some wieners would fall. And it had a little ribbon on it like the dog did so people would think they cut the dog up. I was worried too because I was afraid they had cut the dog in half. Then they had gloves on that had something in them and they would hit each other and it sounded like they hit hard it popped so.

Chapter 27

Less than an Athlete,
but More than a Wimp

Only in my wildest dreams could I have ever been called an athlete. Yet, since my earliest childhood, athletics and physical exercise have been very important to me. As a small child, I especially enjoyed roller skating and tree climbing. I have already described the time when, soon after my illness from which I lost my sight, my mother looked out the kitchen window to see me perched high in a Chinese elm in the back yard.

When I was about twelve, I became enamoured of horses. I will never know what it was that convinced my parents to let me have a horse, but one day we saw an ad in the paper for a mare and colt, and that led to our paying $125 for Star and her six-month-old filly colt Comet. The next three years of my life were, for all intents and purposes, totally oriented toward horses. We eventually even moved to a place in the country so that could care for my horses directly. Previously, they had been boarded at the edge of town, which meant a tedious trip out and back at least once a day. Now I had them right at my elbow, just across the fence in the pasture. They also bought my brother John a horse, but he never took to it with any great enthusiasm. He preferred playing soldier.

For my part, though, I loved horses. I was a charter member of the Rogers Riding Club and rode in many a homecoming parade. On weekends, we would take part in the local pick-up rodeo, where I was too young to compete but was old enough to ride in the opening parade. I even had a girlfriend, Helen Cochran, who shared my love of horses. We covered every square inch of every country road within five miles of Rogers. On one weekend, the riding club rode all the way to War Eagle to spend the night. I didn't enjoy sleeping on a hard wooden cabin floor in a sleeping bag, but I dearly loved the ride.

Of course, there was a downside. I had to shovel manure. I had to groom. I had to clean and treat the tack. And the best character builder of all, I had to go out at 6:00 o'clock on frigid winter mornings to feed. I don't think I ever really resented or shirked these tasks. Whether or not they strengthened my character, I never questioned that my horses were worth it.

Eventually, Comet grew up and I broke and trained her myself. This was a source of real satisfaction. Later, when we moved to Little Rock, the horses moved with us. We even bought a house out of town with an attached stable and rough paddock to accommodate them. But I was moving into my teenage years and eventually my horses had to compete, less and less favorably, with outside activities. The time finally came when it became apparent that my equine phase was over. The horses were sold, but I still remember them fondly and even dream about them on occasion.

I think it fair to say that horseback riding was a form of athletics, but I suspect that the better part of the associated exercise came from cleaning the barn and toting 100 pound sacks of grain. I also had some chickens to feed which added to the chores. I think I was in good shape, though, for a youngster.

Later, when I went to high school, I must concede that I evaded Physical Education (PE). They simply couldn't think of much I could do to participate in the organized sports. In the seventh grade, I did take PE, though, and made a B. The climaxing activity was tumbling and I managed to do that well enough to get a passing grade. From that point on, though, I felt little interest in athletics until college.

As related earlier in these pages, during my first year of law school at the University, my fraternity insisted that I make a contribution in the area of intermural sports. I couldn't think of anything I could do, but they signed me up for wrestling. I had never wrestled in my life and was not particularly keen to do it now. Luckily for me, though, my friend Henry Moore, a member of the football team whom I had known in Little Rock High School, took me under his wing and taught me the rudiments of wrestling, but I only lasted one match. To my credit, I wasn't pinned. To my discredit, I flopped down on my stomach and stayed there until the match was over. The preparation, though, started a whole new chapter in my life. I got interested in exercise and began a regimen of morning calisthenics that I have continued to the present.

Of course, there is also the exercise that I get working with my dog. Walking, particularly at the pace at which dogs like to walk, is not only good exercise for me but also for the dog. In fact, it is essential for the dog's health and training that we work regularly and as much as possible. I have tried to keep this in mind throughout the forty-some years that I have had guide dogs, and I believe that my daily regimen of calisthenics and my almost daily jaunts with my dog have served me well. Many of my contemporaries are heart patients or couch potatoes, while I am still able to walk for miles on end. Of course the back problem which I developed in later years limited me for a while, but even while it lasted I forced myself to exercise as much as possible in spite of the pain. As a result, I was able to continue walking for much longer that I could have expected. In fact, my ability to continue functioning actually worked against me to some extent. I used it as an excuse to put off surgery as long as possible. After surgery, however, my overall good conditioning made it possible for me to get back on my feet sooner than expected. Then, my resumed program of calisthenics and walking had their intended effect. Within a year, I was not only back to normal, I was actually more fit and functional than I had been in years.

I recognize that exercise is not precisely the same as athletics. I am not an athlete. This is not to say, though, that I do not have an interest or even a passion for athletics. I have been a lifelong fan of the Arkansas Razorbacks, both football and basketball, and St. Louis Cardinal baseball. I began listening to the Cardinals about 1946 and remember the names of George Redmunger, Stan Musial, Marty Marion, Enos Slaughter, Murry Dickson, Max Lanier, Walter Cooper, Willie Mays, Joe Garagiola, Jackie Robinson, Yogi Berra, Mickey Mantle, Bob Gibson, Lou Brock, Hank Aaron, etc., etc., and etc.

My brother and I devised countless variations of baseball related games and played whole league series. One of my favorites was to use dominoes as players and then using a pencil as a bat, hit a marble. If a domino was knocked over, it was an out. If it got through, it was a hit. Of course, we had to chase a lot of marbles under the bed, but it passed the time. Later, in our teens, we devised more exciting versions. I could not hit, but I could pitch. I spent countless hours pitching batting practice for my brother. We couldn't always afford a baseball, though, so we used our native ingenuity to provide alternatives. One of these was a cork wrapped with many layers of adhesive tape. It served well enough as a ball, but talk about a rabbit! A solid hit could travel for two blocks. This made ball retrieval sort of tedious.

Another ball substitute was a tin can. After repeated smashings with a bat, it became a solid chunk of ragged metal. It was great for throwing curve balls, but it tore up bats something fierce and occasionally tore up the pitcher even worse. It is a minor miracle that I didn't get tetanus.

I also began listening to Razorback football about 1946. I remember hearing the first radio broadcast while I was visiting the Mortons who boarded my horses. It was the team with Clyde Scott, Muscles Campbell, Ross Prichard, Aubrey Fowler, et al. Later, in college, I had many friends on the football team and attended games regularly. I loved Saturday afternoons, picking up my date, buying her a mum to wear and sitting in the sunshine on the east side Razorback Stadium cheering the Hogs. Our teams during the '50s were only 1954, but greatness was just around the corner. In the '60s, I was in the stands when Arkansas played for two national championships and in 1969 President Nixon attended the game, arriving dramatically in his helicopter.

I was also slightly interested in basketball, having some fraternity brothers who were on the Razorback team. However, it was not until the late '60s when I was back in Rogers practicing law that I began regularly listening to the basketball broadcasts. This interest had actually been born originally in high school when I became an avid fan of the Fayetteville

Bulldogs basketball team. They played for a state championship in1952, and I was elected by the pep squad as an honorary color guard. It was their annual award for the person who contributed the most spirit at games. By the time I moved to Phoenix in 1975, Arkansas basketball was on the upswing with the Eddie Sutton years. By the time I returned to Fort Smith, in 1986, the Nolan Richardson era had begun. Even then, there were clandestine whispers and secret dreams of national prominence. With the beginning of the 1993-94 season, it appears that these dreams may one day come true, perhaps even this year. By the close of the regular season, the Razorbacks had 25 wins and only two losses. They had won the Southeast Championship outright and the whole state was looking forward to the NCAA tournament with unconcealed excitement.

At long last, after years of poverty and procrastination, I have splurged and jointly with my brother purchased season tickets for both football and basketball games. The games that I can't attend I listen to on the radio. I also continue to follow the Cardinals with avidity. An average evening consists of me sitting in my recliner, smoking my pipe, and reading a book accompanied by the broadcast of a ball game on the radio at my elbow. This is my idea of rest and relaxation.

In this brief recital of my interest in athletics, I should also have noted the years I spent working in Little League Baseball, not to mention the multitude of games that Liz and I attended. Then there were the Major League spring training games which we tried to attend each year while living in Phoenix. The highlight of these was the year that John obtained for me an autograph from the notorious St. Louis Cardinals and Chicago Cubs broadcaster Harry Carey. I had become a fan of his when he was a Cardinal broadcaster. By the time I obtained the autograph, he was broadcasting for the Cubs, but it was still a thrill.

Also during the Phoenix years, I became a fan of the Phoenix Suns NBA team. I regularly listened to their broadcasts. I attended as many games as I could, even though they were only mediocre at that time. Now, eight years after I left Phoenix, they have become contenders for the championship. I am now their most avid Arkansas booster, especially since a number of ex-Razorbacks have helped them reach their new eminence, especially "The Big 0," Oliver Miller.

No description of my athletic achievements would be complete, though, without relating my one claim to fame. About the time I was a senior in high school, I decided to take up golf. My mother's cousin, Martha Wetzel, happened to be visiting at the time and was an avid golfer. When I expressed my interest, she undertook to coach me. I showed little promise, and I found that I could not withstand the relentless sun. To accommodate it, I was forced to wear a floppy straw hat which interfered considerably with my concentration and swing. Still in all, I made a few attempts at the game. It wasn't until about 1954, though, that I hit my peak. One summer afternoon, while playing a round with my brother at the old Twin City Golf Club north of Rogers, I got a hole-in-one. Granted, it was on the par three third hole and I bounced the ball off both bunkers before it ricocheted high into the air and came straight down into the cup. Still, I will never forget the deadly silence from my brother who was rattling the pin to give me direction. For a full ten seconds nothing happened. Then, in utter awe, he said, "Son of a bitch...it's in the cup!" That was both my best and last golf stroke. Having reached the pinnacle of the game, I decided to hang up my clubs and go into retirement. With the potential of playing a nine-hole round of golf in nine strokes, there really wasn't any challenge left.

The foregoing just about covers my sporting interests. Oh, I tried fishing, but I didn't like messing with bait and fish. I tried bowling, but after getting my first strike, I decided that I had mastered that game as well. I also went up in a glider once (Liz gave me a ride as an anniversary present) and that was an experience that I will never forget. Having done it once, though, I can't really see any incentive for doing it again. I have always wanted to skydive, but being status post-back surgery, it occurs to me that a hard landing even on my feet wouldn't do me much good. I did try water skiing once, which I described earlier in these pages, and that event is somewhere recorded on film for posterity. I like to swim, but chlorine sets my sinuses off on a binge which isn't worth the price. Finally, I have already described the bicycling which Liz and I did for the last few years we lived in Phoenix. I still have the double bike, but since her death there is little likelihood that I will resume that activity. So it seems that I now limit myself to walking, daily calisthenics, and listening to the Cardinals and the Razorbacks on radio. After all, though, that's about all the excitement that a man of my age can take anyway.

Chapter 28

My Many Lives and My Many Wives

My first step upon the path of matrimony came in 1959. After a courtship, carried out primarily by correspondence, I married Mary Lynn Ellis of Chevy Chase, Maryland. Her father, Clyde Ellis, had been a congressman from Arkansas in the 1940s. I had known him since that time. Indeed, he took a very active interest in my early progress. Although he had left Congress and taken up a job as director of the National Rural Electric Cooperatives Association in Washington, DC, he still considered himself an Arkansasan. I met his daughter at a picnic for the Washington, DC, Arkansas Society in the summer of 1957. I was in Washington with my parents, visiting my sister Carolyn. She and her husband Gene Banks and their daughter Karen were then living in Washington where Gene was employed by the Federal General Accounting Office. I attended the Arkansas picnic and met Clyde's two daughters, Patricia and Mary.

For the next two years, I maintained a desultory correspondence with Mary. It began to pick up in intensity and volume after I returned from England in 1958. By the time I finished law school and moved to Washington at the end of August 1959, we had reached the point where neither of us doubted that we would eventually get married. It didn't take long, either. We were married on Halloween day, October 31st. Our nuptials were conducted in the Chevy Chase Presbyterian Church. I was a Methodist and Mary was a member of no church, but the Presbyterian Church was convenient to her home. It was a very small wedding. My parents and my brother John and his wife Susan flew in from Arkansas, and of course Mary's parents and her sister Pat and her husband Bruce Marti were there. Also present was Ollie Collins, as well as Clyde's sister Jane and her husband Buddy Ransom. I do recall that I was late for the wedding. Clyde had just returned from a fact-finding trip to Russia to look over their efforts in the field of rural electrification. He had some fascinating slides and memorabilia. The men of the wedding party went to Clyde's office to view these and to sample some of the real Russian vodka that he had also brought back. We lost track of time and were almost an hour late getting to the wedding. Mary was not amused.

Mary graduated Summa Cum Laude from the University of Maryland with a degree in English. When I met her, she was working as a librarian with the Bureau of Medicine of the US Food and Drug and Administration in Washington. She continued to work there until we moved to Rogers in 1962. After taking a break to have our children and get them well launched, she returned to work part time at the Hough Memorial Library in Rogers. It did not take long for her talents and abilities to be recognized, and soon she was involved in a wide range of activities.

Over the years she not only participated with me in such activities as sponsoring a senior girl scout troop and membership in a play readers club and a fine arts club, but she also expanded her interests far beyond my orbit. She helped establish the Benton County League of Women Voters. She was a member of the local Girl Scout Council. She was a member and officer of the State Art Association. She was president of the State Mental Health Association. One of her finest hours was when she elected to the Rogers City Council, the first woman to have been so honored. After our divorce in 1975, she first worked as a lay counselor with the Ozark Guidance Center, later returning to obtain her Master's Degree in social work. After receiving her degree, she returned to the Ozark Guidance Center, where she served as a member of the professional staff until she moved to Columbia, Maryland, in 1986. Since that time, she has worked as a clinical social worker for a health maintenance organization and more recently as a social worker for the US Soldiers' and Airmen's Home in Washington, DC

In February, 1975, several months after Mary and I had permanently separated, I met and became interested in a young lady who was working as an office assistant for a dentist friend of mine. Her name was Gail Smith. She had a six-year-old daughter named Delane and I had visions of acquiring a new, instant family. Things progressed rapidly. On April 14, 1975, the same day as Mary's and my divorce became final, Gail and I were married in a small Methodist Church in Florence.

From the very beginning, our marriage was doomed. After a single, rocky year of long separations and brief reunions, we finally went our separate ways in March, 1976. Our divorce became final on the following July 20.

At that time I was living in Phoenix, Arizona, where I was serving as an Administrative Law Judge with the Office of Hearing and Appeals of the Social Security Administration. On March 9th, 1976, I was introduced by a friend to a young lady acquaintance. Her name was Joan Peachy. She had recently gone through a divorce herself and was still trying to sort her life out. For our first date, I took Joan (later to become Liz) to the Playboy Club, which was located two floors above my office.

Liz and I began to see each other regularly and were becoming rather serious by the summer of 1976 when my children came out to visit. That rather put Liz off because at age thirty-two she was not sure that she was ready to become the stepmother of two children approaching their teens. Actually, Diana was eleven and John was almost nine. Still, even after they came to live with me permanently in September of 1976, Liz and I continued to see each other and to grow closer every day. Finally (although I don't remember it) Liz liked to tell the story of how one night I told her that "Babe, we have got to either fish or cut bait." We decided to fish and did so on the following December 29.

Liz was from New York City, having actually been born in Brooklyn, of an Italian father (Tony Alba) and a polish mother (Helen). In her teens, the family moved to Deer Park, Long Island. Liz graduated from John Adams High School in 1962 and went on to earn a degree in History from Hofstra University in 1966. She tried her hand at teaching for a year, but became disenchanted by the New York City school jungle. Whereupon, she applied and was accepted for officer candidate school in the United States Air Force. After commission as a Second Lieutenant, she served in various capacities and at various stations. She completed tours in Okinawa, Thailand, and finally San Bernadino, California. Her most rewarding work in the Air Force was as a Race Relations Officer. When her service ended, she had achieved the rank of Captain. Falling victim to the RIF resulting from the wind down from the Vietnam War, she returned to civilian life about 1974.

Following separation from the Air Force, Liz and her first husband Harold Peachy, who had been a Sergeant in the Air Force and who had also been RIFed, moved to Phoenix, Arizona, where both of them returned to school. Liz enrolled in Grand Canyon College, where she obtained a degree in Personnel Training and Development in May, 1976. She and Harold were divorced in January, 1976. Thus, Liz and I were both fresh from failed marriages when we met in March, 1976.

After graduation from college, Liz went to work for the State of Arizona in its personnel department. Following our marriage on December 29, 1976, Liz continued to work for the state until 1979. In dissatisfaction with her rate of advancement, she resigned from the State to look for more employment more commiserate with her training and experience. Circumstances, however, mitigated against her and she was unable to find suitable employment.

During the next few years, Liz primarily occupied herself with being a wife and coping with the role of motherhood, for which she was ill prepared. They were difficult years. There were high spots, though, including her stint as a Cub Scout den mother and a Little League mom.

In 1983, Liz began doing volunteer work for a friend of hers who was attempting to establish a business as a consultant. She continued in this work until a crisis in my law practice made it necessary for her to embark upon a new career as a legal assistant. She did this with competence and verve, and was an equal partner in our venture when we moved my practice from Phoenix to Fort Smith, Arkansas in June, 1986. She continued working with me in my office until November, 1989, when she entered the final stages of her illness resulting from breast cancer. Liz died in Fort Smith on March

27, 1990. After a combined Methodist/Catholic funeral, conducted at Christ the King Catholic Church, Liz was buried in Calvary Catholic Cemetery on Lexington Street in Fort Smith.

My fourth wife, I firmly believe, was a gift from God. I had been alone for over a year and was finally beginning to put my grief behind me, when my niece Karen Banks decided to introduce me to her friend, Barbara Raines. Barbara was a special education teacher working for the State, whose job it is to teach mobility to blind students who are mainstreamed into the public schools. Of all people, I can appreciate this since I was one of the first, if not the very first, such student in Arkansas. Barbara's territory covers half of the state and this included Fort Smith.

Barbara was born on August 24, 1944, in Sheridan, Arkansas, where her father owned the local Chevrolet dealership. At an early age, she became an automotive enthusiast, learning to fix cars, as well as drive them. She even competed in drag-car races and won the title of Mid-South Champion for 1965.

Barbara became a competition-class baton twirler, being named Drum Major for the Sheridan High School band and being later chosen for Majorette for her college band. She graduated from Sheridan High School in 1962. She must have looked the part of the typical all-American girl as she drove away in her sky blue Chevrolet convertible to attend Henderson College at Arkadelphia. In 1966, she graduated with a BA degree in Health, Physical Education, and Recreation and immediately took a job as a physical education teacher in the public school. She later worked for the School for the Blind teaching mentally retarded blind children. At the Arkansas Enterprises for the Blind, she obtained mobility training and returned to the School for the Blind to set up their first orientation and mobility program.

Barbara then went back to the University of Arkansas in 1977 for her Master's degree in Education with an Emphasis in Orientation and Mobility. After graduation, she became a Certified Mobility Instructor and worked with adults at the Arkansas Enterprises for the Blind. While there, she also taught instructors from all over the world. Today, she is employed by the Arkansas Department of Education as a mobility instructor, teaching visually impaired children who are being mainstreamed in public schools. In addition, since receiving her Master's degree, she has gone on to complete 30+ hours toward her Certification as an Educational Specialist in Adult Education.

In 1983, Barbara served as Secretary for the Society for the Prevention of Blindness. More recently, she has been a member of the Arkansas and American Councils for the Blind, the Little Rock City Women's Club, and the little Rock Business and Professional Women's Club. Currently, she is a member and on the board of the State Association for the Education and Rehabilitation of the Blind and Visually Impaired (AER), as well as the Fort Smith chapter of the American Cancer Society. In February, 1994, she attended the International Conference on Orientation and Mobility for the Visually Impaired, held in Melbourne, Australia. She is some lady!

Chapter 29

The Dogs for Whom I have Worked

Earlier in this narrative, I described how I went to The Seeing Eye in the summer of 1952 to obtain my first Seeing Eye dog. Her name was Binney, and she was an eighty pound black and tan German shepherd. She was my first dog and as such she holds a special place in my memory. However, she was only the first of six dogs that I have had to date. Each of them, though, in their own way, have played a special role in my life. I have often remarked how my life seems to have fallen into segments, and in a similar manner, it seems as though I have been granted a special canine companion particularly suited for each of the chapters.

Binney

Binney took me through college, took me overseas for my English adventure, brought me back to finish law school, saw me married, and got me launched on my legal career. These were busy transient and unsettled years. Binney seemed particularly suited to them. She was a high strung and willful dog, but a very dependable guide. Maybe it was because I was only seventeen years old when I got her, but she always felt as though her judgment was better than mine. Times without number we stood on street comers at the end of the day and disputed our route. After 5:00 o'clock, Binney was intent upon going home for dinner. If I wanted to go in any other direction, it was a battle to the death. Eventually, I might win, but it was a reluctant and sullen bundle of fur that went with me. Also, she hated getting wet and would refuse absolutely to go out in the rain.

On one occasion during college, I was living in a small apartment

Binney

off Arkansas Avenue in Fayetteville. It was pouring rain outside, but the building was so insulated that neither of us were aware of how hard it was coming down. When we opened the door, there was nothing between us and a sheet of water but a thin screen door. Binney, who was on my left side as was proper, immediately turned right around the front of my legs and spun me completely around and back into the apartment. She had no intention of going through that door, and she didn't. Later, when the rain slackened off, she did reluctantly agree to venture forth. She kept her eye on the sky, though, for the rest of the day.

On the other hand, Binney would go out into the snow with zest. Even though as a female she had to squat in the snow in order to relieve herself, it never seemed to bother her. Although somehow over the years she did train me to stamp out a cleared space for her to use.

One thing does occur to me. I wonder if during those years my fellow students' attitude toward me was colored by Binney's personality. I don't think that I was an aggressive, pugnacious, pushy type. However, Binney was all of those things. If she was walking through the campus and a gaggle of girls blocked the sidewalk, as so often happened, she would touch her cold nose to the back of each bare leg in succession until she cleared a path. In fact she didn't like anyone getting in front of me. One of my best friends and fraternity brothers, Aub (Bill) Martin, who was editor of the Razorback year book and an accomplished photographer about campus, happened one day to precede me down the stairs at the student union. As he took his first step, Binney took his ankle, firmly but not damagingly, in her mouth. Aub jumped the rest of the flight of stairs and never again got in Binney's way. My apologies not withstanding, Binney had made her point.

Of course, Binney's biggest trial came when she was quarantined in connection with my trip to England. For six months, she languished and so did I. To my great astonishment, when the day of liberation finally arrived, Binney resumed working as though we had never been interrupted. I don't know whether this had more to do with her basic good training or with our brief but intense training sessions. In any event, I was greatly relieved.

England is a country of dog lovers, and Binney and I had never been out of the limelight from the first day that it became publicly known that I was going to England to study and that my guide dog was going to be quarantined. The British public never forgot either of us. Every time I would visit, I would find cards from pet lovers and dog societies pinned to Binney's special cage.

I do want to make it clear, though, that while I did not relish having Binney in quarantine and having to do without her company and her assistance, I never, at any time, resented the fact that she had to be quarantined. After all, it was the law and there was a good reason for it. England is the center of a world-wide trading empire, involving many countries where rabies and other animal diseases are not strictly controlled. She can not afford to allow animals to enter the country without making certain that they pose no threat to the indigenous animal life. Binney didn't, of course, but there was no way to really guarantee it.

Senator Fulbright, the then-junior senator from Arkansas who had sponsored the Fulbright Scholarship program under which I was studying in England, happened to be in London at the time of Binney's coming out. He graciously consented to help me host a press conference in order to satisfy the inexhaustible appetite of the press for dog trivia. I was worried that Binney would get too excited and not behave herself. The minute I put on her harness, though, and gave her the command to the outside door of the kennel, she knew she was on her way and neither God nor the Queen could have stopped her. I think she was afraid to misbehave lest I change my mind. In any event, she was a perfect lady with all of those flash-bulbs popping and people yelling questions. Then, during the formal press conference with Senator Fulbright, she laid at my feet with complete composure and never turned a hair.

Soon after Binney's release, I availed myself of an offer to visit the British guide dog school in Warwickshire. I had thought that there might be a need for some refresher training and it would also give me an opportunity to play ambassador to the British guide dog movement. As it turned out there was no problem. Binney didn't need a refresher and in fact we ended up giving a demonstration of work. They took us out on the street and subjected us to countless barriers, traffic checks, etc., photographing the entire time with a movie camera (video recorders were not yet known). How proud I was with Binney's smooth and professional performance. What a trooper she was!

Unlike the Seeing Eye's strict insistence upon discipline and control, the British school, at least at that time, permitted socializing between dogs and masters when not working. I was extremely proud of Binney as she lay at my side and studiously ignored the advances of a gaggle of dogs (all golden retrievers, that being the only breed which the British school employed). She would have nothing to do with her British cousins. I, of course, attributed it to good breeding, good training, and good discipline. I am sure that as you start to baby a dog, it begins to lose its edge. Therefore, I can't say that the grief I felt at losing Binney was any the greater because she was a guide dog. However, the very fact of the closeness of our association, the extent of our interdependence, and the many experiences we had shared together made the loss very poignant. I missed her, but this soon faded to fond memories as Wyn took Binney's place.

In the summer of 1961, I returned to The Seeing Eye and

Wyn

Wyn

obtained my second guide dog, a large black male German shepherd named Wyn. I had him until 1968. He was very gentle and was what is termed a "soft" dog. He could not take harsh discipline and severe reprimands and keep on chugging like Binney could. One sharp word, and Wyn would slump in dejection. In some ways, I don't think I gave Wyn a real chance. This is often the case with guide dog users. They are so bonded to their first dog that they never give their second dog an even break. On the other hand, I was young and active and vigorous, and Wyn needed encouragement, love, and reassurance. I don't think he was quite the temperament of dog which I should have had at the time. It finally became necessary for me to have a representative of the Seeing Eye come to Rogers to help me work with him to try to get him to buck-up and do his job. For example, if he was confronted by a barrier which he had never seen before, his first reaction was to turn around and go back the way we had come. It was safer than risking the unknown or risking a mistake.

The other side of the coin was that Wyn was the perfect dog to have when my family began. Diana and John thought he was one of their siblings. Diana still talks about him with nostalgia. At the time, I think she thought of him as one of her best friends. He didn't play nanny too conspicuously, but he did watch the children with a caring eye. I never saw him be aggressive, but I am convinced that if anyone had ever threatened the children, the worm would have turned.

Wyn also shared in helping me through some unique experiences. He weathered the move from Washington to Rogers. He was with me when I started my law practice, began my trial work, and entered into politics. He helped me cope with children in diapers and, near the end, he was at my side through my abortive campaign for Circuit Judge in 1968. I am sure that it was no little test of his composure to face those many audiences before whom I spoke, attend pie suppers, walk around numerous small town squares, and visit countless stores and accost stranger after stranger on the street. These were not the kinds of new and different experiences which Wyn would have preferred. He was a creature who would have been much happier with a simple routine repetitive and untaxing lifestyle. His career came to an end in 1968 when he suffered a disintegrated disc in his back.

Shane

One morning he was simply unable to get out of his basket. His hind quarters were totally paralyzed. Again, I had to part with a good friend. Perhaps we had not been become as closely bonded as I had been with Binney, but we had been through a lot together.

I immediately returned to The Seeing Eye and was assigned to Shane. She, too, was a German shepherd; not as big as Binney or Wyn, but much more dynamic in her personality. Her only problem was that she was somewhat high strung and it affected her physically, particularly her intestinal tract. From day one, she suffered chronic diarrhea. The poor dog never got over it, and we spent the next nine years hunting for patches of grass. I think during that whole time she only had two accidents indoors, which was a commentary upon her self-possession and self-control. The threat was always hanging over our heads, however, and this was a strain on me especially. I ate a lot of Rolaids in those years. Apparently, both of us had stomach trouble. I can only wonder who was picking up on whom.

It was Shane who finally broke my devotion to the memory of Binney. Like Binney, she was independent and self-willed. We could try

anything together and usually
succeed. We had a few quiet
years to get our act together
and then we began the gypsy
period of my life. Shane may
have crapped a lot, but
otherwise she took life in
stride.

First, there was my
separation from Mary, which
included both the kids and
our home. For a while, we
camped out in my office and
later in an unfurnished
apartment down the street.
None of it seemed to affect
Shane much. In fact, I think

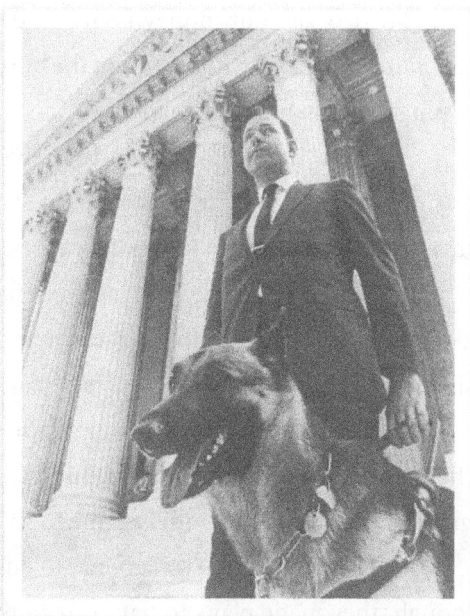

**Davis and Shane being admitted to the
Supreme Court**

she enjoyed the period when I slept on a pallet on the floor. She always liked
to have me down on her level.

Then came my appointment as an Administrative Law Judge in
1975. Shane and I trooped off to Arlington, Virginia, for judge's training
and then took up residence in Florence, Alabama. Six months later, we went
to Fresno, California, by truck. I rode out in the U-Haul truck that I had
rented to haul my household goods. Shane rode at my feet and never made
a complaint. Up to this point, I had held a somewhat lesser position as a
Social Security Insurance (SSI) hearing examiner. Three months after
arriving in Fresno, I received my appointment as a full Administrative Law
Judge (ALJ) and returned to Washington for more training, and thence to
Phoenix, Arizona. In Phoenix, we lived in three different apartments before
I married Liz and the kids came to live with us. Then we bought a house. It
was with Shane that I learned to navigate casinos in Las Vegas, traffic in
California, and survive the heat in Arizona. She went with Liz and me to

visit Mexico on our honeymoon, and while her diarrhetic tendencies remained quiescent while south of the border, Liz and I caught Montezuma's revenge.

Then, out of the blue, in 1977 she was stolen. At least, we think she was. I have dealt with this extensively in a prior chapter, so suffice it to say that it was an extremely traumatic experience.

Next, there came Jenny. I went back to The Seeing Eye in the fall of 1977 and came home with a large, aggressive, eager, joyous female German shepherd. Unfortunately, Jenny had diarrhea worse than Shane. Although it had not shown up during training, the minute we were back in Phoenix, she began to squirt every time I put the harness on her. After only three months, The Seeing Eye advised me to ship her back.

The question then was what to do for a dog. After only a short time, though, they made plans to have one of their senior trainers, Daniel Boeke, travel to Phoenix and bring me a new dog. I had just been through a training session three months before, and the new dog, a fifty pound black Labrador Retriever named Cinder, had just been orphaned by her master. She had only been in service a year or so and was therefore also in good training. In other words, we were two professionals who didn't need a lot of practice.

Cinder

Mr. Boeke brought her out and introduced her to me in my office one afternoon just before closing time. He had plans to spend three days helping us get adjusted. Since there was no time to lose, we decided to walk home the two miles from the office. Unfortunately, though, it was pouring rain, but little things like rainstorms never deter the diehard Seeing Eye instructor. We walked it anyway. From that point on, Cinder and I never looked back. It did take me almost a year to win her complete confidence and trust, but she always worked with diligence and I think even some fondness. She was a very self-contained little dog, though, and not overly demonstrative. It wasn't until three or four years had passed that she really decided that maybe I was a pretty good guy after all, or maybe she had to be sure that I wasn't going to die on her like her first master had.

Cinder carried me through the judicial years. We traveled the country together from Pasadena to Detroit, holding Social Security hearings wherever we went. We struggled through snow and desert heat. She learned to tolerate Little League games, band concerts, graduation exercises, Cub Scout meetings, and girls bunking parties. The only thing she couldn't handle were storms. Binney didn't like rain, because she didn't like to get wet. Wyn was more or less indifferent. Shane didn't like storms and would go to her bed when they occurred. Cinder, on the other hand, was terrified. One crack of thunder and she disappeared. We finally found that she would always head for the interior bathroom where there were no windows. There, she would crouch in the bathtub shivering behind the shower curtain until the storm was over. I could drag her out, but she would go back. Then she would shake for the rest of the day. No amount of reassurance or comforting made the slightest difference.

Other than being terrified of storms, Cinder was Miss Phlegmatic. Even at age twelve, older than any of my previous dogs, she took our move to Fort Smith in stride. By 1988, however, she was fourteen years old and beginning to have physical problems. Finally, when it became obvious that her concentration and energy were flagging, the Seeing Eye helped me make the decision to get a new dog. All over again, I felt like I was betraying a friend when I had her put to sleep, but in view of Cinder's lifelong professionalism, I don't think she would have ever wanted to continue to try to work at anything but her best.

Then came Eddie. In October 1988, I returned to The Seeing Eye. My newest canine colleague was a ninety pound black and tan German shepherd named Eddie. Without a doubt, he has proven to be the best dog I ever had. He has all of Binney's enthusiasm and daring, all of Wyn's gentleness and love, all of Shane's patience and stick-with-itness, and all of Cinder's professionalism. He is one great dog. He is funny. He is competent. He is everything that I have always thought that a Seeing Eye dog should be and like my other dogs he has already shared crisis with me. Soon after he came to live with us, Liz became mortally ill with her cancer and good ole Eddie never faltered in helping me meet each day's trials, and he never failed to give Liz a lick and a snuggle whenever he passed her during

Eddie

her final days as she sat almost inert in her recliner.

Some of Eddie's accomplishments have astounded even me. The evening we came home from Seeing Eye, I showed him his rug on the floor and explained that was where he was to sleep. I turned out the light and left the room. When I returned a few minutes later, he was stretched out on the bed. I scolded him soundly and returned him bodily to his rug. Once again, I explained that the rug was where he belonged. When I returned the next time, I found him again on the bed, this time on top of the rug which he had also brought onto the bed. The solution to that one was a challenge. This incident was actually recounted by one of the other Seeing Eye graduates who was with me at the time I obtained Eddie. Andy Potok is a writer who wrote an article about his trip to The Seeing Eye that was published in the Readers' Digest. We corresponded for some time after our sojourn at The Seeing Eye and he loved the story about Eddie and the rug. He asked me if he could use it as one of his dog Dash's accomplishments in the article. I agreed, of course, and now Eddie is, in a sense, immortalized in print, although under an alias.

On another occasion, I began to worry about just how much Eddie did understand. He was searching through the house for his nylon bone that I had told him to get so that I could throw it for him to fetch. He had looked everywhere downstairs, but could not find it. Then as he passed the door of the study where I was sitting, I suggested casually, "Eddie why don't you look upstairs?" Immediately, he turned around and dashed for the stairs like a freight train going uphill. He found his bone, too. From that day on, I have been careful to not say anything in front of him that I didn't want him to hear.

Seeing Eye identification
cards for each dog

The only thorn in the patch when it comes to Eddie is his problem with applause. Clapping drives him crazy. He can attend a Razorback football game at the University and not be flustered by the screaming of 50,000 fans. He can withstand the deafening roar of the Walton Basketball Arena. Let a dozen people at a dinner applaud the speaker, though, and he comes unglued. At this writing, I am still working on the problem. The Seeing Eye has suggested various techniques to deal with the problem, but none of them have provided a long-term solution. So far, I have desensitized him to the point where he no longer jumps up and I think the barking has been eradicated, but he still whines and groans. It is embarrassing and disconcerting. Mainly, I think it bothers me, though, because it detracts from Eddie's dignity. Still, this too will pass. Together we will overcome it.

What I can say for sure about Eddie, though, is that we have bonded more closely than any dog I have ever had. He works like a demon and in fact shows a precision to which none of my other dogs even came close. There is one thing he insists upon, however. Every morning, when I get up, no matter how badly he needs to go out and pee, we have to lie down on the floor and give each other a big hug and a few licks before we start the day. If I fail to do it, he is in a bad humor until I rectify the situation. Also, I can not ignore him for overlong. He has an old slimy wet chew-bone that he likes to drop in my lap when he wants my attention and it always works. He also has a well-shredded throw rug with which he would rather play than eat. I don't dare say the word "tug-a-rug" because it sets him off to frantically searching throughout the house for his rag of a rug. I don't have to invite it, though. Sometimes when I am merely sitting and smoking my pipe, he brings the rug to me and dumps it in my lap. Then, with his teeth damped on one end, he growls ferociously until I grab the other end and go at it with him toe to nose. He also does this to total strangers who visit us, but they are not nearly so understanding as the family. We try to hide his tug-a-rug if we know company is coming. In fact, Eddie believes anyone who visits us has really come to see him. It has been a constant struggle to keep him from greeting people at the door, not with a bark and growl like other dogs, but with open arms and an obvious offer of hospitality. I think he would even play receptionist at the office if I didn't order him to stay in my office on pain of death.

Perhaps one's current guide dog is always considered to be the best dog one has ever had. This may be why I feel as I do about Eddie. One thing I can say for sure, far more people in Fort Smith know Eddie than me. If I didn't take him with me, I just wonder how many people would know who I was. I can only hope that all of my future dogs come even close to the standards set by those who have preceded them, especially, Eddie the Great, Prince of Tails. His greatness can best be attested the little boy who was recently overheard at church saying to his dad, "Hey look, there goes that dog with his lawyer!"

Chapter 30

Politics—A Never Ending Pageant

Except for the three times I sought election to political office, I have had only a passing interest in state and local politics. Indeed, I was even living outside the state when Bill Clinton, now our President, was elected Governor of Arkansas. I did have occasion to meet him, though, when he was still a nobody. While running for Circuit Judge in 1968, I attended a political rally where all candidates gathered to speak. It was held over in Carroll County under a tent in the middle of a field. The spectators sat on metal chairs and the stage was made of planks laid across saw-horses. After the meeting was over and we candidates were all circulating among the crowd, shaking hands and handing out cards and the like, a young man came pushing through the chairs to introduce himself as Bill Clinton. I don't remember whether he was running for anything or just out getting a feel for country politics, but there he was. If I had only known, I would not have washed my hand.

Local politics aside, however, I have been blessed by living through and to one degree or another participating in national politics as far back as the tenure of Franklin D. Roosevelt as President. I was not born when he was first elected and I have no memory of anything much until the War Years (1941-45) when he was the great war leader. At the time, the name President Roosevelt was synonymous with God. He was something more than human, an almost supernatural being who everybody listened to on the radio and who everyone knew would save us from the Nazis and Japs. I guess the first time I was made to really think of him as a man was the April day in 1945 when he died. My then-best friend John Fred Hawkins greeted me as I came up the alley to his back door with the news that President Roosevelt had died. I also remember that church bells rang. Gloom seemed to hang over the entire town for days. I think that in many ways it was the end of innocence. Up to that time we could look to a great and noble leader. After that, we have had mere mortals to follow.

By contrast, Harry Truman began as almost too human, but ended revered. I well remember such comments as "Harry Who?" Even as young as I was at the time (eleven), I remember the surprise I felt upon hearing President Truman's stumbling speech. It seemed all the worse by comparison with the flowing eloquence of Roosevelt. Still, by 1948, when he actually ran for President the first time, Give 'em Hell Harry was slipping into myth. His speeches were becoming smooth and decisive. We were getting used to his midwestern drawl. Since television was in its infancy, most of us heard him only by radio. One wonders if public reaction would have been different if he had been subjected to the rigors of television. There was simply something calming and reassuring in the way he spoke. It was sort of like listening to one's grandfather telling you that everything would be all right and that he had everything under control. His surprising victory over Wendell Wilkie in the 1948 election affected a lot of people more as a sense of relief that everything was still under control and there would be no big changes. We were still healing from the war and weren't ready for changes or excitement. After that, I think Harry had it made.

The extent to which he had achieved acceptance by the public is most evident in the fact that he took us to war in Korea and through it to a reasonably satisfactory conclusion without the foot dragging and controversy which would plague Lyndon Johnson and Richard Nixon just a few years later. The Korean War was not a particularly popular war, but we still trusted our leaders. Even when Harry retired General MacArthur for insubordination, we trusted his judgment. After all, as popular and charismatic as MacArthur was, Harry Truman represented the well-established principle of civilian control of the military, and we had faith that our President knew what he was doing. I fear that nobody believes this anymore, whether justified or not. Instead of following our leaders, once elected, we immediately begin tearing them down and undermining public confidence in them. Historically, such loss of confidence in the system has too often led to totalitarianism.

Then came Ike. Who could not like Ike? He had won the War in Europe. He was a military hero. He never seemed to say anything particularly brilliant. In fact, he seemed to have difficulty expressing himself. On the other hand, he had a fantastic smile. He was a threat to no one. In truth, Ike represented the new mood of America. We were tired of responsibility. We wanted freedom from pressure and freedom from the need to accomplish great things. The '50s had dawned. The choice was quite plain in the 1952 election. It was between Ike who represented peace, prosperity, stability, and a chance to lay back as contrasted by Adlai Stevenson who challenged the nation to continue moving forward and to continue to strive upwards toward greatness. What America wanted was not to avoid greatness, but to take a break from the struggle. As a matter of fact, one of Ike's telling promises during the campaign was that he would go to Korea and stop the war, and that was precisely what he did. Of course, the fact that the war was already over anyway was beside the point. The gesture was what counted.

For the next eight years, we had our recess. During this time I was in college and there was little talk of national goals, of world leadership, of social reform, etc. It was not until the Russians put Sputnik in space in 1958 that we were suddenly jolted out of our lethargy and complacence. One moment we were lazing on the beach. The next we were picking up our toys and getting back down to business. That was when John Kennedy emerged on the scene.

President Kennedy was elected in 1960 with a challenge to move forward and sacrifice if necessary. From that point on, our nation began to address the many issues which have been with us since. We have tried to deal with racial inequality, war, feminism, poverty, disease, development of the third world, hunger of the masses, and now a reshuffling of the world political structure. For a short time during the early '60s, the whole nation was caught up in the good feeling of national altruism. We had goals. We were concerned about real problems. We wanted to do something. The problem was that objectives were sometimes unclear and it was not always possible to achieve them even when they were. Then, of course, John Kennedy was assassinated in Dallas. The whole nation went into shock. It was not just that a promising young president had been killed. Our new-found self-appreciation and dedication was deprecated. Without the magical leader, we began to feel insecure and devoid of direction. On this note, Lyndon Johnson assumed the throne.

From a polished, poised charismatic leader in John Kennedy, we went to a crude man of the soil who wielded naked power with zest. We had to follow him. He was all we had. At least he seemed to be going in the same direction that Kennedy had pointed. Unfortunately, though, it led into the Vietnam War. Many of the social and human issues were side-tracked. Even if Johnson had had the wisdom and the courage to pursue the Camelot dream, Vietnam killed it.

Kennedy's new frontier and Johnson's great society were overwhelmed by the preoccupation with Southeast Asia. The irony was that there were many, mostly the young, who opposed the war, going so far as to incite civil unrest. But, their motives were primarily selfish and had to do with a misguided sympathy for the Viet Minh. Charlie wasn't right. He was wrong. I never doubted for a minute that South Vietnam had a right to defend itself and to prefer a republic over communism. The problem was that we never really made a commitment to guns over butter. Whether or not the war in Vietnam was just, too many were not willing to give up any of the good things in life for an abstract principle. They just couldn't get enthused.

Johnson himself must have recognized the quicksand for he sought no second term in 1968. We had become a nation adrift, ineptly prosecuting a war in a far away land, for people with whom we could not identify. As a result, we found ourselves being humiliated by a second rate military power and with gnawing problems at home which were long overdue for solution. Thus we turned to Richard Millhouse Nixon.

President Nixon was elected, I believe, primarily because he proposed to either win the war or get out or Vietnam. All else was secondary.

Ike had offered to go to Korea and stop the war, but it was merely an offer to let the nation off the hook for a while. Nixon offered something more specific: a chance to shake off the evil genie of Vietnam. Then, of course, he was confronted with rampant inflation, war protestors, and the MIA question. As I mentioned before, we have never been tolerant of our leaders. We build them up only to tear them down after they are elected. There is something in the nature of Americans which believes that if someone is elected, he must not deserve it and at the very least he must be cut down to size lest he be convinced of his own importance. Whatever the reason, Nixon did not achieve miracles at once, and the nation was almost gleeful when he was caught engaging in less than savory political maneuvering. We were a frustrated nation and only needed a failed tyrant to set us howling for his head. I don't think Richard Nixon was a good president, although there have been worse. He was probably not even a very good man. But I believe that his major error was in being caught doing what others have done in the past and therefore he believed was acceptable. If politicians live on the edge, they must not forget that one step too far can mean disaster. Nixon had nobody to blame but himself, but we the people should not feel too sanctimonious for having brought down a presidency. The nation paid a much higher price than did Richard Nixon.

So was it surprising that we scuttled back to a brief flirtation with the Eisenhower syndrome as embodied in Gerald Ford? Once again, we were frustrated, tired, and needed a break. It was time to stick our heads back in the sand. When Richard Nixon was forced to resign under threat of impeachment and his recently acquired new Vice-President Gerald Ford (Nixon's elected Vice-President Spiro Agnew had been forced to resign even earlier by evidence of criminal activity) was sworn in as President, the nation heaved a sigh of relief. With Gerald Ford, we could relax again. Things were back to normal. The Vietnam War was over, although many of the side issues were not resolved. It was a time, though, to let go and enjoy the prosperity and leisure of the mid-'70s. It was back to the '50s, but with a twist.

Next came Jimmy Carter. Again, it was a pale imitation of the Kennedy phenomena. After several years of indolence, the nation was challenged to again face real life issues. There was inflation, an energy crisis, tension in the Middle East, and the continuing MIA controversy. Jimmy Carter helped us focus the issues, but he was not John Kennedy. He lacked the staying power and he lacked the focusing power. Once in office, he became indecisive. Some said he was too intelligent and saw the merits in every argument. This was bad enough, but when the hostages were taken at the Embassy in Tehran, Iran, and President Carter was unable to achieve a resolution, much less take decisive action, he lost credibility. Then, when he finally did act, the bungled rescue mission sealed his fate. It merely became a matter of waiting for Carter's successor.

Then we got Ronald Reagan. He rode into town on a white charger, promising a stronger military and a stronger economy. The nation bought it hook, line, and sinker. Still smarting from the loss of self-esteem in Vietnam, the voters wanted to stand tall again. John Wayne was a movie idol, not because of his acting, but because of the heroic image he portrayed. It was the image that most Americans want to see in the mirror each morning—tall, strong, forceful, courageous, dedicated, and patriotic. We were tired of failures and feeling bad about ourselves. So, we elected Ronald Reagan to be our President. What a joke! He was nothing but a second rate actor. He succeeded well enough in portraying a president, but it was only an image without substance. I am proud to say that I did not vote for him. I also confess that I did not vote to re-elect Jimmy Carter. Mr. Carter had lost his mandate. I voted for John Anderson of Illinois. While I knew that he could not win, I truly felt that he was the best qualified of the candidates. I kept telling myself it was not a protest vote, but under the circumstances, it probably was.

To give Ronald Reagan his due, he did restore our sense of national pride, and probably because of the relentless pressure placed upon Russia resulting from our military build-up, Reagan's so-called "evil empire" eventually crumbled. They simply could not compete economically with the resources of the United States. I do not believe that Ronald Reagan had the slightest idea what he was doing with the economy and was no great mental giant when it came to international affairs. However, he got one thing right. He put on the pressure and kept on the pressure. For two generations we had tried to treat the Communists as reasonable human beings. They weren't. They were as implacable as John Wayne. They only understood strength and that's what President Reagan brought to bear. It is his one true contribution to our heritage. Perhaps it was worth the price.

On the other hand, the Reagan economics, generally referred to as Reaganomics, were a disaster. You can't spend, cut taxes, and live. It was the old guns and butter argument all over again. The end result was a quadrupled national debt, a weakened dollar, and the threat of bankruptcy hanging over the nation. We had a terrific military establishment, but truth to tell we couldn't afford it much more than could the Russians. We just had enough to out-last them. Then came time to pay the piper.

During his tenure, Mr. Reagan played the part of President with consummate skill. Being an actor, it probably came easy. I always felt that he never stopped playing the part and never even really took himself seriously as president. In other words, I don't believe that he ever got past the part itself to become seriously involved substantively in the office.

Unfortunately, he was not bright enough or astute enough to prevent the inevitable corruption of power which can accrete around a weak president who will not or cannot retain control.

Some of the abuses were intentional and some simply resulted from greed. Brush-fire wars broke out in Nicaragua and the Middle East. We tried to back our friends. In the interest of the economy and in light of our uncertainty about who our friends were, limits were placed upon such support. Therefore, bureaucrats who were cleverer than they were moral (Colonel Oliver North being a case in point) devised ways to circumvent the law. Consequently, like Nixon and his Watergate scandal, Reagan had his Iran-Contra scandal. Munitions were secretly sold to the Islamic fundamentalist regime in Iran and the funds diverted to the anti-Sandinista

Contra rebels in Nicaragua. It was a classic example of individuals thinking they knew what was best and were convinced that the end justified the means. The problem, though, was that it was not only morally wrong and illegal, it also didn't work. Mr. Reagan said he knew nothing about it, but whereas nobody believed Nixon's protestations of ignorance concerning the Watergate break-in, nobody wanted to believe that Mr. Reagan was guilty. By silent acquiescence, the nation looked the other way. We had already had one president brought down in disgrace. It was too soon to have another. Besides, hadn't Ronnie suffered enough with the wound he sustained in 1984 at the hands of the would-be assassin John Hinkley? He was just too likable and too vulnerable for anyone to want to cause him harm. After all, his term of office was about over and after that he would be nothing more that a footnote to history. Nice old guys fare far better than shifty looking old guys.

It was with a sigh of relief that Reagan was finally succeeded as President by George H. W. Bush. Bush was an attractive and articulate man and an accomplished politician. Having been Reagan's Vice-President, as well as having served both as director of the CIA and in Congress, he appeared to be eminently qualified. At the outset, there was every indication when he took office in January, 1989, that George Bush would be recorded in history as one of our more outstanding presidents. Progressing events seemed to bear this out. Unemployment increased, but inflation appeared to be under control and the economy seemed to be growing. On the international front, two significant events took place. The Russian empire began to disintegrate, suddenly leaving the United States alone on the world stage as the last of the super powers. The military, economic, and political threat of communism went poof and overnight seemed to have vanished. George Bush was in a position to lead the establishment of a new world order.

While all the foregoing events were taking place, the growing tensions in the Middle East came to a head. The protracted war between Iran and Iraq was settled, and Iraq's president Saddam Hussein was free to turn his formidable military machine upon less formidable neighbors. With very little warning, he made a grab for the tiny nation of Kuwait and formally announced its annexation. Not only was this seen as naked aggression, but it also put Iraq in control of vast, new oil resources; and of equal concern, it placed Iraq in direct confrontation with Saudi Arabia. For once, world opinion coalesced in opposition to Iraqi imperialism. Arab nations, such as Saudi Arabia, Egypt, and Syria, which had never been able to agree or cooperate on much of anything, joined the western nations led by the United States but also including Britain and France to establish overnight a military response.

After months of military buildup in Saudi Arabia while Iraq postured and threatened and launched Scud missiles indiscriminately against Saudi Arabia, but mostly against Israel, the Allies in early 1991 launched an all out air assault upon Iraq, followed by Operation Desert Storm. Massive armored columns swept across Kuwait and into Iraq. The Iraqi army was for all intents and purposes crushed. George Bush had what every president dreams of: a successful war. By the time the cease fire had been ordered and the combatants had settled down to hammer out an uneasy peace, George Bush was at the peak of his popularity. It was inconceivable at that time that anybody could possibly derail his bid for a second term. But the impossible happened.

The year 1992 began with a hoard of aspiring presidential candidates, both Democrats and Republicans, spreading out across the land to test their viability in the state primaries. No one thought George Bush had anything to worry about. Most observers were predicting that Senator Gore of Tennessee, or Senator Tsongas of Massachusetts, or even Senator Ted Kennedy would cop the democratic nomination and only serve their party selflessly as cannon fodder in a losing struggle.

Without warning, out of the New Hampshire primary emerged a new name, Governor Bill Clinton of Arkansas. He had entered the primaries, probably hoping at best to begin developing a national following, perhaps with an eye toward the 1996 election when George Bush's two terms would end. When he won the New Hampshire primary, Bill Clinton suddenly became a viable political force. He went proceeded to roll-up one primary victory after another. The other candidates, for one reason or another, fell by the wayside. By the time of the Democratic Convention in Atlanta, the Bill Clinton Express was unstoppable. He was nominated almost as an afterthought and chose Senator Albert Gore of Tennessee as his Vice-Presidential running mate. Then they tore into the Republicans like starving wolves into a flock of fat sheep. Almost at once, Clinton took the high ground and George Bush found himself frantically defending his presidency on all sides.

The only exciting element of the campaign came from the third party candidacy of Ross Perot. This millionaire industrialist, misplaced conservative Republican, and gadfly politician not only split the conservative vote, taking support away from Bush, but also caused such a distraction that Bush could never regain the stage. His campaign verily fizzled. Bill Clinton, former Governor of Arkansas, had been elected as the 42nd President of the United States. Who would have dreamt it?

At first, there was considerable doubt as to whether Clinton had the stature to be President. Actually, I am not sure he did at the beginning. Indeed, his wife Hillary seemed to overshadow him in both maturity, suavity, and charisma. As the nation moved through 1993, however, Bill Clinton, like Harry Truman before him, seemed to grow with the job. From a young man who wanted to be President, he became President. His presidency has thus far been characterized by direct assaults upon some of the most pressing issues of our time. He practically forced through Congress by his will alone a budget, which, for the first time in living memory, cut spending from some of the most sacred of sacred cows. Even social programs felt the crunch, but the major target was the defense budget. Bases were closed which had been kept open through pork barrelling since the Revolutionary War. The Star Wars initiative was all but dismantled. B1 and B2 (Stealth) bomber production were curtailed. All branches of the service were cut back. It was evident from the outset that President Clinton was determined to restructure the national effort to accomplish the most possible, within our means, and lead the new world order in facing the social crises confronting us not only at home but all over the globe. He has sought to lead and assist, but has resisted military intervention.

Closer at home, President Clinton and, even to a greater extent, First Lady Hillary Clinton have taken on the almost insoluble health care problem. Health

Davis, President Bill Clinton, Barbara, and Izmir

care costs have escalated beyond all reason. Almost 40 million people cannot afford health insurance and thus must do without health care or obtain it through charity programs which increase the burden on the taxpayers. As of this writing, the outcome is anything but clear. The Clintons have proposed a health care plan. The Republicans and those with vested financial interests such as insurance companies are putting up a desperate fight to retain the status quo. The President has taken the position that something must be done and that if his proposals are not acceptable then the opponents have the obligation to devise more palatable solutions. So far, it seems apparent that the President will probably accomplish some health care reforms, although their nature and extent are still uncertain. They will probably not be all that we need, but they will be better than we have.

The important factor, though, is that this young, new President, obviously influenced by the anti-establishment attitudes of the '60s, is breaking with the tradition of business as usual and is attacking head-on some of the most daunting social and economic problems which have ever confronted any nation or any president. I know Bill Clinton personally, although not intimately. I like him, and I respect his courage and independence. The searchers for skeletons in the closet may diminish his effectiveness. He may not reach his exalted goals, but I applaud his willingness to try. If he succeeds, he will be remembered as a truly great President and his wife Hillary as the prototype for a new breed of First Lady. If this comes to pass, our nation and its citizens will be the real beneficiaries.

Chapter 31

Contemplations

As a matter of historical interest, I am reprinting herein the following brief essays which were originally prepared as thirty-second radio spots for use in my 1968 campaign for Circuit Judge of the newly created 19th Judicial District of Arkansas. They contain in summary my thinking on various matters which I believed were, or at least should have been, of intimate concern to America during the third quarter of the 20th century. Without exception, they deal with principals and problems which are, or will become, fundamental to the individual's way of life in this nation. Although it is often the policy of political candidates to first discover the people's interests and then espouse them as their own, I thought it was more appropriate to promulgation of a free society founded on republican principals that those who would be leaders point to the road ahead, despite the hazards, and seek to mold the future, not molder in the past.

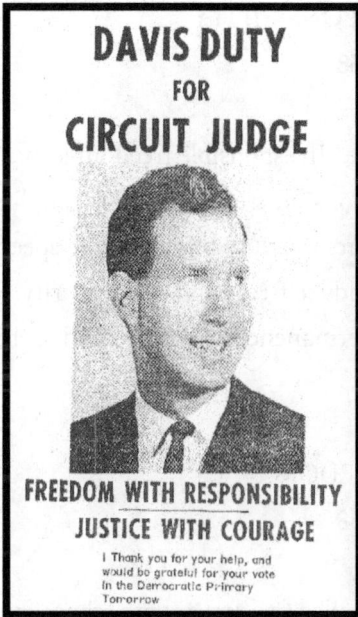

DAVIS DUTY
FOR
CIRCUIT JUDGE

FREEDOM WITH RESPONSIBILITY
JUSTICE WITH COURAGE

I Thank you for your help, and would be grateful for your vote in the Democratic Primary Tomorrow

I do not present these thoughts as immortal, philosophical insights. It is merely my intention to disclose my political perspective at a particular point in time. And ironically reading the essays again twenty-six years later, I must confess that my thinking has not substantially progressed. I hope that this is because my ideas were sound to begin with.

EQUALITY
July 15, 1968

No one can claim that all men are born exactly equal; therefore there must be equality of opportunity. Political equality cannot vary; but social and economic differences do exist and are wrong only if improvement is denied. Democracy survives just so long as the opportunity to participate and advance are equally enjoyed.

FREEDOM WITH RESPONSIBILITY
July 16, 1968

Freedom and responsibility are inseparable. Irresponsible freedom leads to tyranny of the strong over the weak. Responsible freedom means coupling a duty to each right. The right to vote bears the duty to vote. Free speech requires speaking responsibly. This demands self-restraint and maturity. It means getting involved. But it offers permanence to liberty and is the keystone of our republic.

LIMITS OF FREEDOM
July 17, 1968

Freedom under control blesses; uncontrolled it curses with chaos and anarchy. The death of liberty leads to political death and oft-times to personal death. Yet, unrestricted freedom is no freedom. Liberty is not license. Each man's freedom ends where another's begins. This requires individual self-restraint as well as strict law enforcement.

VIOLENCE UNCHECKED
July 18, 1968

Recent events have shown with tragic vividness that liberty or death is still a choice which every free man must make. Today we must repudiate the growing idea that violence is justified in the name of protest. America must remain a nation of laws, not of men. If elected, I pledge a court dedicated to these principals.

JUSTICE WITH COURAGE
July 19, 1968

Justice demands courage to deny human prejudice and emotion. Thus tainted, justice ceases to be just. But with courage, justice surpasses those who serve it and proclaims fairness and equality under law without consideration of race, color, creed, sex, or social condition. This is the mainspring of America, a nation of laws, built by men, for men, but not of men.

HANDCUFFING THE POLICE
July 20, 1968

The United States Supreme Court is criticized for its decisions "handcuffing" the police. Reading these cases, however, you find that the Court has actually not restricted the police, but instead has bolstered the rights of the individual. True, these cases have worked to the immediate benefit of the outlaw element -the communists and the rioters. But in the long run, the fortress of freedom for us all is made ever more impregnable.

POLICE BRUTALITY
July 22, 1968

Police brutality and over-restriction of the police both stem from a conflict between the true enjoyment of individual rights and the need for strict law enforcement. Proposed remedies are: higher police pay and standards, self-restraint in exercising rights, respect for the rights of others, and support for law and order. Our future lies in the efficient, legally-restricted and self-restrained policing of a law-abiding people.

AUTOMATION
July 23, 1968

Automation is the most ignored problem facing America. Machines must not enslave us, but if controlled they can help man realize his true potential. Still, machines will inevitably infringe upon human work. This requires three areas of adjustment: population control, discovery of new frontiers for man, and emphasis upon creative leisure. Let us not fear automation, but treat it as a challenge.

AMERICA'S MISSION TO THE WORLD
July 24, 1968

Domestically, America faces grave new problems: over-population, technological displacement, and economic disparity. One may dispute the solutions, but can anyone decry the objectives? Internationally, America stands as the pillar of freedom. We cannot police the world, but we must guard the portals of liberty and reasonably assist those who seek its shelter. Although our mission is dangerous, it is vital and we shall persevere.

PERSONAL INVOLVEMENT
July 25, 1968

Personal involvement is the key to democracy. America is blessed in this respect, from charitable giving to political participation. While actual evasion of duty exists, apathy is the real danger. We must conscientiously seek personal involvement, for without it tyranny enters by default.

Tomorrow I will summarize the first five of my series on America.

SUMMARY, PART I
July 26, 1968

For two weeks, I have discussed ten areas of freedom for America. In the first five, I suggested that equality and opportunity are synonymous, that freedom and responsibility are inseparable, that liberty is not license, that violence is utterly intolerable, and that justice requires courage to prevail.

If you agree with these principals, I ask your vote in the Democratic Primary next Tuesday for me, Davis Duty, for Circuit Judge. Tomorrow I will summarize the second five of my series on America.

SUMMARY, PART II
July 27, 1968

For two weeks, I have discussed ten areas of freedom for America. In the last five, I suggested that individual rights are superior to police authority, that police brutality and "handcuffing" the police are equally wrong, that automation can be a threat or a challenge, that domestically and internationally America cannot escape her destiny, and that personal involvement is the key to democracy.

FINAL APPEAL
July 29 and 30, 1968

In the past two weeks, I have discussed my views on matters basic to the American system. These ideas are summed up in my campaign theme of Freedom with Responsibility, Justice with Courage. If elected your Circuit Judge, I pledge a court dedicated to these principals. With trust in your judgement and faith in our domestic process, I ask your vote in the Democratic Primary for me, Davis Duty, for Circuit Judge.

Chapter 32

Me-n-God

I don't remember a time when I did not go to Sunday School and Church. Scrubbed and in our Sunday togs, mother delivered us faithfully to Sunday School every Sunday morning and, during the summer, to Vacation Bible School at the First Methodist Church in Rogers. I well remember the day when I was about ten years old that I went down front and joined the church. It was not a spontaneous act, though. It had been scheduled in advance. Still, I was moved.

When we moved back to Rogers in about 1954, it was a matter of course to return to my home church. I had some choir experience in high school, so I joined the Methodist Church Choir and thus began an itinerant church choir career which lasted about twenty years. I sang in the church choir on Sundays. I sang in Christmas and Easter cantatas. On one occasion, we put on a performance of the Messiah with orchestra and all. I became a member of the University Choir (then called the Collegiate Singers). I sang in the Methodist Church in Fayetteville while at the University and I took part in the Wesley Foundation Choir. Later, I joined the Rogers Community Chorus during its brief life in the mid-'60s. It took time and energy and I made a minimal contribution talent-wise, but, like any form of recreation, it enervated me both physically and mentally, and perhaps even spiritually.

I was a good Methodist until age twenty-two. On one occasion, I even went down front after a service to rededicate my life. I felt a strong spiritual pull, not to enter the ministry or a church-related career, but to make the Lord an anchor point in my life. Like most people, though, I did less thanking and more asking, and less praying when things went well than when they went bad. Still, I was drawn.

In 1958, I went to England. They have Methodist churches there, but none were readily at hand. So when Binney finally came out of quarantine and I could go when and where I pleased, I began attending Sunday morning services at St. Pancreas Parish Church, which was on Southampton Road about three blocks from where I lived in Passfield Hall just off Endsleigh Square. St. Pancreas Church was Church of England. It was located in a section of London which was becoming industrialized and commercialized. Very few parishioners remained. I doubt that there were more than a hundred people present in that imposing edifice on Sunday mornings. I became very comfortable in the Church of England services, though, and when I returned to Arkansas in 1959, I continued to attend the Episcopal Church for some time. In fact, I got my sister and her husband Gene interested and they eventually joined and became very active Episcopalians. Later still, with our combined influence, we brought my parents from the Methodist Church to the Episcopal Church. They remained quite active until their early eighties. Then they began to feel somewhat alienated by the brash younger generation who moved in and took over St. Andrew's Church where they attended in Rogers. In the meantime, having gotten all of the deadwood out of the Methodist Church, I returned to it.

Throughout my time in Rogers from 1962 to 1975, it could be said that I was a pillar of the Methodist Church. I was a member of the Board of Stewards. I was on numerous committees. I sang in the choir. It was a comfortable time, but I experienced very little spiritual growth during those years. Indeed, I was almost alienated from the church in connection with President Kennedy's assassination in 1963. The minister at that time was anti-Kennedy and refused to even acknowledge the assassination in his sermon on the following Sunday. The nation was in shock. I was in shock. We desperately needed explanations and reassurance. Kennedy's assassination on Friday left the nation adrift, with a weekend before it to think and weep. On Sunday, people went to church in unprecedented numbers for the solace and comfort they could find nowhere else. We were in grief, but our minister chose the opportunity to make a political statement by ignoring the incident. I was so incensed that I almost walked out of the service. I finally decided, though, that the church was bigger than the individual and that I wasn't going to allow one bigot to run me off.

I had always loved the Methodist Church because of its tradition of free thought and enlightenment. It is deeply ingrained in me that spiritual growth is inhibited by narrow mindedness. I love the Methodist Church and will probably die a Methodist, but I had broken out of the rut during my time in England.

When I married Liz, she was a Catholic. We were married in the Episcopal Cathedral in Phoenix, though, by a Bishop no less (Joseph Hart, who later resigned after multiple accusations of sexual abuse of young boys). Liz' first marriage had been in the Catholic Church. Therefore, even though she and Harold were divorced, she could not remarry in the Catholic Church unless the prior marriage was annulled by the Church. We settled on the Episcopal Church as a compromise. I felt good and married, but Liz considered herself excommunicated from the Catholic Church, and although we attended the church regularly, neither of us took Communion. She would not be reconciled with her church until Harold's death in 1988.

The nearest church to our home in Phoenix was St. Gregory's Catholic Church, only a block away on Osborn Road. We began attending there, and I didn't see the inside of a Methodist Church again for ten years. Liz and I did not take an active part in parish life, but never felt out of place in the Catholic environment. I was made to feel like a part of the family by both Monsignor Gordon and Father Frank Fernandez. Both Diana and John were, for all intents and purposes, raised as Catholics. In fact, Diana was eventually confirmed.

When Liz and I moved to Fort Smith in 1986, I decided the time had come to return to the Methodist fold. However, I had developed a deep affinity for the Catholic Church. Therefore, we decided that we would double-dip. We attended the anticipatory mass on Saturday night at Christ the King Catholic Church and the Sunday morning service at the First United Methodist Church. I joined one, Liz joined the other. My church accepted Liz as an honorary Methodist, and most Catholics at Christ the

King are unaware that I am not part of the flock. They probably wonder why I don't take Communion, but they probably just put it down to unremitted sin.

Finally, Liz' ordeal with her church came to an end. Harold died in the summer of 1988, and Liz and I were married in Christ the King Catholic Church by Father John Connell on September 19, 1988. Although the church had never said a word to Liz, she felt herself to be out of step. At long last she was back in her fold. I could not help but note how much happier and positive she became thereafter. It also meant that when she died in March 1990, she did so in the bosom of her church and with the knowledge that she would not be alone in crossing over to the other side.

After Liz died, I continued to attend both churches and the members of both churches rallied round to see that I had rides and did not feel the isolation which the death of a spouse too often produces. It was probably foreordained, therefore, that when I began to re-emerge into the world and was ready for another relationship, it was, of course, a good Catholic girl who caught my eye. On the other hand, Barbara was a converted Catholic, having started out as a Baptist. It was probably less of a culture shock for her to slip into my double-dipping regime than it was even for Liz. She, too, had a living ex-husband, so on May 26, 1991, we were married in the Methodist Church. The ceremony took place in the Roebuck Chapel of the First United Methodist Church in Fort Smith and was presided over by Reverend Joe Taylor. True, we have talked about getting an ecclesiastical annulment of Barbara's previous marriage so that we can be married in the Catholic Church, but I don't think it is as urgent with Barbara as it was with Liz. I think that she is quite satisfied that a Methodist marriage is binding.

Over the years, I have became quite involved in the activities of both churches. In the Methodist Church I was a member of the Board, a member of Methodist Men's Club and have served as Chairman of both the Race Relations Committee and the Memorials Committee. From the beginning, I have taught Sunday School classes on a substitute basis. My most meaningful activity, however, involved three years of services as a Stephen

Minister. This is a caring ministry in which trained church members provide long-term caring support for those in need. It provides more intensive support for the care receiver. It relieves the burden of the professional ministers. Most importantly, though, it offers the caregiver a channel for spiritual growth through love, compassion, and selflessness.

I didn't stint the Catholic Church, either. For three years I participated in the RCIA program, which meets for several months in the fall and spring of each year to introduce non-Catholics (especially spouses of Catholics) to the Church and its beliefs and rituals. I must have been one of the only Methodists who have ever helped teach Catholicism. Father Tom Marx introduced me each year as either a Cathodist or a Metholic. Truth to tell, as with the Steven Ministry, I got more out of the program than I gave.

Besides the Episcopal, Catholic, and Methodist Churches, I have also attended church in numerous other denominations and faiths. I have attended Bahá'í services. I have been to Jewish Temple. I have participated in services in numerous Christian denominations, including Christian, Presbyterian, Lutheran, Church of Christ, Assembly of God, Baptist, and numerous others. I found God in all of them. One thing that I never felt, though, was John Wesley's strange warming of the heart or any other sudden manifestation of salvation or conversion. For me, it has been a long and gradual process of spiritual growth. The end result is a very Methodist and yet very Catholic view point. I crave the freedom of thought inherent in Methodism and I equally value the dedication and concentration of worship which is inherent in the Catholic Church.

The bottom line is this amorphous thing called Salvation. Although I have never experienced a spiritual rebirth and cannot qualify as a "Born Again Christian," I don't feel unsaved. I like to think that I started life in a state of grace and have grown enough spiritually over the years to hang on. Yes, I have slipped on more than one occasion. My inner, spiritual self, however, has always provided me with the essential life line to regain safety. It is my conviction that one starts life connected to the Holy Spirit and this connection will remain intact throughout life unless severed by one's own actions. I also believe that it takes a lot of what some call sin to shake the Holy Spirit loose. It hangs on to us for dear life as long as there is any possibility of our salvation. In my case, though, probably like many others, I was never a saint, but I never strayed so far that I could not with confession, remorse, and a lot of prayer, regain the spiritual track. Indeed, I recently heard someone ask what had been the effects of life events upon one's faith. This made no sense to me at all until I reversed it to ask how my faith had affected my life. I am convinced that my life has, from the very beginning, been directly molded by my faith. For instance, I believe that faith can bring about miracles. I believe that through faith petitions will be answered and, if it harms no one else, requests will be granted. Also, I don't think this is a matter of predetermined spiritual value. The most trivial of requests will be considered by God, not just the biggies like life and death, healing, etc. I may never be "born again" because I believe that I am already one of God's children.

In addition to my strictly church related activities, I have also tried to extend my spiritual life out into the community. On Saturday mornings, I attend meetings of the Christian Business Men's Committee, which is a Christian group of businessmen dedicated to introducing Christ into the lives of other businessmen in the community. We sponsor periodic outreach luncheons and dinners, as well as putting on the annual Fort Smith Mayor's Prayer Breakfast. The latter has become an event of some status in this part of the state. On Saturday mornings, we pray together and study scripture together. As a result, we grow as we serve God in the community. I was honored to be elected chairman of the Saturday Morning Committee for the years 1993 and 1994. I don't expect to do better than my predecessors, but I hope to do as well.

In summary, I am not a proselytizing, Bible-thumping born-again-type Christian. But I want to live my life according to the teachings of Christ and I love the Lord with all my heart. I don't wear my religion on my sleeve. I suppose I will never aspire to sainthood. I would like, though, to be remembered as a good, socially aware, concerned person. I have learned that the more you give of yourself, the richer your life becomes without the necessity for ego enhancement or material acquisition, although God won't forget the latter if you will.

Being a good Christian makes sense, because it makes our life ever so much more bearable. It doesn't make the rough spots smoother, but it makes it easier to get over them. The only really rough spot I have had occasion to employ it on, though, was Liz' death. I think it helped.

Hopefully, my road ahead will remain reasonably straight and even, but if rough terrain lies ahead, I at least have a staff to lean on. It is rather comforting to feel that even when you are by yourself, you are not alone and uncared for.

This leads me to my very amateurish view of God. It is apparent to me that God is either infinite, omniscient, and omnipotent, or he is finite, compassionate, loving, and even super powerful, but not all powerful or all knowing. On the surface, I would prefer the former. However, it leads to a view of a God who may care for us but doesn't really need us or need to interact with us. The other type God would be one who is still growing and expanding. Although he has knowledge and power beyond human comprehension, he still needs us humans as a contact with the physical universe in order to affect it and learn from it. This would, of course, presuppose a very close relationship between God and man and our inter-dependence. It would explain why sin and evil can exist and why good and beauty can often come out of failure and disaster. It can perhaps even explain why we are so seldom allowed to rest on our laurels. God must be a God of change. Since only through change and experimentation and the knowledge and experience gained therefrom and through us as his instrumentalities can God grow and strive toward ultimate dominion over the universe.

Then, how does Jesus fit into all this? I suggest that there are only two logical views. Jesus is, as the Muslims and many Jews contend, a holy man or even prophet. On the other hand, there is the view to which I personally subscribe that Jesus is the Christ, God as human, who is the portal to salvation (whatever that is) through his sacrifice of himself to atone for our sins. Ironically, forgiveness may be of little importance to God. He may love us enough that forgiveness becomes irrelevant. It is, however, important to us. We have an infinite capacity for guilt and self-flagellation. These are disruptive to positive action. Thus, even if God doesn't need to forgive, we need it from him in order to free us for constructive thought. It has been rightly said that if Jesus had never existed, we would have had to invent him. Without any doubt, he was the key which unlocked human potential, at least for the Gentiles.

There is no solid evidence other than human experience upon which to choose between treating Jesus as God or man. I can see that my choice is purely subjective, based entirely upon emotion, and, I hope, the promptings of the Holy Spirit. When all is said and done, however, it makes no real difference whether one believes that Jesus was the Christ or prophet. What counts are his teachings. For the first time in human history, Jesus articulated a moral code designed to permit a new social compact based on love, truth, and decency. I suggest that a conviction that Jesus was also God incarnate enhances the credibility of his doctrine. And for that reason, provides greater impetus to its implementation than would a view of him as merely mortal.

So, the answer to Jesus' role is that he can either occupy the center of our focus, or he can be at some remove from the center as merely a force for good. I submit that he cannot be totally ignored in view of his historical impact. I prefer to place him at the core of my faith, but this is simply my choice. Whether I believe that he is God or not changes nothing, except perhaps for my own intensity of dedication. I do, however, believe that faith in Jesus as the Christ can provide the focus necessary for spiritual growth. I do not say that he is the only door to salvation, but I do believe that he is a major one.

The foregoing does not preclude a life after death or the ultimate triumph of good over evil. It only helps to explain what they are and why they are. I would hypothesize that man is a physical creature hosting a spiritual essence (call it the soul) which is a part of the God entity sent by it as an emissary to interact with the physical world. At death, this spiritual essence returns to the God plane. If it has reached maturity, it can re-unite with the God head, thus enhancing God. If it is a young soul or has not achieved maturity, it can, after reflection or perhaps debriefing, return to the physical plane. This is how I see and why I believe in reincarnation. I hope it exists, because I don't believe that my soul is anywhere near maturity yet.

I can see that the theology which I have so blithely spouted is probably laughingly naive and even more probably way off the mark. Still, I'll bet that there are some seeds of truth in it. I don't think any human is capable of comprehending the big truths, but I think that each of us is capable of seeing part of the truth, and these glimpses of glory are what motivate us to hope, to have faith, and to keep trying.

The bottom line is that the spiritual approach makes me feel better. One thing that I have learned, though: You can't grow spiritually without conscious effort on your part. Professing to be a Christian or a Jew or a Moslem or whatever is not enough. You have to actively seek and participate. One can go to church, serve on committees, sing in the choir, teach Sunday School classes, read the Bible, take part in Bible study classes, in fact do anything that searches out spiritual truths and directs the awareness outward and away from the inner I. This isn't guaranteed to work, but it is more likely to work than remaining passive and expecting God to come looking for you. At least this is what seems to have worked for me.

I don't know how much I have grown over the years, but I do know that I feel that I am more whole and have it more together now than I did a year ago or five years ago or ten years ago and certainly more than I did twenty years ago. I offer my ideas not as a guide to anyone, but merely as the observations of an amateur religious.

Chapter 33

Life and Death

It is presumptuous for me to start pontificating on the unanswerable questions of life and death. To some degree or another, though, everyone has an opinion. The degree to which they come to terms with the answers as they perceive them, has, I believe, a significant bearing upon the degree to which they find tranquillity or even happiness during their lifetime. In this respect, one's view of the ultimate plays a vital role in determining outlook and perspective. I do not ask that you buy into my construct. I only ask that you respect it and read it so that you can understand better where I come from.

With the foregoing in mind, I will try to briefly state my views on life and death and their ramifications. First, I think I have to deal with death before I can deal with life.

I firmly believe in the concept of reincarnation. Admittedly, my evidence for this is skimpy. I refer to the church convocation back about the fifth century which established many of the theological precepts of modem Christianity. Interestingly, it did not reject reincarnation, although it did not embrace it enthusiastically. I also understand that Jewish theology makes room for reincarnation interspersed between periods of forgetfulness when the facts of prior lives are erased. Then there is the evidence of hypnotic regressions, two of which I have observed. Finally, in a taro card reading which was done for me at a psychic fair in Phoenix about 1982 or 1983, past lives were emphatically and in some cases vividly described. True, this is not empirical evidence, but then it is a subject which cannot be proved scientifically. I find it reassuring, though, and with no good reason to reject it, I choose to believe it.

The alternative is that death is the final end. In that case, there is really noting to fear except the end of life and awareness.

Then, there is the belief that once a person dies he crosses over into the spirit world where he spends the rest of eternity. I find this view depressing since it means that there is no opportunity to correct one's mistakes. With reincarnation, one, at least, has the opportunity to correct mistakes, balancing one's karma so to speak.

Reincarnation also implies a process of spiritual growth which suggests that repeated reincarnations are a tool by which the individual develops. I like to think that this means growth into the kind of person which one is capable of being. When this spiritual state is achieved, it would probably no longer be necessary to be reincarnated. Perhaps this suggests a pure state of grace or inclusion in the circle of saints. Whatever, it does strongly imply eventual merger with God. Whether this is a joining with God of an independently evolved consciousness or is an enhancement of God by the re-incorporation of spiritual essences which sprang from God in the first place, it makes no real difference. The former, of course, suggests the concept of an infinite God while the latter suggests a finite, evolving God. In either event, though, I accept that God is so much wiser, more powerful, and superior to me and to anything I know that it makes Him\Her\It essentially incomprehensible.

Whether one is reincarnated or his essence springs into being at conception, what is its purpose or does it have a purpose? In other words, what is the purpose of life? I believe that it has a two-fold purpose.

First, I believe that it is a means by which God embodies the spirit in the physical universe to gain knowledge and experience which is of value both to the individual and to the God-force. Second, I believe that it is a renewable opportunity for the individual to achieve the spiritual growth noted above. I do know, from my own experience, that life can be a growing process. I have grown spiritually. Of this, I am absolutely certain. I have done more spiritual growing in the past five or six years than in the previous fifty, and the more I grow, the faster I grow. It doesn't mean that I have achieved any degree of spiritual stature. It may only mean that I had a long way to go to start with. Still I feel spiritually stronger and closer in awareness to an understanding of God than I did when I was younger. Primarily this is manifest as simply being more comfortable with spiritual awareness. This then is what I believe life is designed to accomplish.

The question then arises, do I fear death? Yes and no. Yes, I have twinges of anxiety when I think of dying, especially of ceasing to breathe and my heart stopping. I don't fear the intellectual transition. I do fear the physical. I think one of the reasons I fear it is because of my slight tendency towards claustrophobia. Somehow I seem to equate dying with being confined in a smaller and smaller space and losing contact with the reality around me. Intellectually, though, I believe that once the physical barrier is passed, I will have an even greater awareness of the universality of existence. I do believe that it is a fear which I can handle. Then, too, there is the accompanying confidence that I will have a chance while on the spirit plane to sort through my life experiences and make those karmic adjustments which may be indicated.

I also look forward to the opportunity of meeting with those who have gone before. I have friends and relatives whom I would like to see again. I believe in the words of Jesus in the Bible that we are not married in Heaven. Therefore, I don't anticipate resumption of any kind of permanent housekeeping relationship with Liz or anyone else. Still, I sincerely hope that there is an opportunity to see and communicate with those who precede me.

I also hope that I will be able to get past the immediate problem of continuing to be bound by my past life and move on into a more purely spiritual element. I was deeply impressed upon reading about some of the Buddhist views of death and its relationship to light. I practice constantly, in a form of meditation, to make myself withdraw from physical ties and face the light. I do this particularly when kneeling during Communion in the Catholic Church. Since I don't go down to Communion, it gives me an extra allotment of time to meditate. The more I meditate, the brighter the light becomes and the harder it becomes to face it. Maybe this is what the Quakers refer to as the sea of light. If I can maintain this perception after death, it might be that I will have a shorter road or a swifter passage from physical attachment to spiritual awareness. I hope so.

Finally, there is the question of the continuing relationship between the living and the dead. I believe that such a relationship does continue. Like most people, though, I suspect that those who have passed on have a clearer awareness of the living than the other way around. I think they can hear us, see us, and help us. I see nothing wrong with talking problems over with them and asking their guidance. It is only courtesy to recognize them upon occasion and say hello when you feel them close. On the other hand, it is a disservice to them to create a myth around their memory and put them in a shrine on a pedestal. Let them go. Remain friends, but respect their freedom.

I was much taken with a passage which was quoted, without attribution of authorship, in a novel which I recently read entitled "September," by Rosamunde Pilcher, published by St. Martin's Press, 1990.

"Death is nothing at all. It does not count. I have only slipped away into the next room. Nothing has happened. Everything remains exactly as it was. I am I, and you are you, and the old life that we lived so fondly together is untouched, unchanged. Whatever we were to each other, that we are still. Call me by the old familiar name. Speak of me in the easy way which you always used. Put no difference in your tone. Wear no forced air of solemnity or sorrow. Laugh as we always laughed at the little jokes that we enjoyed together. Play, smile, think of me, pray for me. Let my name be ever the household word that it always was. Let it be spoken without an effort, without the ghost of a shadow upon it. Life means all that it ever meant. It is the same as it ever was. There is absolute and unbroken continuity. What is this death but a negligible accident? Why should I be out of mind because I am out of sight? I am but waiting for you, for an interval, somewhere very near, just 'round the corner. All is well."

I do not subscribe to the foregoing in every respect, but I do think it contains a lot of truth. At the very least, it sets the right tone. It is helpful in giving us a proper perspective on the relationship between the here and there.

What I am trying to say is that I do not fear death. Rather, I welcome it, but no less than I welcome life. Both have their purpose and both are valuable. Indeed, one cannot exist without the other. In the same vein, whether or not you subscribe to my views, I ask you not to fear my death or grieve for me when I am gone. Remember that you grieve for yourself, not for me. If death is the end, I will be already be beyond it all. If there is a life after death, I will have begun a new adventure.

Do not to let the event of my death and memorial service create a depressive reaction. Be joyful. If one is a good Christian, or Jew, or for that matter religious in any sense, death is not to be feared but something in which to rejoice. Rejoice with me. I will, if it is at all possible, remain aware of those I leave behind and offer whatever assistance I can, even if it is just a nudge now and then. I will not haunt and I will not follow anyone around to spy. Your lives are yours and mine is mine. Our lives are inextricably entwined, however. If I die before you, I will be there to greet you when you come across. I will be upset, though, if you allow my death to scar you mentally or emotionally or if you erect some sort of mental or physical shrine in my memory. I am not the material of myth or legend. Let me remain what I am, an ordinary human being.

Of course, I will also be cross if you don't miss me just a little. Try to miss me fondly, though. Those mistakes which I made, I ask you to forgive and try to forget. After all, I will be having to deal with them on the other side or in future lives as it is. Don't let resentment or regret mar our relationship after I am gone and can do nothing about it. Just remember that I love you all deeply and will be missing you as much as you miss me. But the separation is only momentary in terms of the passage of eternity. In other words, I will see you before you know it, and hopefully I will have learned enough to give you a hand adjusting to the next stage in your life process. Go with God and go with joy.

Chapter 34

Relatively Speaking

My purpose in this book was to describe in as straightforward a manner as possible the history of the Duty family up to the time of my birth and then a summary of my life. While I feel reasonably competent to relate the history of the family and to describe the events of my own life, I am not in a particularly good position to describe any other branch of the family. On the other hand, the story which I have tried to tell would not be complete without mentioning family members outside my direct line and each of them possess stories of their own. These stories have no direct bearing upon the information which I have tried to impart, but they do cast some light upon it and provide an expanded background upon which the main events can be seen more clearly. I have, therefore, decided to include brief sketches of the more immediate branches, listed in alphabetical order. I have not researched these areas as closely as I have the facts of my own story. Thus, information I relate may not be quite as accurate. Still, it is an aspect of the story which should be reported. To enhance both accuracy and detail, I submitted the material to each of the concerned branches, who provided additions, corrections, and comments. Accordingly, I exit stage, and surrender the rest of the narrative to others.

Babe Duty and Carolyn

The Banks Family

My sister Carolyn Beth Duty was born on May 11, 1932. She was the second, but first surviving, child of Lois and Jeff Duty. Her early years were spent in Rogers, Arkansas. Except for a year and a half when she attended St. Mary's Catholic Girls' Academy in Little Rock in the third and fourth grades, she attended Central Ward Grade School and then Rogers High School through the ninth grade.

At the end of Carolyn's ninth grade year, the family moved to Little Rock so that Jeff could take up an appointment as Assistant State Attorney General. There, Carolyn enrolled in Little Rock Central High School, from which she graduated in 1950.

After high school, Carolyn attended the University of Arkansas, where following in the footsteps of her

8A • ARKANSAS GAZETTE, Tuesday, Jan. 13, 1953.

Women's + Society ...NEWS

—Photo by Fleeta Wood Mitchell.
Mrs. Warren Eugene Banks Jr.
The marriage of Miss Carolyn Beth Duty and Warren Eugene Banks Jr. was solemnized December 27 in the Prayer Chapel of the Central Methodist Church of Fayetteville. She is the daughter of Mr. and Mrs. Jeff Duty of Fayetteville. The bridegroom is the son of the late Mr. and Mrs. W. E. Banks of Hot Springs.

mother and her Aunt Mary she became a member of Delta Delta Delta sorority and was elected to Phi Beta Kappa. After an interruption to get married and raise a family, she earned a Bachelor of Arts Degree in political science. Receiving a Ford Foundation grant, she did graduate work in

history at Kenyon College in Ohio and at the University of Arkansas. All the course work for a Master's Degree was completed when the University decided to cancel the program and the degree was never awarded. She then transferred to the College of Education, where she did two years' postgraduate work to obtain teacher's certification.

Midway in her junior year in

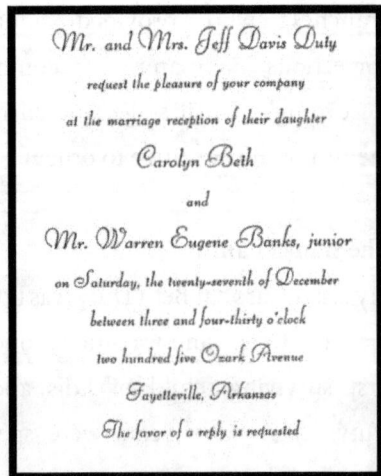

Mr. and Mrs. Jeff Davis Duty

request the pleasure of your company

at the marriage reception of their daughter

Carolyn Beth

and

Mr. Warren Eugene Banks, junior

on Saturday, the twenty-seventh of December

between three and four-thirty o'clock

two hundred five Ozark Avenue

Fayetteville, Arkansas

The favor of a reply is requested

college in 1952, Carolyn married Warren Eugene Banks of Hot Springs. She met Gene when, with two fellow law students, he rented an apartment from her family, which was located over an old garage behind their home in Fayetteville. It was a stately, southern-style house, located on Fairview Drive where the UofA College of Business now stands. Carolyn first dated one of the other boys in the apartment, but eventually began seeing more and more of Gene until they finally became engaged. They were married in the chapel of the Central Methodist Church in Fayetteville on December 27, 1952. Her brother Davis was honored to be Gene's best man.

Grandmother Lois Duty with Karen and Keith Banks

Following their marriage, Gene graduated from law school, where he was an honor student and editor of the Law Review. He also received an ROTC commission and upon completing college entered the Air Force Judge Advocate General Corps. After completing his tour of active service, he returned to civilian life, but remained in the Active Reserves, eventually achieving the rank of Colonel.

While the couple were stationed at Selfridge Air Force Base in Michigan, Carolyn gave birth to her first child, Karen Marie Banks, on June 14, 1954. On September 5, 1958, she was delivered of a son, Keith Randolph Banks. Both were beautiful, intelligent, and exceptional children.

Upon leaving full time active duty, Gene enrolled at Georgetown University and took a job with the General Accounting Office in Washington, DC. After completing two Master's Degrees and a PhD, he returned to Fayetteville to teach at both the Business and Law Schools of the University of Arkansas. He rose to the rank of Distinguished Professor and

Chairholder and was Head of the Department of Finance in the School of Business, as well as holding the rank of Professor of Law in the Law School. Simultaneously, he was counsel to the prestigious law firm of Kincaid, Home & Trumbo, where he became well known as an expert in taxation and estate planning. He had approximately 100 articles published in the field and was a nationally known consultant.

It was during this period that Carolyn returned to college and obtained her degree. Afterward, she taught in the Fayetteville public schools for a number of years, as well as working on the University staff for several years. She became an active member of the Daughters of the American Revolution and St Paul's Episcopal Church in Fayetteville. For many years, she did extensive travel and counseling for the Anglican Franciscan Order.

Daughter Karen attended the University of Arkansas and joined the Navy, where she served as a Navy nurse. After returning to civilian life, she went back to the University and earned a Bachelor's Degree in Communications and a Master's Degree in Education, as well as completing a degree in Nursing. At the time of this writing, she is employed as a nurse by the Springdale Memorial Hospital in Springdale, Arkansas.

Son Keith proved to be both a joy and a tragedy. He was the All American boy, active in the church, lettering in football, becoming an avid body builder and scoring at the top of his class in chemical engineering at the University of Arkansas. He found time to indulge in rock climbing and to serve as Rush Chairman for his fraternity, Pi Kappa Alpha. He was to enter medical school in September, 1980. Just before graduation in spring 1980, however, he died by gunshot wounds under extraordinarily mysterious circumstances. The unresolved facts of his death, as well as its untimeliness, continue to this day to cast a shadow over the lives of the rest of his family.

Keith Banks

Soon after Keith's death, Gene was

diagnosed with cancer. He survived for seven years, undergoing repeated major surgery and extensive chemotherapy, despite which he continued to write, teach, and practice law until his death on August 18, 1987. In 1990, the University Board of Trustees paid him a singular honor by conferring on him the posthumous rank of Distinguished University Professor, the highest honor that can be paid to a faculty member.

Carolyn continues to live in the family home at 1109 Sunset Drive, Fayetteville, Arkansas. In 1993, she also was honored by the University Board of Trustees, being designated to Emeritus ranking.

**Davis, Lois, Carolyn, and Gene at
Davis' home in Phoenix, 1984**

-4-

This Memorial Resolution was unanimously adopted by the Washington County Bar Association on August 24, 1988.

By order of the undersigned for their respective Courts, on August 24, 1988, the foregoing Resolution is accepted, approved and ordered to be spread of record upon the records of these Courts.

THOMAS M. [illegible]

JOHN [illegible]

MAHLON G. GIBSON

KIM M. SMITH

The Collins Family

Ollie Collins, although not actually of the Duty line, has for as long as I can remember been the touchstone of the Duty family honor and tradition. She has defended the name fiercely, and the love and support which she has given unstintingly to four generations of Dutys has at least earned her the right to honorary family membership. Of course, this is not to say that she is unrelated. Indeed, she is a cousin at some remove.

Ollie's great grandparents were Butler and Eliza Margaret Dotson Bond, who were the parents of Ollie's grandmother Evelyn Bond Collins, born in 1849 in Tyler County, Virginia. She was the younger sister of my great-grandmother Helen Bond Duty. Evelyn's son Alph married Jettie Gains. The couple had three children: Ollie, her brother Francis, and her sister Bessie.

Ollie was born in West Union, West Virginia, on January 25, 1904. In 1922, she and her parents moved to Rogers, Arkansas, no small incentive being the proximity of her paternal great-aunt Helen (Mammy) Duty. Among the many coincidences which have since entwined Ollie's life with my family was that the house in which the Collinses lived during those early years in Rogers was later purchased by my maternal grandparents, Nonnie and Granddaddy White. They made it their home from the time they moved into town soon after World War II until Nonny's death in 1974. The world is small indeed.

Immediately upon settling in Rogers, Ollie went to work as a legal secretary for the law firm of Duty & Duty, in which capacity she continued until 1933. Over the years, Ollie applied herself to the law, under the tutelage of my grandfather John R. Duty. By still another coincidence, she took her Arkansas Bar exam at the same time as my father Jeff in June, 1930. Both of them passed. Ollie remained with Duty & Duty until she at last felt ready to fly the nest. When she did finally decide to do it, though, she did it in style, going to Washington, DC, where she obtained a legal position with the Public Works Administration. She remained there for six years before moving to the Justice Department, where she served as an attorney in the

Civil Division until she retired in 1976. Since then, she has lived in retirement in her beloved Washington, where she can keep an eye on the Government, while continuing to monitor Duty family doings around the country.

It is no exaggeration to say that Ollie has served as the mentor for one Duty after another. She helped my Uncle Ralph get settled in Washington while he was in the process of getting a job with the Treasury Department. She help smooth the way for my sister Carolyn and her husband Gene Banks when they moved to Washington, where Gene worked for some years for the General Accounting Office. Ollie played a key role in helping me to get settled in Washington when I moved there following law school in 1959. In fact, it was directly due to her good offices that I found employment with the Justice Department. I have often wondered how many IOUs she called in for that one. Still later, she was there, ready with advice and support for my son John when he was awarded internships with Representative John Hammerschmidt and Senator David Pryor. In like manner, she was there for my niece Laura Duty during her internships with Arkansas' Senior Senator, Dale Bumpers, and Representative John Hammerschmidt. I can only summarize by saying that never have so many Dutys owed so much to one dear lady.

Today, Ollie at ninety years of age, although frail in body, exudes the same razor-sharp intellect, common sense, humor, and indomitable will which have ever been her hallmark. I best remember her, however, during those years when I was in Washington, always encouraging and always supportive. Then, at the height of her powers, she was a slim, elegant, stylish figure, whom I will always picture in her magnificent mink coat, charming all those about her with her wit and grace. A dinner party at Ollie's apartment was always a memorable occasion. I believe I speak for the Dutys over the years in expressing our gratitude and love for our dear cousin Ollie.

The Davis Family

Lois' sister Eleanor left the family nest to move to California and establish another branch of the family. First, though, she attended teachers college in Manhattan, Kansas. Then, Sunday, October 20, 1929, she married Zelbert Davis of San Francisco, where the couple made their home. Zelbert was a respected photographer and exterior decorator, providing decorating for buildings and parades. Eleanor became known in the community for her many good works.

Zelbert Davis, 1915

Eleanor and Zelbert produced three children: Patricia, Rheem, and Elden. Zelbert died about 1955. Eleanor passed away about 1958.

Patricia lives in Belmont, California, where she has worked for many years in the elections department of San Mateo County. She and her ex-husband Bill Flaherty have two children, Danny and Kelli. Kelli married to David Grey and now resides in Boston, Massachusetts. They have two children, Zachery and Kevin. Danny and his wife Debbie live in Hayward, California, and they have one daughter, Katie. Danny works as a supervisor for a freight line.

Eleanor Beatryce White Davis

Above: Eleanor White Davis (age 8)
wearing an Indian costume
Right: Her daughter Patsy Ann Davis
(age 12) wearing the same costume

Mr. and Mrs. Will J. White

announce the marriage of their daughter

Eleanor Beatryce

to

Mr. Zelbert Louis Davis

Sunday, October the twentieth

one thousand nine hundred and twenty-nine

Ely, Nevada

at home
after November 15
1119 Market St.
San Francisco, Calif.

Zelbert Davis with his
parents and brother

Rheem has had a colourful 30 year career with the Pacific Gas and Electric Company. He retired in 1992. He currently lives in Scottsdale, Arizona, where he married Dr. Pamela George on February 13, 1994. She is a child psychologist in practice in Phoenix. Rheem and his first wife Rosie have two children. They are Scott, who lives in San Francisco and just graduated with a degree in graphic arts, and Jimmy, who is attending college of San Mateo and studying movie film production.

After an early triumph in amateur golf, Elden turned to a career in insurance, in which he has been eminently successful. Currently, he owns and is the president of his own company, providing health insurance for pets, primarily in Arizona. Elden and his wife Carolyn (called Kelly) have two children, Troy and Lance. Troy works in the carpet business. He and his wife Marie have four children: Steven, Tania, Blake, and BJ and live in Phoenix. Lance is attending college and studying restaurant and hotel management. He and his wife Jody also live in Phoenix.

The Elden Davis Family

Carolyn, Davis, Elden, Rheem, and Nonny at her 100th birthday

The Dean Family

The story begins with Helen (Mammy) Bond and Andrew (Pappy) Duty of Doddridge County, West Virginia. They were married in 1878 and had two sons, John Randolph and Cla ude Joseph. About 1890, they moved to Marietta, Ohio, where they adopted a daughter, Laura Blake. In 1900, they began a classic covered wagon migration westward, eventually settling in Benton County, Arkansas. At first, they lived on and operated a family farm near the town of Garfield, which is located a few miles south of the Missouri line.

Jeff Duty and his Aunt Laura Blake
(the pig's name is not known)

Mammy's and Pappy's sons John and Claude later moved to Rogers, where they became attorneys. Their daughter Laura married Walter Dean of Avoca who served for many years as the Chief of Police of Rogers. They had two children, Mary and Lee Andrew. Laura died in 1927 while her children were still young and Lee was raised for all intents and purposes along with Jeff, Ralph, Charlie, Ireland, and Baby John (Babe) as one of the sons of his Uncle John R. and his wife Rella. Mary Dean later wed Andrew Dumas, a career serviceman. After retirement, they resided in Colorado until Mary's death about March, 1991, and Andrew's death in the fall of 1992. Andrew and Mary are survived by two sons: David, who lives in Cottonwood, Arizona, and Lee, who lives in Albuquerque, New Mexico.

Lee attended medical school. After receiving his MD, he enlisted in the United States Navy, where he served as a medical officer, including extensive tours at sea, until the end of World War II. After the war, he returned to Rogers to establish a medical practice. At the outset, he joined forces with Dr. Guy Hodges, the town's venerable old family doctor, who incidentally had earlier presided at the births of Jeff Duty's children, Carolyn, Davis, and John. (How the treads do interweave!) Later, Lee set up an independent practice in which he continued for many years, becoming one of the community's most prominent physicians in his own right. In his middle years, he closed his practice and resumed medical studies to become a psychiatrist. Upon qualification, he moved to Pine Bluff, Arkansas, where he devoted still more years to treating the mentally ill through the state mental health system. He died in retirement in Rogers in November, 1986. He is survived by his widow, the former Mary Jane O'Brien, and five children: Marilyn, Lee Ann, Virginia, Helen, and Christopher.

Mary Jane lives with three pet horses on an acreage outside of Rogers. She leads an active life, which includes selling real estate and keeping up with her grandchildren.

Marilyn married Richard Lanford and has three children, Allison, Patrick, and Andrew. Allison married Bruce Schratz and has two children, Caroline and Conner. They live in Memphis, Tennessee. Marilyn's husband passed away in April of 1988, and she now makes her home in Rogers, Arkansas, where she has a successful real estate business.

Lee Ann married Frank Ward and has two children: Frank III and Paige. Paige married John Alan Smith and they live in Vero Beach, Florida. Lee Ann, Frank, and Frank III live in Ft. Pierce, Florida.

Virginia (Ginger) married R. David Scruggs of Little Rock where they make their home. They have three children: Nicole (Coco) and Bradford, who are twins, and R. David Scruggs, Jr. It should be noted that Ginger's son R. David Scruggs, Jr., married Ellen Phillips, who is the daughter of Liz Phillips who, in turn, is the daughter of Mary Melton, sister of Lois Duty. Thus is the family bond further cemented. David and Ellen have a very new son named R. David III. Daughter Helen Jane lives in Rogers, and teaches special education in Pea Ridge. Son Christopher makes his home with his mother in Rogers.

The Charlie Duty Family

Charlie Ross Duty, the second son of John R. and Rella Duty, was born in Mountain View, Arkansas, on February 16, 1908. His name was taken from a current sensational newspaper story about a young child, Charlie Ross, who had been kidnapped. Charlie graduated from Rogers High School and later attended diesel mechanics school in Chicago. He led a carefree and adventurous life, traveling about the country and the world. For a number of years he worked on oil pipeline construction jobs in the Middle East.

Lois Duty and brother-in-law Charlie Duty

Charlie married Lucy Daily of Bentonville and became the step-father of her son by a prior marriage, Tommy Emmanuel. Lucy, a beautiful

Lucy Daily Duty

and talented musician, suffered poor health for many years and died young at the age of 46 in 1952. Charlie later married Hattie Mason. This marriage ended in divorce some years later. In his latter years, Charlie moved back to Rogers and took up residence in a small house deep in the country. There, he lived a secluded life with his dogs and nature. He died on September 14, 1972.

Tommy Emmanuel married Phyllis Patterson of Rogers. The couple make their home in Las Cruces, New Mexico, where Tommy works as a game warden for the White Sands Proving Grounds. They have three children: Keith, Tommy, and Brent. All are married.

The Ireland Duty Family

Ireland was the third son of John R. and Rella Duty. Born on December 29, 1909, he graduated from Rogers High School and qualified as a Certified Public Accountant. He enjoyed a full career as an accountant for the Air Force.

In his youth, Ireland married Rose Marie Herndon of Rogers. They had one child, James Ray. Ireland and Rose Marie were divorced and Ireland

Left-right: Jeff, Lois, Davis, Liz, Thelma, Ireland, and Cinder

later married Thelma Gelzer of Chicago. After retirement, Thelma and Ireland made their home in Sun City, Arizona, just outside of Phoenix. Ireland died in Sun City on March 13, 1985. Thelma died April 23, 1989.

James Ray (Jimmy) Duty is married and lives in Plainview, Texas. He has been active for many years in directing and counseling in drug rehabilitation programs.

John Ellis Duty

John Ellis Duty was born in Rogers, Arkansas, to Mary and Davis Duty on October 4, 1967. Like Diana, his early years were spent in Rogers, where he attended Westside and Eastside Elementary Schools. In 1976, he moved with his sister to Phoenix to take up residence with their father.

In Phoenix, John enjoyed a very busy and successful adolescence, earning the rank of Eagle Scout six months before reaching the minimum required age of 13, playing the trumpet in his junior high band and the bugle for his Scout troop. In fact, he was the bugler for the Arizona troop at the National Scout Jamboree, held in Fredericksburg in 1981. He was also very adept at baseball and played for the Little League All-Star team. Later, he lettered in baseball in high school.

John enjoyed a well-rounded high school career, involving sports, membership and presidency of the German Club, and induction into the National Honor Society. In his junior year, he was chosen to participate in the Hugh O'Brian Foundation. His efforts culminated in being awarded both a Flynn Foundation scholarship and a Regents scholarship to attend college. He graduated third in his class out of many hundreds.

John attended the University of Arizona in Tucson. Not only did he maintain a 3.5 grade point average over four years, but he also found time to join the Sigma Alpha Epsilon fraternity and was selected for membership in both the prestigious Bobcats and Arizona Allegiance. The Bobcats (known as the Bobcat 13) is a highly exclusive senior honorary society. Only 13 students are inducted each year. The Arizona Allegiance is a student group which functions as a liaison between the Athletic Department and the Student Body. John graduated in May, 1990, with a degree in Political Science. Probably the accomplishment which would have the most permanent effect on John's live in college was his meeting Melissa (Missy) Berkowitz. This occurred during John's junior year, and from that day on there were no other girls in his life.

Returning to Arkansas, John enrolled in the University of Arkansas School of Law for the fall term in 1990. After one year of law school, however, John made the difficult decision that the law was not for him. He thereupon moved to Miami, where Missy lived and soon found temporary employment as a copy reader for an advertising agency. During the course of the next year, John made two major decisions. He and Missy became engaged in December, 1992, and soon thereafter, he applied for admission to the prestigious graduate program in Public Relations at Northwestern University in Evanston, Illinois. He was one of only 25 successful candidates chosen from thousands. So, by the time he had seen his sister Diana married in May, 1993, John was making final preparations to enroll at Northwestern in September and marry Missy in December. With the former, he settled into a year and a half program, which would lead to an MBS (Master of

Business Science) in Integrated Marketing.

On December 18, 1993, in Miami, Florida, John and Missy were united in marriage in a sumptuous wedding. Immediately following the reception, they left for a honeymoon in Aruba. After a week of fun and sun, they returned to Miami and began the long trek north to Evanston. As of this writing, they are well settled into matrimonial bliss. Missy has returned to work as a sales representative for men's formal wear lines, and John is well on his way to his own career in public relations. Not only has he maintained an outstanding high grade average, but he has already to serve as Assistant Editor to the program's national newsletter. John's and Missy's future beckons brightly in the near distance.

The John White Duty Family

John White Duty was born on November 10, 1938, in Rogers, Arkansas, the youngest child of Lois and Jeff Duty and the brother of Carolyn Duty Banks and Davis Duty. He began his schooling at Central Ward Grade School in Rogers. When his father Jeff became Assistant State Attorney General in 1948, the family moved to little Rock, where John attended the Centennial Primary School. While at Centennial, John made his mark as center fielder for the Centennial Wolves baseball team.

When the family moved to Fayetteville, John attended the Fayetteville schools through the tenth grade. His primary interest at this stage in his life was athletics. At Fayetteville High School, he earned the position of second string quarterback on the football team. At the end of his sophomore year, the family moved back to Rogers. He intended to continue his football career, but suffered a separated shoulder which spelled the end of that ambition. He then went out for basketball and as a senior he played on the Rogers State Championship contender basketball team of 1955-56.

After graduating from high school, John attended the University of Arkansas where he earned a Bachelor of Arts Degree in Business Administration. On January 23, 1959, he married Susan Jane Dubbell of Rogers. After graduating from college in 1961, John went to work in the credit department of the Ralston Purina Company. Finding this line of work unpalatable, and having always had an interest in military affairs, John volunteered to serve in the United States Air Force in 1964 and qualified for Officer's Candidate School. He received his commission as a Second Lieutenant and was sent for navigator training. After completion of this course, he was assigned to the Strategic Air Command, where he served for eight years. Most of his service was during the Vietnam War and involved navigating KC-135 tanker aircraft. After flying over 100 combat missions during the war in Vietnam, John transferred to the Tactical Air Command, where he was assigned to navigate C-130 aircraft.

During his term in TAC, John frequently found himself flying resupply missions into firebases in the jungles of Vietnam. On one occasion, late in the afternoon and conditions being unsafe for takeoff, the crew was forced to spend the night in the base's bunkers. Whiling away the hours in forced idleness, John picked up a copy of the Armed Forces Stars and Stripes newspaper. To his astonishment, on the front page was a picture of his brother Davis with his guide dog Shane descending the front steps of the Supreme Court Building in Washington. It was the occasion of Davis' admission to practice before the High Court. John commented later that it was a frustrating world where a man could join the Air Force and remove himself by 5,000 miles to escape his brother, only to run into him in the jungles of Vietnam. Apparently, the world is really nothing more than a neighborhood after all.

Following 250 combat missions over Vietnam, John was returned to stateside duty where he was assigned as a development navigator on the AWACS (Airborne Warning and Command Systems) project being conducted by the Boeing Aircraft Company in Seattle, Washington. This assignment lasted four years, after which he served a tour of duty at Tinker Air Force Base in Oklahoma. Then in 1979, he was assigned as a United States Liaison Officer with NATO in Mons, Belgium. Completing this tour,

John White Duty after completing 100 combat missions in Vietnam (1969)

he returned to the United States where he finished out his career at Sheppard Air Force Base, at Wichita Falls, Texas, ultimately achieving the rank of Lieutenant Colonel. John retired from the Air Force in 1985.

Following retirement from the military, John tried his hand at several retirement careers, including mortgage banking, real estate sales, and restaurant management. In 1989, he moved from Wichita Falls back to Rogers, where he established a franchise of the Golden Fried Chicken restaurant chain. He continues in this business at the time of this writing, with increasing success.

John's and Susan's four children are spread out across the land. Steven and his wife Kim live in Washington, DC, where he has a position in hotel corporate sales, employing his degree in hotel and restaurant management. Stuart attended Occidental College and later earned an MBA degree from Harvard. He and his wife Mary (called Amy) live in San Francisco, where he is a vice-president with an investment banking company.

The 1989 John White Duty family
(left-right): Lisa, Susan, John, Laura,
Steven, Stuart

The 1993 John White Duty family
(top left-right): John Vargas, John,
Stuart, Steven; (bottom left-right): Lisa,
Matthew, Susan, Laura, and Kim

After graduating with a degree in interior design, daughter Lisa married John Vargas, a computer engineer. They make their home with their sons Matthew and Scott (Jeff's and Lois's first great-grandchildren) in Colorado Springs, Colorado.

Daughter Laura is nearing completion of her undergraduate work at Indiana University of Pennsylvania (IUP). In the summer of 1990, she served an internship with Arkansas' Senior Senator, Dale Bumpers, and Representative John Hammerschmidt in Washington, DC. She will be taking a degree in Social Psychology in December, 1994.

The Ralph Duty Family

John R. and Rella Duty's fourth son Ralph Wendell Duty was born in November of 1913. He graduated from Rogers High School and attended the University of Arkansas, where he received his law degree. He married Jo Bramer of Rogers and had two children: Jolinn and Mike.

Ralph served as a lieutenant in the Second Marine Division in World War II and participated in the landings on Sai Pan and Tarawa. After the war, he became a special agent for the Federal Alcohol Tobacco and Firearms Division of the Treasury Department. He was a real-live T-Man.

After leaving Government service, Ralph practiced law for a time in Rogers. Jo passed away in October, 1958. Around 1966, Ralph moved to

Ralph Duty, 1928

Ralph Duty, 1968

Clovis, New Mexico, where he later married Lucille (last name unknown). He qualified to practice law in New Mexico, and established a successful practice in Clovis. In 1967, he was elected to the post of Municipal Judge and served in this capacity, with distinction, until his death in March of 1981. Lucille passed away in 1984. Ralph is survived by his daughter Jolinn Deason, son Mike, and step-daughter Paula Beech.

Ralph was a brilliant, considerate, gentle, and funny man. One of his favorite observations about life was, "It's a great life if you don't weaken." He was also an avid fisherman. At one time or another, he wet a hook in every body of water in Benton County and floated every river in five counties. His only aversion was to snakes. A story is told (probably apocryphal) how on one occasion he and Buddy Whitlow were floating the War Eagle river. Dusk was coming on as they drifted beneath an overhanging tree limb. Without warning, a snake (which grew larger with every telling) dropped off the limb and fell with a plop in the bottom of the boat. Instinctively, Ralph grabbed a shotgun, which they always carried for emergencies, and blew the snake to smithereens. Unfortunately, he also shot the bottom out of the boat. All their fishing gear sank with the boat, but

Jo Bramer Duty

**Mama Duty with Davis,
Carolyn, Jimmy, and baby Jolinn**

**Mama Duty with Davis (4.5),
Jolinn (2), baby John
(6 mos), and Carolyn (7),
1929**

Ralph never once bemoaned its loss. No price was too high for killing that snake.

Jolinn was born on July 5, 1937, and on June 1, 1956, married Jack Deason of Rogers, where the couple still make their home. Jack has enjoyed successful careers as a builder, turkey farmer, and currently as a dog breeder. In his younger days, he was a prominent member and officer in the Jaycee movement. Jolinn, true her family's legal tradition, worked for many years as a legal secretary and currently holds a managerial position with the legal department of the Wal-Mart stores. Jack and Jollin have two daughters, Amy Jo and Melinda. Amy Jo married Douglas May and lives in Maumelle, Arkansas. They have two children, Katie Leigh and Sean Andrew. Melinda married Michael Linehan. They have two children: Colin Sean and Conner McKenzie. The Linehan family live in St. Louis, Missouri.

Mike graduated from the University of New Mexico with a degree in architecture. He married Janet Carmac in 1967 and has two children, Dustin and Chamblee. Mike and Janet make their home in Santa Fe, where he has a very successful architectural practice. Chamblee is attending the Oxford University in England and Dustin is living in Santa Fe.

Mike Duty and his family

The Melton Family

Lois Duty's sister Mary Emily White attended the University of Arkansas, where she was a member of Delta Delta Delta sorority and met and later married William Oren (Doc) Melton of Yellville, Arkansas. In their early years, the couple lived in small towns in northcentral Arkansas (Harrison and Conway) where Doc employed his degree in agriculture as a county agent for the State. Later, he joined two of his brothers, Marvin and Oscar, in a farm implement business operated in Jonesboro and Truman. Doc managed the Truman store and later a third store in Malden, Missouri. He moved to Jonesboro, Arkansas, and continued in the partnership until he retired. After his wife Mary's death on October 30, 1988, he remained in Jonesboro until 1991 when he moved to Little Rock and resided until his death on June 20, 1993.

Mary was a quiet spoken, very ladylike, and gentle woman. She had a huge capacity for love, expressed in concern and compassion for others. If you had a problem,

Lois (left) and her sister Mary (right)

you could talk it over with her and never risk rejection. On the face of it, one might wonder how people so different as Mary and Doc could get along so well. It must have been an example of opposites attracting. Doc received his sobriquet when in attending the university. His brother, Dr. Garland Melton, had established an optometric practice in Fayetteville. It seemed to follow that his younger brother would be known as "Little Doc," later shortened to "Doc." Doc was a big, outgoing, friendly man, who could talk to anybody. He was interested in all sports, but especially the St. Louis Cardinals, to whose broadcasts he tuned religiously over the years. He kept an immaculate yard and was a source of family wisdom on horticulture. His most notable trait, however, was his raucous and contagious laughter. All of the Melton brothers—Oscar, Russell, Marvin, Garland, and Doc—shared this trait. And when two or more were together, they would feed off of one another, making their surroundings rock with their mirth.

Mary and Doc had three children: Thomas, Mary Elizabeth, and Sarah Jane. Thomas attended the University of Arkansas, where he was a member of the Sigma Alpha Epsilon fraternity, and earned a degree in Business Administration. He married Garlanda Green of Forrest City, also Delta Delta Delta, and had two daughters, Susan and Allison, who followed the family's Delta Delta Delta tradition at the University of Texas. The family makes their home in Houston, Texas, where Thomas is an executive with International Business Machines Corporation (IBM).

Mary Elizabeth attended the University of Arkansas, where she was a member of Delta Delta Delta Sorority and met and later married John Duffee Phillips (Sigma Nu from Little Rock). After graduating from the University, John joined the Air Force and received pilot training. With test pilot credentials, he participated in development of the F-111 fighter bomber. John retired from the Air Force in 1988 and they returned to make their home in Little Rock. They have three children: Scott, Craig, and Ellen. Scott is married to Denice Smith of Oregon and they have two children, Kyle and Kaitlynn. Craig is married to Marsha Andrews of Dallas, Texas, and they have one son, Austin. Ellen is married to R. David Scruggs, Jr., who is the grandson of Lee Dean, Jeff Duty's first cousin. They have three children: Nicole, Bradford, and R. David Scruggs, III.

Sarah Jane also attended the University of Arkansas and followed her mother, sister, Aunt Lois, and Cousin Carolyn as a member of Delta Delta Delta sorority. While at the University, she met and later married Tommy Ray Polk of Hope who graduated with a degree in Architecture. The couple lived in New York and Memphis before making their home in Little Rock, where Tommy pursued his architectural career with notable success. Sarah taught school, was Training Director for Maritz, Inc., at Southwestern Bell's Corporate Research Center, and later was Director of the Arkansas Bar Association's Continuing Legal Education department. The couple divorced in 1994.

Sarah Jane and Tommy have two children, Natalie and Elizabeth. Natalie is a University of Arkansas graduate and Delta Delta Delta. She is married to James Mitchell Hoffmann of St. Louis and makes her home there. They have one son, Jackson Mitchell Hoffmann. Elizabeth attended the University of Arkansas, but graduated from Memphis State University. She is married to Paul Edward Barzizza of Memphis, where they now live.

Diana Duty West

Diana Lynn Duty was born to Mary and Davis Duty on August 8, 1965. (By one of those astonishing coincidences which make life fascinating, her birthday was the same as Liz Duty, Davis' third wife.) Her early years were spent in Rogers, where she attended West Side Elementary grade school through the fourth grade and Eastside Elementary grade school through the fifth grade. In 1976, she and her brother John Ellis moved (with the help of their grandmother Lois Duty) to Phoenix, Arizona, to live with their father.

After Davis' remarriage to Liz Alba Peachy on December 29, 1976, the family established their home on 18th Avenue, just off of Osborn Road in Phoenix. Diana attended West Side High School, and later, when it closed, Central High School where she graduated in 1983. The substance of these years has been described earlier in these pages.

Following high school, Diana attended Northern Arizona University in Flagstaff. At the end of two years, she took a break from school to enter the business community. Until 1987, she worked as a secretary in Phoenix and took night school courses at Arizona State University.

In 1987, Diana moved to the east coast, where she initially made her home with her mother (Mary) in Columbia, Maryland. For the next four years, she continued working as a secretary and attending night school at the nearby Howard County Community College. It was during this period that Diana was selected to be the United States candidate for a Management Training Program for her British-owned company. As such, she was sent to London, England, to compete through a series of examinations against the other international finalists for five positions. Unfortunately, her competition was more knowledgeable in matters of mathematics and she was not selected. Back in States, she graduated summa cum laude from HCC in May, 1991, with an Associate of Arts degree. She then enrolled at the University of Maryland at Baltimore County (UMBC), where she is slated to receive her Bachelors Degree in Psychology in the spring of 1995.

To this point in Diana's life, she had scrupulously avoided long-term amorous involvements. However, with a little bit of finagling from her father and future mother-in-law Sharon West, she was introduced to Bradley Alan West in 1991. As described earlier in this book, the early months of their courtship were conducted solely by mail and telephone. They finally met in person, though, at Christmas of 1991, when both of them returned to spend the holidays with their respective parents.

After Christmas, they both returned home, Diana going east and Brad traveling west to his home in Los Angeles. For a time, then, Diana's life was devoted to work, school, and pursuing an ever progressing long-distance relationship with Brad. On her birthday, August 8, 1992, they became engaged. The clock began ticking. With a wedding planned for May, 1993, Diana set herself to complete as much school as possible and to get her professional life organized. By Christmas 1992, both she and Brad converged on Fort Smith and wedding plans were well underway. When she returned to Maryland, it was for only three months so that she could tie up all the loose threads and be ready to move to California to be with Brad.

On May 8, 1993, the big event took place. Brad and Diana were wed in the First United Methodist Church in Fort Smith, in a ceremony which Diana had herself carefully orchestrated. The reception was held at the Hardscrabble Country Club and involved a sit-down brunch to the music of a classical quartet. It might be interesting to note that a substantial number of the persons mentioned in this book were present at the Duty-West nuptials. Following the reception, the bride and groom departed in a horse-drawn carriage for a honeymoon in Sweden. Needless to say, the horse and carriage were only employed for a very short first leg of the trip.

Diana and Brad spent two weeks in Sweden and then returned to California where they made their home and both worked in the Los Angeles area. This, however, was only an interlude. By the fall of 1993, they were preparing to move to the east coast. They made the move over Thanksgiving and set up housekeeping in Gaithersburg, Maryland. Brad had arranged for a transfer with the same company for which he worked in California. At this point, however, he encouraged Diana to stop working temporarily in order to devote herself to attending school full-time. This she did with a vengeance. As of this writing, she has established a 3.63 grade point average, has been inducted into the National Honor Society in Psychology, Psi Chi, and is already beginning to think and talk about pursuing her doctorate in organizational psychology.

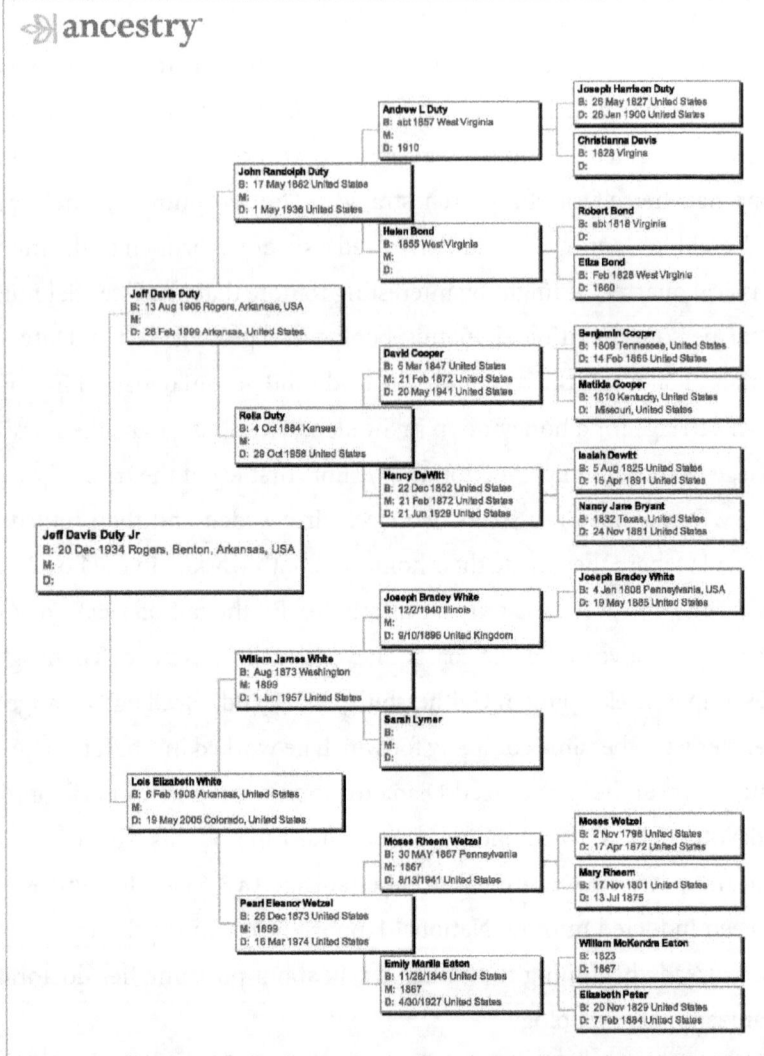

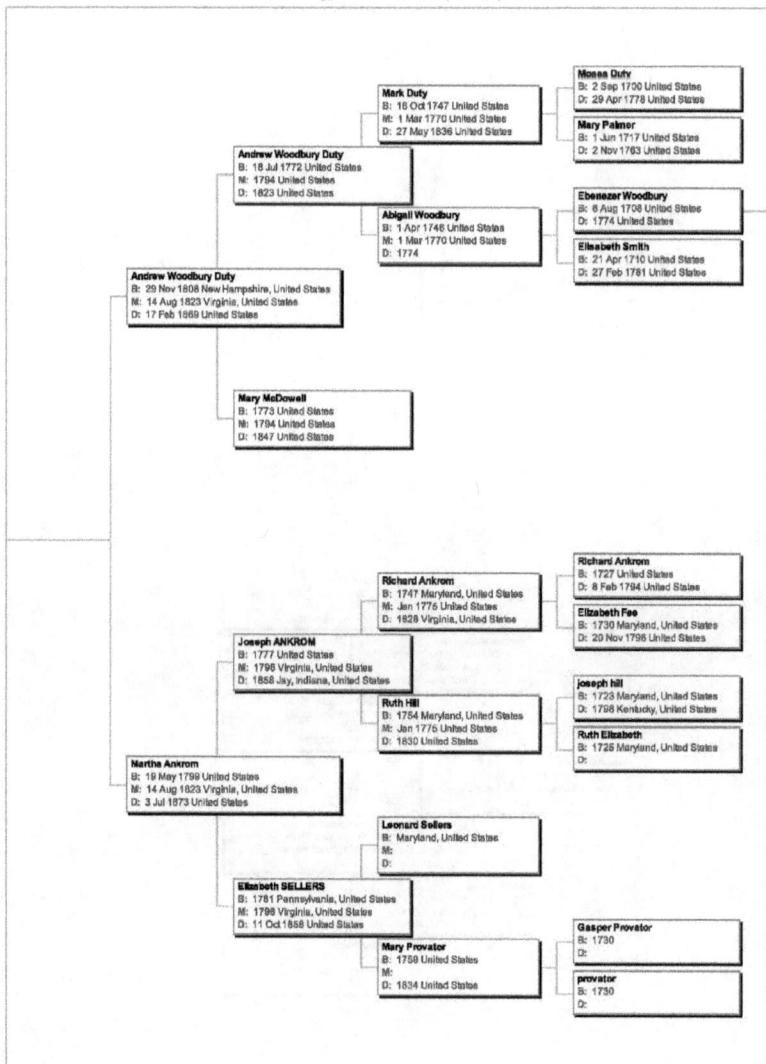

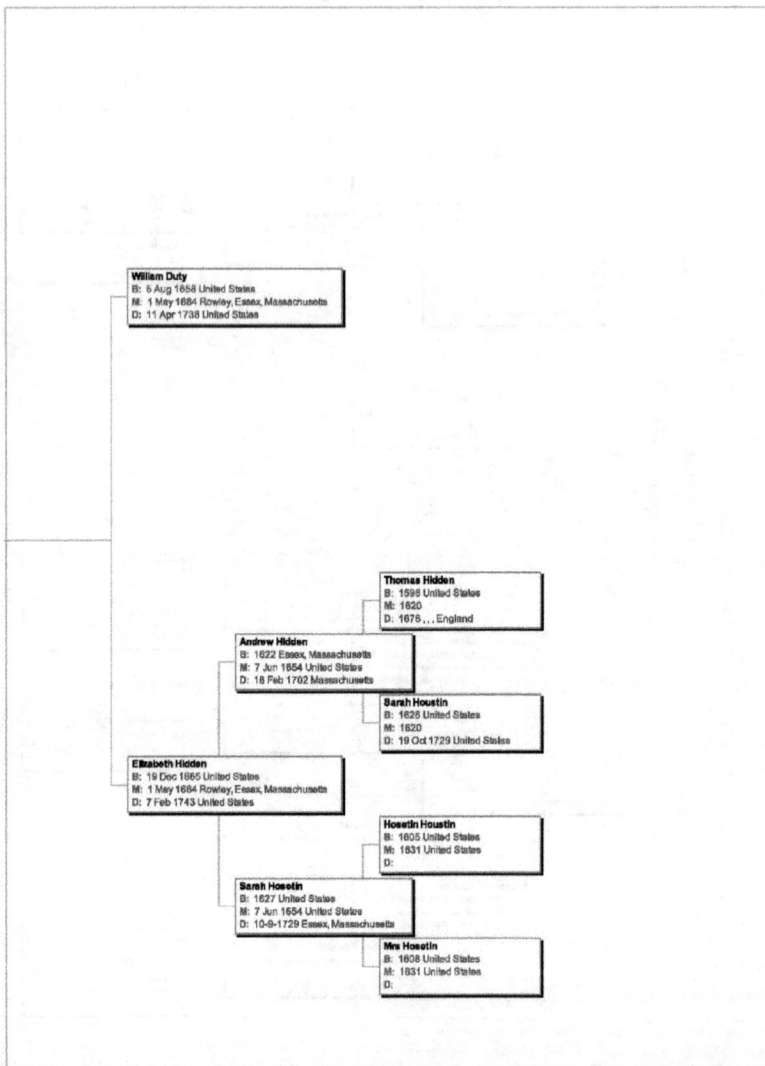

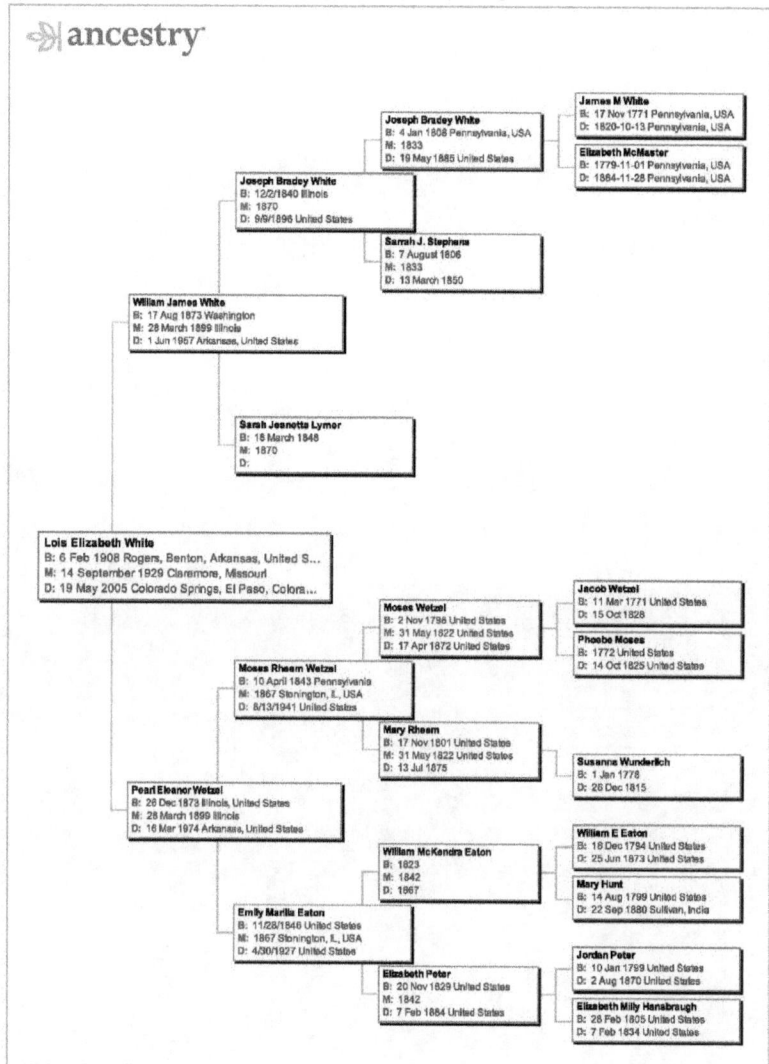

Chapter 35

Index of Cemeteries

Index of Names